The Social Construction of Dementia

of related interest

Perspectives on Rehabilitation and Dementia
Edited by Mary Marshall
ISBN 1 84310 286 2

Dementia and Social Inclusion
Marginalised Groups and Marginalised Areas
of Dementia Research, Care and Practice
Edited by Anthea Innes, Carole Archibald and Charlie Murphy
ISBN 1 84310 174 2

Dancing with Dementia
My Story of Living Positively with Dementia
Christine Bryden
ISBN 1 84310 332 X

The Simplicity of Dementia
A Guide for Family and Carers
Huub Buijssen
ISBN 1 84310 321 4

Training and Development for Dementia Care Workers
Anthea Innes
ISBN 1 85302 761 8

The Perspectives of People with Dementia
Research Methods and Motivations
Edited by Heather Wilkinson
ISBN 1 84310 001 0

Explorations in Dementia
Theoretical and Research Studies into the Experience
of Remediable and Enduring Cognitive Losses
Michael Bender
ISBN 1 84310 040 1

A Guide to the Spiritual Dimension of Care for People
with Alzheimer's Disease and Related Dementia
More than Body, Brain and Breath
Eileen Shamy
Forewords by Richard Sainsbury, Robert Baldwin and Albert Jewell
ISBN 1 84310 129 7

The Social Construction of Dementia
Confused Professionals?

Nancy Harding and Colin Palfrey

Jessica Kingsley Publishers
London and Philadelphia

First published in the United Kingdom in 1997
by Jessica Kingsley Publishers
116 Pentonville Road
London N1 9JB, UK
and
400 Market Street, Suite 400
Philadelphia, PA 19106, USA

www.jkp.com

Copyright © Nancy Harding and Colin Palfrey 1997
Printed digitally since 2005

Library of Congress Cataloging in Publication Data
A CIP catalog record for this book is available from the Library of Congress

British Library Cataloguing in Publication Data
Harding, Nancy
The social construction of dementia: confused professionals?
1. Dementia – Great Britain 2. Dementia – Patients – Services for – Great Britain
I. Title II. Palfrey, Colin, 1939–
362.1'968983

ISBN-13: 978 1 85302 257 9
ISBN-10: 1 85302 257 8

This book is dedicated to
Iorwerth Harding, Gareth Harding
and to Rose Palfrey

Contents

Acknowledgements

Thanks are due to Dr Ceri Phillips and to Rhiannon Urquhart at the University College of Wales, Newport, both of whom made significant contributions to the original research projects.

Acknowledgements, with thanks, also to current and former staff of the Institute for Health Care Studies, University of Wales, Swansea: Patricia al-Salahi, Clive Mulholland, David Rea, Michelle Steel and John Wilkinson.

Others who contributed just by listening sympathetically were Pauline Crossman, Sylvia Godfrey, Colin Murray and Sandra Thomas.

Preface

This book has been developed out of an extended evaluation of an innovative community care scheme funded originally by the Welsh Office and subsequently by the Department of Health. We were involved as Director and Research Officer in two projects designed to maintain elderly people in their own homes who, in other circumstances, would have been assessed as requiring residential or hospital care.

The particular Project which forms the basis of the book was evaluated over a period of three years according to specific criteria set out by the Welsh Office. These were: quality of service, inter-agency collaboration, cost-effectiveness, and the capacity to delay substantially or prevent entry into residential or hospital care. The Appendix describes in some detail the progress and *modus operandi* of the Project.

One of the salient features of the process of this community care programme was the emergent dominance of a bio-medical model which came to inform the Project's approach to maintaining elderly 'mentally infirm' people in their own homes. Despite the emphasis laid by the Welsh Office on the need for close collaboration among health and social services and voluntary agencies, a prevailing model of medical 'care' was applied.

This prompted us as researchers to enquire into how this had happened during the life of the Project. The aim, in the context of the evaluation, was to describe, record and report as accurately as possible the interesting dynamics of professional interaction. But once this final report was produced the question, 'why did this happen?' gave way to the more searching concern of whether it was right to have happened. How do some older people come to be referred to statutory agencies as in need of care? In particular, why were the subjects of intervention on the programme identified as suffering from a generic condition called 'dementia'? Can what is diagnosed from a medical viewpoint as a clinical illness be amenable to forms of 'intervention' that are alternatives to a nursing, care-oriented approach?

We considered the behaviour of those referred to the programme as a manifestation of 'abnormality', and wondered whether an apparently pathological condition could be construed differently viewed through an alternative conceptual lens.

Scepticism about the validity of bio-medical discourse as a pervasive interpretive paradigm is, of course, not new. But with dementia as a focus, certain theoretical perspectives – social constructionism, post-modernism and labelling, for example – offered us the means to analyse the 'career' of dementia as a physiological, psychological and social phenomenon. In particular, the 'discovery' of Alzheimer's disease in the early 1900s and the eventual merging of this 'disease' with other forms of dementia into a near homogeneous diagnostic category, prompted us to examine how and why a relatively wide array of presenting patterns of behaviour could so readily coalesce as a group of symptoms which could in future, without any cogent physiological evidence, be classified as a pathological syndrome. Previous distintions between pre-senile dementia, senile dementia and senile dementia of the Alzheimer's type have increasingly become unified under the diagnostic term 'Alzheimer's Disease'.

Our interest does not lie in attempting to dispute the fact that many older people display signs of mental dysfunction in the form of memory lapses and disorientation over a mild to severe spectrum. The purpose of this book is to examine the credentials of those predominantly bio-medical theories and compare them with other theoretically based interpretations; to consider whether, for example, there is an unsubstantiated move towards stereotyping certain observed behaviours according to an ageist formula. The potential problem, as we see it, has to do with cultural imperialism, which forces phenomena into a kind of theoretical procrustean bed.

What we offer in the succeeding pages is a discussion of ideas. Most adults, we could argue, live out their lives in a state of intermittent or more persistent confusion. The human response has been to impose order legitimised through religious and scientific doctrines. The argument implicit in this book is that confusion is the enemy of dogma and those who appear to be exhibiting signs of confusion may be revealing one aspect of human-ness which has yet to be adequately defined.

CHAPTER 1

Evaluating the Care of People with Dementia
Beyond the Bio-Medical Paradigm

In 1887 in Edinburgh a tuberculosis dispensary was opened to which people were referred and from which a staff of nurses visited the homes of patients, collecting information which enabled the building of a complete picture of the community, its members, and their habits, networks and contacts. It became 'a clearing house and a centre for observation from which patients could be directed to the most suitable place, home, hospital or sanatorium' (Armstrong 1983, p.7). This dispensary is in many ways reminiscent of the small, experimental, community care Project for people with dementia which provided the inspiration and, albeit tentatively, the empirical basis for this book. The Project[1] was one of a number of schemes set up with the aid of government funding at the end of the late 1980s and early 1990s in order to assess the capacity of a collaborative approach to social care provision to maintaining vulnerable people in their own homes. Our particular involvement was as researchers commissioned by the Department of Health to evaluate over a three year period several such demonstration projects.

Methodologically, the evaluation of this particular Project was problematic. Although a range of data collection methods were used in the process of evaluation, attempts at identifying any factors which undeniably contributed to the prevention of admission to residential or hospital care were fraught with problems centring on possible intervening variables. What became evident, however, was the prevailing medical interpretation of people's behaviour and resultant methods of 'control'. Apparent deviance from the norms of acceptable

---

1 It would be invidious to identify the scheme, and therefore we will refer to it as 'the Project'. Details of it are included as an Appendix.

social behaviour came to be construed as symptomatic of a disease. Forgetfulness and poor orientation in time and space were interpreted not as lapses of
concentration or of selective memorising, but as indicative of a specific
syndrome associated with pathological defects.

In our role as evaluators we and our colleagues as a matter of course reviewed
the literature about confused states amongst elderly people and, in particular,
those texts which offered a clinical description of dementia and Alzheimer's
disease. We noted that, despite the absence of any medical research evidence
capable of explaining the aetiology of confused episodes amongst elderly
people, the assumption conveyed in the literature was, nevertheless, within the
mainstream of orthodox medical praxis – that is to say, that by prescribing
drugs to the 'sufferer' the condition might be controlled until the cause of the
disease could be unequivocally established (it should be noted here that, as we
shall show in Chapter 3, the cause of the disease can be established only with
difficulty before a person's death). The 'theory' which prompted such an
approach appeared to be derived from a fairly simplistic analysis of the human
being as a quasi-machine which was amenable to repair once the single cause
of the problem had been isolated. One of our main concerns, therefore, from
quite early in the evaluation was the lack of any robust theoretical basis for the
regimen of care designed for the scheme's participants.

In reviewing previous evaluations of other such schemes we found that the
theoretical basis, or absence of one, of services to people with dementia had
never been questioned, despite increasing awareness of the need to cope with
the 'problems' such people present to community care. As social scientists we
felt it necessary to explore this absence. We wondered whether confusion
amongst some elderly people could be explained solely by a bio-medical
diagnosis; that because human beings are not machines many different factors
might combine to lead to an apparently confused state of mind; that since being
in advanced years appeared to be strongly correlated with various types of
'dementia', lapses of memory were construed to be the first stage of a phased
disease amongst older people but interpreted as normal behaviour amongst the
rest of the population. We needed, in short, alternative conceptual frameworks
in order to explore the phenomenon of dementia.

This book presents such a framework, but it was not arrived at without a
very long process of gestation during which various theories were tested and
rejected as inadequate. In a process with which researchers will be familiar, we
began with a search to establish the extent of the knowledge base about
dementia (the results of this are contained in Chapter 3, which provides a
summary of current knowledge about dementia), and this led to questions
which we later discovered to be naive and simplistic. We began, for instance,
by noting that one of the key criteria pre-selected by the commissioners of the
research – the effectiveness of inter-agency collaboration – should persuade us

that, at least potentially, there was likely to be more than one professional perspective that could apply to the interpretation of the presenting behaviour of those elderly people assigned to the Project. We speculated about the possible effects of drugs on the recipients of domiciliary care and, in particular, upon the potential for a mixture of drugs to instigate or exacerbate confusion. This is a domain which remains to be explored. The anecdotal evidence we have gathered about drug-induced dementia in older people is impressive, but could not be explored in sufficient detail for inclusion in this book. We received reports from friends and colleagues of older relatives whose initial diagnosis with one debilitating illness had led soon after to the diagnosis of a 'dementia' which reduced in severity once the drugs for the original illness had been withdrawn. We are not qualified to explore the realm of drugs, but such tales did lead us to explore one of the domains which our qualifications as social scientists have equipped us to enter – 'labelling theory' – for the experiences of friends' and colleagues' relatives suggest that if an older person develops a drug-induced confusion they will then be labelled as 'demented' and the trajectory of their lives from then on will be determined by that label.

Labelling theory

The idea that certain behaviour and conditions are labelled 'deviant' derives from Durkheim's seminal writings. He claimed that deviance serves to remind the social group of the importance of certain values (Freund and McGuire 1991). Durkheim observed that the very existence of social norms means that there will be deviance in all societies. The labelling of a person's characteristics or behaviour may, therefore, be said to be a social product (Becker 1963). Those who exercise considerable power and authority in any given society are able to impose their mechanisms for control over other people and to define what is acceptable or deviant.

While the 'sick role' – as Parsons (1951) depicted it – can be legitimated by society provided that the sick person behaves in culturally prescribed ways (such as consulting a doctor; trying to get better) certain social labels constitute *stigma* (Goffman 1969). Leprosy, epilepsy, AIDS and mental illness have all carried this condemnatory cachet. The increasing influence of the medical profession over many aspects of Western society is exemplified in the tendency to accept clinical diagnoses in order to delineate the boundaries between 'madness' and 'badness'. Persons guilty of criminal offences, for example, may be subjected to psychiatric analysis in order to establish whether they are fit to plead. Potential moral culpability may, in this way, be avoided and there is a powerful rationalisation of non-certifiable perpetrators of highly repellent crimes as being still, in some way, 'sick'.

Our reading of labelling theory led us to one of the currently most influential theories in the sociology of health: social constructionism.

Social constructionism

Labelling theory suggests that key players in the social structure become 'moral entrepreneurs', capable of distinguishing in an officially accepted way between good and bad behaviour, between sickness and health. An extension of this particular theoretical approach asserts that the apparent scientific basis on which medical practice is founded is only one way of interpreting the world. The paradigm of scientific knowledge is one in which reality is depicted as facts waiting to be discovered 'out there'. Yet, some sociologists would argue, these facts are mental constructs which are influenced by social and cultural values. What feature as undeniable facts today or in one society may be discredited later or in another culture. The portrayal of knowledge as value-free is questioned by those who would contend that epistemologies gain acceptability and authority only by dint of their being compatible with prevailing beliefs and value systems.

In Europe the Renaissance heralded an era of discovery, of enlightenment, the division between mind and body as distinguishable entities and the sublimation of reason over other human faculties. The emerging sciences became influential in determining a dominant mode of perceiving and interpreting experience, and medical practitioners allied themselves to this paradigm and authenticated their profession as an authoritative social institution. Yet their claim to functioning as social luminaries has come to be challenged: 'The forces shaping the "discovery" of disease categories are not purely objective, scientific factors; rather, value judgements, economic considerations, and other social concerns frequently enter the process' (Freund and McGuire 1991, p.206). Funding for research, for example, is largely dependent on what is socially defined as a serious problem at any one time.

Our initial forays into social constructionism have led to this book, for social constructionism seems best to explain the reality of the Project as it appeared to us (a model of social constructionism is outlined in some depth in Chapter 2). This is, so far as we are aware, the first book-length treatise on the social construction of an illness. Its length allows the exploration of particular issues in some depth. We will argue that dementia or Alzheimer's disease is an example of a socially constructed disease, and that the major players in such a construction – its architects as it were – are the medical profession. We need therefore to explore how medical knowledge is constructed.

The social construction of medical knowledge

Berger and Luckmann (1967) argued that knowledge is unevenly distributed in society and that access to specialised formal knowledge such as medical knowledge is particularly uneven. The growth of professionalism and specialism within medicine serves to control who enters the profession. Somewhat ironically, as Berger and Luckmann point out, the extent of knowledge required by medical practitioners is 'recipe knowledge', that is, 'knowledge limited to pragmatic competence in routine performances' (Berger and Luckmann, p.47). Furthermore, medical ideas are the product of social processes and are continually changing, not necessarily because of more detailed knowledge but as a result of cultural concerns and practices. Bell (1987), for example, cites the menopause as a normal biological process which has come to be defined as a medical problem in most Western societies, whereas in other countries this stage represents a form of liberation from many restrictions affecting women in those particular societies (Davis 1996). Menopause, through an experience that is capable of being variably construed according to the individual and cultural context, has come to be medically constructed as a disease because it has been interpreted in the bio-medical paradigm as a pathological configuration.

The need to search for one cause–effect relationship in order to explain the presence of disease typifies the bio-medical construction of the human condition. This process relies on the classification of 'symptoms' into a taxonomy of clinical labels. This process of 'medicalisation' is the means by which medical control over an area of life is legitimated by asserting the primacy of a medical interpretation of that area (Conrad and Schneider 1980; Illich 1975). Childbirth is another example of a natural process which has been medicalised. The specialisations of obstetrics and gynaecology have been developed so that even uncomplicated reproduction is seen to be the rightful province of medical supervision. Conversely, but by the same process and paradigm, perceptions of illness can only be authorised as having an objective reality if they are categorised as diseases. There is no ambiguity about feeling pain and realising that we are unusually lethargic. Yet these conditions personally experienced as real may not be recognised as having an authentic existence until they have been defined as repetitive strain injury or myalgic encephalomyelitis. Having satisfied ourselves and, we hope, our readers, that medical knowledge is socially constructed (we show how the medical model of dementia has been constructed in Chapters 5 and 6), we need to show how medical knowledge can become social knowledge, or how society comes to accept the labels of diseases arrived at by medical scientists, learned by medical practitioners and applied to the bodies of those members of society who come into contact with the medical profession. This led us to the sociology of the body, the school of thought specifically concerned with understanding how we, as individuals and societies, understand our bodies. The body, too, is socially constructed.

The social construction of the body

The Western notion of the body as a machine quite separate from the mind is culturally determined. The body as a metaphor fits with beliefs that are dominant in a society. Oriental constructs of the body as a system of energies and spiritual channels determine how various ailments are dealt with both personally and professionally in terms of therapeutic practices. Because there are a number of beliefs about how the body and mind 'work', it is reasonable to assert that 'the body', as the domain of medical interest and intervention, is the creation of a set of deep-seated beliefs. The Western mediaeval world view was of a universe originally created out of nothing and ordered by God. The original state was one of ineffable harmony in which the music of the spheres bore testament to a preordained hierarchical structure in which every part of the universe had its appointed place.

The four elements of earth, air, fire and water were correspondingly innate in the human being and were realised as the four humours or fluids: yellow bile or choler; black bile or melanchole; blood and phlegm. Excess of any humour would lead to an imbalance of fluids with characteristic manifestations in physical appearance and behaviour. Other cultures used other metaphors. Ancient Egyptian societies adopted the image of a river while Chinese tradition and yogic beliefs conceived of the body as the repository of elemental forces or energies.

In our society, the metaphor of a machine capable of being maintained in good order and repaired at the point of breakdown is a powerful symbol of a rational, technological world view. The search for a specific aetiology that will identify the cause of disease also leads to a fragmentation of the patient as an aggregation of interconnected but distinct parts, each the province of a specialist physician. This physical reductionism plays down the possible socially and psychologically induced states of the ill-health and continues in its quest for a 'magic bullet' to 'shoot and kill' the disease (Dubos 1965). Orthodox medicine seeks answers to the question: 'What kind of disease does this patient have?'. Alternative therapeutic approaches are more likely to enquire: 'What sort of person is it who has come for treatment?'. The sociology of the body takes us beyond the medical domain into the wider social world. We will show in Chapter 7 how society *needs*, because of the embodiment of its individual members, dementia to be seen as a disease which can, eventually perhaps, be cured. If a cure for dementia can be found then a cure for ageing itself may be found.

Conclusion: the theoretical basis of this book

In exploring the phenomenon called 'dementia' we draw upon the paradigms of post-modernism (readers of Armstrong's (1983) post-modernist analysis of health services will be familiar with the dispensary which was the subject of the opening paragraph of this chapter – it will be returned to in the conclusion) and social constructionism. Both of these perspectives challenge traditional thinking which has, at least since the seventeenth century in Western cultures, extolled rationalism as the pathway to truth. According to this doctrine, any phenomenon that is not verifiable by scientific observation, experiment or mathematical formulae cannot be credited with the term 'fact'. Laws governing the natural world are waiting to be discovered. The advance of science and technology has led to an explosion in our knowledge of how things work. The essential model in which scientific enquiry proceeds is one of cause and effect.

It is a small step conceptually to transpose this model to all aspects of human experience. By so doing, other avenues of perception come to be assigned a lower rank in defining the meaning of what we perceive and experience. The human being, after all, is *Homo sapiens*.

The more relativist thesis that we develop here questions whether this dominant mode of interpreting the world is sufficient and appropriate. In particular, we examine the claims of the medical profession to speak with any authority about a condition which has been labelled 'dementia'.

We note that diagnosis of apparently aberrant behaviour or states of being changes according to dominant 'discourses'. Possession by evil spirits becomes schizophrenia; hysteria alters from a disorder of the womb to a manic depressive illness; homosexuality is a sin or a genetically determined or environmentally shaped disposition; epilepsy – once the sign of divine inspiration – turns into a neurological affliction. Less dramatically, 'battered wife syndrome' and 'child abuse' remain stubbornly resistant to exclusively bio-medical explanations. The cause–effect odyssey is incomplete.

Against this background of diverse explanations for what are regarded at any one time in society as undesirable states, we discuss in Chapter 3 current knowledge about the 'causes' of, or factors correlated with, 'dementia'. Progressive loss of memory, impaired ability to think and reason, disorientation, breakdown of personality – do these add up to a pathological syndrome, as medical literature would assert? Where is the evidence for such an interpretation judged by the medical profession's own criteria of validity? Some of the 'symptoms' of dementia may be construed differently. For example, in certain old people, 'distant or remote memory remains longer and may serve as a refuge from present day worries' (Barker 1991); the dementing process should be viewed as the outcome of a dialectical interplay between two tendencies: neurological impairment and the personal psychology an individual has accrued, together with the social psychology with which he or she is surrounded

(Kitwood and Bredin 1992), could mean dementia is part of the normal ageing process (Pollitt, O'Connor and Anderson 1989).

These views of, respectively, a pharmacist, psychologists and social scientists, diverge from the more influential medical typology relayed in a range of literature including clinical journals and voluntary groups' newsletters for carers of dementia sufferers. The prevailing version of what constitutes dementia claims not only that it is a set of characteristics made manifest through behavioural dysfunction, but that it stands as the fourth leading cause of death in the Western world (Sonder 1993).

We will in this book show that the variety of 'explanations' of dementia are no more than speculation dressed up as theories which thus confuse the professional persons concerned with providing care, hence the book's title. We must ask at what point and for what reasons may confusion be allowed to masquerade as dogma? Whose confusion?

CHAPTER 2

Methodological Framework
Social Constructionism

Introduction

In this chapter we will be concerned with establishing the theoretical perspective which will allow us to gain a non-medical understanding of dementia. We must, if we are to gain such an understanding, approach our study in a similar spirit to that recommended in Wiener and Marcus's (1994) study of depression, that is as cultural anthropologists, attempting both to stand outside our own culture and remember all the while the impossibility of leaving behind our own 'enculturation'. We need to do the same; to stand outside our deeply embedded beliefs in the rationality of medicine and Western culture; our understanding of being 'old' and the processes of ageing.

Social constructionism is our chosen tool in helping us develop a theory of what it is like to be a person with dementia, for social constructionism examines how we *make* our worlds and are in turn made by our worlds. Already we have hinted at the tenor of our arguments, for in using the word 'enculturation' we are suggesting that dementia is primarily the result of a sociological or psychological process rather than of the physical deterioration depicted in the medical model.

We do not here deny the importance of the biological aspects of ageing. In social constructionism the issue is not whether biological processes are important or relevant, but, 'whether [their] contribution to action is pre-eminent in the remarkable diversity of human actions'. Whatever the constraints of biological processes, 'the "world" and how it becomes known, incorporated, perceived, transformed, modified, enhanced, emended, mutated, transposed, converted, metamorphosed, recast, or whatever, is presumed to be a construction embodying the sociocultural matrix of that individual. Transactions are in a socially constructed world, however and whatever becomes known' (Wiener and Marcus 1994, p.216). Indeed biological processes themselves become social constructions when our understanding of how they will affect us determines how we act in response to them.

What is 'social constructionism'?

This, it will soon become clear, is not a question which is easily answered, or perhaps it has an answer which cannot readily be conveyed through the medium of words. Constructionism is, for Waters (1994), a type of sociological theorising built on the assumption that the social world is *subjective* and consists of the, 'creations, interpretations, meanings, and ideas of thinking and acting subjects' (p.5), with individuals being competent and communicative agents who actively create or construct the social world. Understanding of the social world can therefore be gained through understanding the individual's meaning of the world. Waters traces the origins of constructionism to George Simmel and Max Weber, German theorists of the late 19th and early 20th centuries, from whose works several schools of subjectivist, interpretive thought have emerged. It is defined by the editors in a series entitled *Inquiries in Social Construction* as an, 'emergent dialogue within the social sciences' which draws its participants from a broad range of disciplines, which involves 'profound challenges' to a range of existing theories, and which has a common thread in its, 'concern with the processes by which human abilities, experiences, commonsense and scientific knowledge are both *produced in*, and *reproduce*, human communities' (Semin and Gergen 1990).

The definition of social constructionism, it will be shown, appears confused by its being influential both in sociology and psychology, and with its having a distinctly temporal, geographical and disciplinary split: the symbolic interactionism which was extraordinarily influential amongst sociologists in the USA until the 1970s, and the European school of social constructionism which has its roots in sociology and psychology and which emerged as an influential, if under-developed, body of theory in Europe in the late 1980s. Both social constructionism and symbolic interactionism are part of a general constructionist mode of thought in sociological theory.

The theme developed here is that whilst symbolic interactionism is essentially non-critical, social constructionism is a merger of symbolic interactionism with feminism and post-modernism/post-structuralism which thus has taken a critical turn. Where symbolic interactionism assumes an unproblematic and essentially pluralist dialectical relationship between the individual and society, social constructionism examines power relationships and renders the relationship between society and individual non-dialectical. Where symbolic interactionism primarily focuses on the way in which individuals build self-identities from the meanings they bring to categories of experience (such as gender, sexuality, male and female), social constructionism examines how meanings are formed and then reflected on to and into the individual. The boundaries between symbolic interactionism and social constructionism are sometimes unclear: some readings which claim to be social constructionist can perhaps more properly be regarded as symbolic interactionist in their approach, whilst American writers attempting to inform symbolic interactionism with feminism and post-modernism continue to use 'symbolic interactionism' as a rubric. This chapter will therefore first discuss symbolic interactionism and then explore the influence of the post-modernist movement.

Symbolic interactionism

Simmel's work was influential in the evolution in the USA of symbolic interactionism. This 'unique American sociological and social psychological perspective' (Denzin 1992, p.xiv), unique in the sense that it was developed, and continues to be claimed, by American sociologists and social psychologists as their own, enjoyed an extended heyday from the 1930s to the 1970s, after which it continued to be influential, if not so dominant.

Symbolic interactionism was primarily influenced by the work of G.H. Mead (Meltzer, Petras and Reynolds 1975). Mead was critical of the dominant 'realist' conceptions which, at the turn of the nineteenth century, had argued that there was one universal reality, which existed independently of the human mind, which science and philosophy could mirror faithfully, and which all would comprehend with few variations in their picture of the world. This view of the world involves a 'dualistic commitment', with the objective, physical world on one side and the mental world of the individual on the other (Gergen and Semin 1990). Building on Simmel's influence, Mead developed the concept of 'dual systems', which stated that the individual belongs to a system which in part determines him/her, and at the same time to a system which he or she determines. In Mead's conception, the individual has no reality outside of the social group. Mead argued that relationships between individuals are established in patterns of linguistic communication: 'Communication is the medium by which society gets inside each actor and is thus why understandings come to be shared and society emerges' (Waters 1994, p.7). The self thus develops through communication with others and interpretation of their intended meanings.

Influenced by Mead, a variety of interpretations of symbolic interactionism evolved, the variations being determined as much by methodology as content. The 'Chicago school' led by Blumer held to an interpretive methodology, whilst the influence of Kuhn led the 'Iowa school' to laud the merits of an empiricist approach (Meltzer et al. 1975). The field labelled 'symbolic interactionism' became so divergent (see Meltzer et al. 1975 and the quite formidable bibliography in Denzin 1992) with a variety of debates and critical currents that any attempt to summarise its main arguments may deserve the accusation of reductionism. With this danger in mind, we will offer a summary of the picture of society drawn by symbolic interactionists. All schools have the following ideas as their basis:

> The influence that stimuli have upon human behavior is shaped by the context of symbolic meanings within which human behavior occurs. These meanings emerge from the shared interaction of individuals in human society. Society itself is constructed out of the behavior of humans, who actively play a role in developing the social limits that will be placed upon their behavior. Thus, human behavior is not a unilinear unfolding toward a predetermined end, but an active constructing process whereby humans endeavor to 'make sense' of their social and physical environments. This 'making sense' process is internalized in the form of thought; for thinking is the intra-individual problem-solving process that is also characteristic of inter-individual interaction. In thinking, then, there occurs an interaction with oneself. In light of the foregoing, *any complete understanding of human behavior must include an awareness of this covert dimension of activity, not simply the observation of overt behavior.* (Meltzer *et al.* 1975, p.vii, emphasis added)

Society and the individual are inseparable and interdependent. Behaviour is constructed and circular, as the environment's influence is experienced as social meanings, which in turn are learned by individuals in social interaction. The self originates in social relationships or, more simply, human beings construct their realities in a process of interaction with other human beings.

These ideas can be more easily understood if we examine two works which can be regarded as seminal in this context: Erving Goffman's (1959) *Presentation of Self in Everyday Life*, and Berger and Luckman's (1967) *The Social Construction of Reality*.

The work of Erving Goffman

Goffman's thesis is built on the metaphor that life is a stage (Manning 1991). He argued that individuals (in his example whilst at the workplace) present themselves to others as if they were performing a play, but with two important players: the individual and the other actors. The other actors seek information about the individual, who tries to control the conduct of the others by communicating an impression of him/herself, both consciously and unconsciously, which will cause the others to accord with his/her wishes. Each 'other' is, of course, an actor in their own right, so the members of any group feed signals to other members and receive signals from them in turn, to which they adjust themselves. All this will occur in and through a working consensus or a desire to avoid an open conflict of definitions of the situation. So individuals effectively project definitions of a situation when they enter the presence of others, and have an expectation that they will be treated in the manner that persons of their kind have a right to expect. This prevents loss of face with its accompanying damaging of sensitive social selves. The 'interaction order' in which this occurs is highly durable, operating even within those total institutions which may try to eliminate it (Goffman 1968).

In this and his later work, Goffman showed that the interaction order is a domain in which meaning is produced, that is, meanings arise from the mutual involvements of participants in particular situations and their definitions and negotiations. These meanings are distinct from those that can be extracted from institutional objectives or role expectations. There is within this a strong emphasis on a moral dimension within social interaction, in which trust, tact and a willingness to take on the responsibilities of involvement with others play a central part (Rawls 1987). General resources, such as language and shared cultural knowledge, are used by people when managing encounters with others. Although such given 'resources' may be modified during a social contact, the 'knowledge base' itself reaches beyond particular situations (Layder 1994). In Goffman's framework, people create meaning in face-to-face encounters. The self is therefore a social product which can only be understood in relation to its social context.

However, Goffman's work contains, 'no explicit theory, but a plausible and loosely-organized frame of reference; little interest in explanatory schemes, but masterful descriptive analysis; virtually no accumulated evidence, but illuminating allusions, impressions, anecdotes, and illustrations' (Meltzer *et al.* 1975, p.71). This is, for later writers drawing upon more recent developments in sociological theorising, a traducement of Goffman's work which should rather be seen in the context of a process of an evolutionary development of theory (Manning 1991). Indeed the dramaturgical perspective is now one of the major tools in the researcher's kit (Mangham 1987).

Berger and Luckmann

Goffman analyses society at a micro level. Berger and Luckmann's thesis is based at the macro level. Writing as sociologists of knowledge, they provided the academic world with a theory which has been variously claimed as an important founding argument by several intellectual paradigms. Waters (1994), for example, allocates Berger and Luckmann's thesis to a chapter discussing phenomenology, or that body of theory which argues that 'reality' comprises appearances and experiences brought to us via our senses and then categorised as social phenomena. In phenomenology, subject and object are inextricably fused, as the separation of the experiencing agent from the object of experience is artificial and misleading (Gergen and Semin 1990).

Berger and Luckmann assert that 'reality' and 'knowledge' are socially relative, that is, 'what is "real" to a Tibetan monk may not be "real" to an American businessman' (1967, p.15) and that, 'specific agglomerations of "reality" and "knowledge" pertain to specific social contexts' (*ibid.*). The 'taken-for-granted "reality" [which] congeals for the man in the street' is socially constructed, originating in his or her thoughts and actions, and maintained as real by those very thoughts and actions. Subjective processes and meanings are objectified and thus construct the 'intersubjective common-sense world'. The more that meanings are shared, the more they come to be seen as having an external, real existence which constrains individuals (Waters 1994).

Society, claim Berger and Luckmann, has both an objective and a subjective reality. The former is made out of:

- ° *Humankind's biological status*, and its capacity for making its own environment.

- ° *The urge to habitualisation of human actions*, which then allows predictability and thus institutionalisation, which occurs, 'whenever there is a reciprocal typification of habitualized actions by types of actors' (p.72). The social formations which are institutions are humanly produced through externalisation and objectivisation (that is, what is externalised becomes made into an object) and are thus experienced as having an objective reality which controls human conduct by channelling it in one direction. However, the relationship between the human and the institution is dialectical – 'the product acts back upon the producer' (p.78) through the process of internalisation. Institutions become legitimated through the socialisation processes by which new generations recognise the institutions, thus giving them historical status. The 'edifice of legitimation' is built upon language, which allows the institution to become part of the socially available and taken for granted stock of knowledge within a subjectively meaningful universe. Knowledge about institutions occurs at the pre-theoretical level, being the, 'sum total of "what everybody knows" about a social world, an assemblage of maxims, morals, proverbial nuggets of wisdom, values and beliefs, myths, and so forth'. Different institutions may provide different definitions of meaning to participants, which allow socially segregated sub-universes of meaning.

- ° *Sedimentation and tradition* which, facilitated by language, allow us to share and to build up a body of knowledge from others' subjective experiences. These 'symbolic universes' allow access to realities other than those of everyday meaning.

○ *Roles.* 'In the course of action there is identification of the self with the objective sense of the action; the action that is going on determines, for that moment, the self-apprehension of the actor' with, eventually, 'an entire sector of self-consciousness' structured in terms of roles. The stock of knowledge that is available in society provides us with the information of how we should act in these roles. 'By playing roles, the individual participates in a social world. By internalizing these roles, the same world becomes subjectively real to him' (p.91). Roles are related to a socially defined appendage of knowledge specific to particular roles, and to a wider range of socially distributed knowledge necessary to an understanding of how one is to act within a role.

The subjective reality of society is established and maintained through:

1. *Socialisation*, or the, 'comprehensive and consistent induction of an individual into the objective world of a society or a sector of it' (p.150) through which one learns how to understand another's manifest subjective processes so that they become subjectively meaningful to oneself, as the other's subjectivity is objectively available and can become more or less meaningful to me. Primary socialisation is the first socialisation one undergoes, which naturally occurs in childhood; secondary socialisation is the process of induction into new sectors of the objective world of one's society. In both, language is of prime importance, as it constitutes both the most important content and the most important instrument of socialisation (p.153).

2. *Procedures of reality maintenance* at the level of individual consciousness. The reality of everyday life and one's position within that reality as a person with a self-conscious identity are confirmed and maintained by being, 'embodied in routines, which is the essence of institutionalization'. Further, they are continually reaffirmed or adjusted in the social process of interaction with others, significant or secondary, who give us information about who we are. The most important vehicle of reality-maintenance is conversation (p.172). Conversation maintains, modifies and reconstructs subjective reality. Speech is privileged as a form of communication.

3. *The achievement of a high degree of symmetry* between objective and subjective reality, and identity, which is deemed to be 'successful

socialisation'. Its opposite, unsuccessful socialisation, opens up the possibility of the question: 'Who am I?'.

4.   *The formation of identity* through a dialectic between individual and society, through social processes and social relations which crystallise, and then maintain, modify or reshape identity. Identities can be engendered through specific historical social structures, and allow orientation and conduct in everyday life.

5.   *A dialectic between nature and society*, that is, between the individual as animal and the social world, and between the biological suborganism and one's socially produced identity.

6.   *Language*, which objectifies the world, transforming experience into a cohesive order, and realises the world, in the double sense of apprehending and producing it.

In sum, society should be understood in terms of an, 'ongoing dialectical process composed of the three moments of externalization, objectivation and internali- zation' (p.149). These are not sequential, as society and each part of it are simultaneously characterised by all three. The individual is constructed in the same way, through simultaneously externalising his/her own being into the social world and internalising it as an objective reality: 'In other words, to be in society is to participate in its dialectic' (p.149). For Berger and Luckmann, individuals do not create the world in the solipsist sense of imagining its existence; they become part of the world already created by others (Turner 1991).

Recent developments in symbolic interactionism

Denzin (1992) has recently sought to rescue symbolic interactionism from the desuetude into which it fell in the 1970s. He argues that it has from its birth been, 'haunted by a double-edged specter': the inability to merge an interpre- tive, subjective study of human experience with the objectivist requirements of a science as dictated by the natural sciences. Social constructionism, we shall see, overcomes this problem by following the prescriptions of post-modernism where, at one level, the natural sciences are seen as but one way of knowing about the world, thus allowing 'non-scientific' methods of knowing about the world equal credence with 'scientific' methods, and at another level refusing an ability for anyone other than the individual subject to know anything about his/her reality. He argues that interpretive and symbolic interactionists:

°   see society as an emergent phenomenon, always changing and therefore incapable of being understood through a grand theory.

They therefore believe they should write about how people are constrained by the constructions they build and inherit from the past

- describe the recurring meanings and practices which persons produce when they do things together

- focus on actual, lived emotional experiences of interacting human beings

- believe that persons make history, but that power intervenes so that the histories made by individuals are not always of their own making: 'This means they study the micro-power relations that structure the daily performances of race, ethnicity, gender and class in interactional situations' (p.24)

- believe that each individual expresses in his or her lifetime the general and specific features of a historic epoch

- ask not 'why?' but 'how?'

- abjure science; grand theory; grand sociology; overly rational, cognitive theories of human behaviour

- assume that people create the worlds of experience they live in through the meanings gleaned through interaction. Symbolic interaction is the merger of self and social interaction.

Symbolic interactionism, then, is a subjective, interpretive social psychology which assumes that individuals create the worlds of experience they live in by acting on things in terms of the meanings things have for them. The central object to be negotiated in interaction is personal identity. This is achieved through the process of communication and thus of cultural meanings. However, the relationship between the individual and society writ large (rather than the small societies of local mutual interaction), with its seemingly external, objective and constraining realities, are ignored (Waters 1994).

Waters (1994) charges constructionist theories with being incapable of analysing much more than interpersonal interaction. Symbolic interactionism, he writes, is, 'acomparative and ahistorical, a social psychology with sociological sympathies but not remotely a complete sociology' (p.51). Now, our thesis implies that society 'produces' dementia through the messages sent to older citizens, which they assimilate into their self-identities. Symbolic interactionism deals only with the second of these two inter-related processes: the way in which the individual builds a self-identity through messages given by others in his/her immediate locale. We need a theory which can explain how the messages are themselves constructed. This theory will show how society in general targets a sub-group within that society. Can social constructionism do this?

Social constructionism

Let us begin this section with a critique of social constructionism. Social constructionism has been accused of relativism: 'We are,' when using social constructionism, 'left to choose between accounts on the basis of intuition', Bury (1986) has argued. Nicolson and McLaughlin respond by arguing that the sociology of knowledge *requires* relativism, for:

> ...to say a proposition is true or false is only to say that it does or does not coincide with one's own beliefs about the world. To make such a judgement is to say something about one's own knowledge but little about why the knowledge under study arose or was sustained. ... Far from relativism being an 'abyss' to be avoided, proper standards of sociological scholarship imply and demand that sociologists of knowledge be methodological relativists. Anything less unnecessarily detracts from the scope and power of sociological enquiry. (1986, p.117)

Social constructionism is not good knowledge, Bury has further argued. Nicolson and McLaughlin (1987), on the other hand, argue that the judgement as to whether knowledge is 'good' or not should depend on whether or not it is fruitful in practice, not on how the knowledge arose. Bearing in mind these criticisms and their rebuttal, we will now analyse the current state of theorising about social constructionism, and then attempt to make good some gaps in the theory.

Inadequate theorising in social constructionism

A review of literature presented by academics writing in the social construc-tionist mode reveals a proclivity for the label of 'social constructionism' to be applied without an explanation of what is meant by this approach (see, for example, Helman (1988) and Barley (1988), both of whom provide fascinating accounts to which they have applied the title 'social constructionist' without defining what they mean by it). Others give a very brief outline of what they mean. Wright (1988), for example, whilst beginning his paper with a warning that social constructionism can be easily misunderstood, limits his definition to two things: a statement of what it is not (that is, it does not render that which is studied as illusory, and it is not a foray into absolute relativism), and the assertion that social constructionism starts from the recognition that all knowl-edge, 'is the product of human social activity and is used by human beings to bring into existence their own lives and experience' (p.300). Others reduce social constructionism to but one concept: Mangham (1987), for example, uses dramaturgy as social constructionism.

This tendency could be indicative of a marked confusion surrounding the concept. Alternatively it could be seen as representing a fear amongst writers of entering too far into the realm of theory in a period when the theoretical world, already accused of disciplinary inwardness, closure and thus exclusivity (Seidman 1992), has been further turned upside down by the advent of post-modernism, so terminologically complex that books attempting to explain it have to carry their own glossaries.

Given this paucity of theorising, we need to explore what is meant by social constructionism, as it is the foundation upon which our analysis of dementia is built. Briefly, and perhaps simplistically, we can commence by saying that social constructionism follows symbolic interactionism in asserting that:

- ° social objects do not have their own objective existence

- ° they do, however, exist, and if they are not objective they must be subjective

- ° if social objects are subjective, they must be constructed out of the perceptions of people, that is, they must be constructed in the social, subjective realm

- ° people are themselves social objects, and they construct their selves, their perceptions of themselves and the self they portray to others.

However, symbolic interactionism does not allow room for the influence of society in general, nor for the accretions of ideologies and other overarching beliefs upon the individual. It is essentially ahistorical, apolitical and non-critical. All these taken together result in enormous difficulty in encompassing the impact of ageing in industrialised societies which, we will argue, is central to a sociology of dementia. We therefore need a theory which retains the core of symbolic interactionism, but allows for these wider influences to be felt and analysed. Social constructionism, in the mode developed here, meets these requirements.

We shall commence our explication of social constructionism with a relatively comprehensible, if somewhat deterministic, model of the social construction of the sciences, identified by Eisenberg (1988). From this we can tease out the theory which it subsumes, that is, a social constructionist perspective of science assumes that:

1. All scientific concepts are inventions of the imagination which, in introducing order into the 'chaos of appearance', take on the appearance of reality. Thus within the human sciences there can be no such thing as a universal truth.

2. The human sciences therefore develop belief systems which are current for a particular time or a particular place. These beliefs are transferred from the scientific to the wider community, resulting in the paradox that that which is believed to be true about behaviour affects the very behaviour which the sciences attempt to explain.

3. This is as true in the medical as in the other sciences, where the trajectory of illness is influenced by the beliefs patients and doctors hold about the course and prognosis of the illness, which are compounded by the self-fulfilling nature of medical prophecies.

4. This is reinforced by the roles people adopt, such as patients and physicians, who operate on boundaries where each group is constrained by socially constructed roles which each must play out for the other.

It follows that there is no 'natural history' of a disease or of medicine, as there is no unfolding of intrinsic biological determinants; but there is a 'social history', determined by the meaning a culture ascribes to a disease. Whereas 'scientific' explanations of diseases, at least in Eisenberg's view, have greater power for prevention and cure, their internal coherence is no greater than that of 'magical' explanations. (Fox's (1993) observations of ward-rounds in hospitals suggest 'cure' is also a socially constructed phenomenon, based upon the doctor's *need* to see the patient as cured and thus proving his/her success as a doctor, and the patient's *need* to return home, a journey which can be undertaken only when 'cured'.)

Eisenberg's statement is important for us at two levels: first for what it says about illnesses, and second for the advances it makes beyond symbolic interactionism, that is:

○ structures of beliefs evolve out of attempts to bring order to an extraordinarily messy and complicated reality

○ these belief systems can, through a reflexive mechanism, become structures in their own right

○ these structures then affect individuals so that they carry out the roles dictated by the beliefs

○ in carrying out these roles, people incorporate them into their self-identities.

Thus, it seems, social constructionism involves a two-stage process: construction by society, and construction by the individual. Let us borrow Goffman's metaphor of the stage and show how this develops that metaphor. A playwright (society) writes a play, outlining the roles of each actor and the words the actor must use. Actors learn these words, and if they do this well enough, the words become as second nature to them: as soon as they walk on stage, they lose their individuality and identify themselves as 'that' part. Away from this artificial stage, and in the 'real' world, as we go about our lives each of us carries out various 'roles' – as parent, lover, friend, employee, colleague, shopper, commuter, sportsperson, club member, and so on, and each of these contexts carries within itself certain 'lines' and 'roles' in which we find ourselves. We 'construct' ourselves just as the actor constructs him/herself into the role fashioned for them by the (at the time) invisible hand of the playwright. However, where the playwright gives the actor the role and the words, 'society' gives us our various and varying roles and the accompanying words. Rather than a conscious process of learning our lines, we have absorbed them as by osmosis, through our daily interactions within our societies. We behave as we *expect* to behave, and act as we *expect* to act within each societal role. The fundamental difference between this perspective and Goffman's is that for Goffman actors write their own lines in such a way as to present particular impressions of themselves. In this perspective, the lines have been written for the actors, who are constrained to mouth them.

From this analysis we can see that social constructionism overcomes the problems of ahistoricism and aculturalism inherent in symbolic interactionism, for it allows the possibility of building an understanding of how wider societal and cultural processes at different times and in different societies contribute to the construction of the self.

Social constructionists can be divided into two schools. In the first of these can be found post-modernists, who see language as the sole form of communication on which the self may be constructed. The second school dwells in the realm which recognises forms of communication above and beyond language as conveying the signals which lead to the construction of the self. Both regard the social realm as the location in which reality is constructed.

Post-modernist social constructionism

The necessity of language in constructing identity has been a constant thread throughout constructionism since Mead (1934). The emphasis upon language in the construction of the self has been given a new emphasis by the post-modernist turn. Post-modernism, 'is a useful term designating a profound mutation in recent thought and experience' (Sarap 1993, p.xi). This brief discussion is based upon Sarap's analysis.

There are affinities between the constructionist paradigm and post-modernism. The latter argues that the human subject has no unified consciousness but is structured by language. This assumption is found in the works of Lacan (1968), who sees no separation between self and society, with language allowing human beings to become constituted as subjects and to become social. For Lacan, society inhabits each individual. Lyotard (1971) is critical of Lacan's identification of the unconscious as a structure of language. Fascinated by the non-linguistic, he strives to give it a place in the understanding of the self. However, language, in the form of language games, characterises the self for Lyotard and represents the social bonds which hold society together. For Derrida (1970), too, the individual is constructed out of language. Language in Derrida's thought is unstable, so it becomes impossible for the individual, constructed out of such an unstable foundation, to be seen as a stable, unified entity. Derrida sees thought and perception as culturally produced, thus preventing an ethnocentric bias (Sarap 1993).

There is a tendency amongst some post-modernists to define away the role of power, Sarap (1993) argues, and he wishes to restore it to a central position. In tracing the origins of societal institutions in a process which involves starting with the present and working backwards, Sarap argues that knowledge is a power over others which gives the power to define others, an argument which has resonances for Eisenberg's analysis quoted above. Power, for Foucault (1973), has the characteristics of a network, its threads extending everywhere, so much so that the individual subjects are constituted by the power of others to define subjectivity. Power and knowledge are two aspects of the same question, Lyotard argues, the question being: who decides what knowledge is? Who knows what needs to be decided?

In post-modernist texts, the role of cause or explanation is seen to lead to evolutionist conclusions and, along with the possibility of grand theory, it is therefore virtually banished. The emphasis is upon the individual. The result is an emphasis upon diverse forms of individual and social identity, with an autonomous subject, 'dispersed into a range of plural, polymorphous subject-positions inscribed within language' (Sarap 1993, p.130). The role of metaphor in language assumes major importance, with metaphor as a rhetorical device which shapes our experience and serves to allow certain kinds of action and exclude others. 'Reality' therefore becomes problematic. It becomes a purely discursive phenomenon produced from the various language systems which provide the only means of interpreting experience. 'Reality' is reduced to the relativism of the neo-solipsism of the fragmented individual.

In sum, post-modernism bans grand theory and focuses upon the individual subject, who is an unstable entity constructed out of language. Language is precarious, its meaning slipping and changing and subject to determination by, in Foucault's terms, those with that knowledge which gives them power.

Where symbolic interactionism allowed the individual the power of defining society, or at least that part of society in which the individual interacts with others, there is in post-modernism a conception of the individual as a relatively powerless product of that which is a highly inefficient carrier of meaning: language.

Shotter writes as a post-modern social constructionist. An explication of his work will demonstrate the post-modernist turn as it is applied to social constructionism. Shotter follows post-modernist lines in arguing that we are constituted as persons through language. He argues that:

> our understanding and our experience of our reality is constituted for us, very largely, by the ways in which we *must* talk in our attempts (to put the matter almost tautologically) *to account* for it – where our experience and understanding of ourselves is a part of that reality. I say *must* because there is a morally coercive quality to the situations in which we use such talk: In accounting for ourselves we must always meet the demands placed upon us by our status as responsible members of our society, that is, we must talk in ways that are both intelligible and legitimate to others, in ways that make sense to them and relate to interests in which they can share. If we do not meet these demands we will be sanctioned; we will fail to maintain our status as autonomous persons, able to give satisfactory justifications for our actions when requested to do so; we will be treated as socially incompetent in some way. Thus my interest is not just in how we talk about ourselves, but in the problem of how we *must talk* about how we must talk about ourselves. (1985, p.168)

He says this double or reflexive concern is crucial:

> Our ways of accounting for ourselves, our accounting practices, work both to create and maintain a certain pattern of social relations, a social order, *and* to constitute us as beings able to reproduce that order in all of our practical activities. In other words, such tellings work to structure our mental capacities, our psychological makeup, as the persons we are. (1985, p.170)

These practices work by reference to exemplars or paradigms which function as 'anchor points', rooting our accounting practices within the ecology of our everyday lives. These paradigms may, however, render:

> …many important processes 'rationally invisible' to us, that is, they can work in practice to make them unreportable as organizations of commonplace events. They become unreportable because the way of talking required for their description lacks currency, either because it is treated as illegitimate, or as unintelligible, or because experience of the appropriate paradigms required to root it is lacking, or because of any combination of these factors. (1985, p.171)

In other words, we follow certain rules of action without realising these rules even exist, and in so doing we remain unaware of the wider world or the world around us. (There is a passing similarity here with Marx's concept of 'false consciousness'.)

Language is, however, indeterminate: '[E]very utterance constitutes only *an attempt* (which is hardly ever completely satisfactory) to "develop" a sensed thought-seed into an utterance-flower. What we try to say, and what we are understood as meaning, are often at odds with each other' (1985, p.109). We translate our thoughts into words, for thoughts, 'do not have an orderly form before they are realized' (*ibid.*) in speech. If thoughts are not 'real' before being translated into words, then it follows that for the human animal the very nature of being is to be found in communication. Without communication we cannot 'be'. 'Being' is to be found through our interactions with others, which means that, 'atomic individuals, possessing an inner sovereignty, each living their separate lives, all in isolation from each other – the supposed experience of the modern self – is an illusion' (1985, p.110). Language and thought, therefore, are heterogeneous sets of means or devices which help us link ourselves to our surroundings and, furthermore, embed us in a 'common sense of our own making' whereby, through the, 'creative work of semiotically linking ourselves, meaningfully, both to each other and to our surroundings…we also socially construct our identities' (1985, p.135).

The individual is therefore constituted through talk, in the manner advocated by the most famous post-modernists. How is this then turned into social constructionism? In 1993 Shotter could write that social constructionism's central assumption:

> …is that – instead of the study of the inner dynamics of the individual psyche (romanticism and subjectivism), or the already determined characteristics of the external world (modernism and objectivism), the two polarities in terms of which we have thought about ourselves in recent times – it is the contingent flow of continuous communicative interaction between human beings which becomes the central focus of concern: a self–other dimension of interaction. (1993b, p.12)

Here we have post-modernism. There are similarities, too, with Berger and Luckmann's thesis for:

> …in this scheme of things, then, the ways of 'being ordinary' available to us in our society, are just as much socio-historical constructions as our ways of being a scientist, or a lover. In other words, not only do we constitute (make) and reconstitute (remake) our own social worlds, but we are also ourselves made and remade by them in the process. It is the dialectical emphasis upon *both* the contingency *and* the creativity of

human interaction – on our making of, and being made by, our social realities – that is, I think, common to social constructionism in all its versions. (1993b, p.13)

He continues:

What in particular social constructionists want to explore, is how speakers and listeners seem to be able to create and maintain between themselves, in certain of their 'basic' communicative activities, an extensive background context of living and lived (sensuously structured) relations, within which they are sustained as the kind of human beings they are. In other words, social constructionists are concerned with how, without a conscious grasp of the processes involved in doing so, in living out different, particular forms of *self–other relationships*, we unknowingly construct different, particular forms of what we might call *person–world relations*: the special ways in which, as scientists, say, we interact with the different worlds of only theoretically identified entities; the routine ways in which as ordinary persons we function in the different 'realities' we occupy in our everyday social lives; as well as the extraordinary ways in which we act, say, when in 'love'. In this sense, a number of person–world dimensions of interaction can be seen as produced *within* the self–other dimension of interaction in a society. (1993b, p.12)

Here we have introduced the concept of the 'world', notably in the form of 'only theoretically identified entities'.

Shotter (1993a, b) develops what he calls a, 'rhetorical-responsive version of social constructionism'. The rhetorical-responsive version is, he argues, distinct from the other strand in social constructionism: the representational-referential strand which focuses upon already spoken words (e.g. Derrida) and which can therefore be objective, standing outside of the person being studied. This, 'rhetorical-responsive version of social constructionism' involves the researcher not in the 'onlooker standpoint' but in an 'instrumentally mediated involvement'. The differences between this and the objective method of observation are:

- a shift from theories to practices or accounts
- a shift from an interest in things to an interest in activities and the uses to which we put 'mental tools'
- a shift away from what goes on inside the heads of individuals to the largely social nature of individuals' surroundings
- a shift from procedures conducted on one's own to their negotiation with others

- ° a shift from starting points in reflection (when the flow of interaction has ceased) to local starting points embedded in the historical flow of social activity in daily life

- ° a shift from language being primarily for the representation of reality, to it being primarily for the co-ordination of diverse social action

- ° a shift from reliance upon our experiences as a basis for understanding our world, to a questioning of the social world. (1993a)

This rhetorical-responsive theory of meaning means that, 'in realizing the degree to which one relies upon one's responsive relations with others in being oneself, one cares about establishing a common ground with them when required' (1993b, p.201). This is different from a referential theory of meaning. It allows access to a 'knowledge of the third kind'. Knowledge of the third kind differs from that of the first two kinds of knowledge, which are concerned with why we do things and how we do them. It is a knowledge which tells us how to become part of society. It:

- ° is linked to people's social and personal identities, and is of a moral kind, 'for it depends upon the judgments of *others* as to whether its expression or its use is ethically proper or not – one cannot just have it or express it on one's own, or wholly within one's self. It is the kind of knowledge one has *only from within a social situation*, a group, or an institution, and which thus takes into account (and is accountable to) the *others* in the social situation within which it is known' (1993b, p.7). This it seems allows us to analyse the role of ideology, of belief systems, of the areas of the world which are closed off to our knowledge.

- ° can be discovered through studying how people 'shape' the everyday communicative activities in which they are involved in practice, that is, people 'see' and 'act' through their use of words, just as much as through their use of their eyes and limbs (1993b, p.15). And, just as important, we can therefore focus on what is *not* communicated, what is taken for granted, what is different (Moore 1994).

- ° explores, rather than grand narrative, local narratives, which, 'supply the set of pragmatic rules that constitute the social bond, and thus provide a framework for showing the relevance of the knowledge "discovered" by [academic] disciplines to our *social identities*, that is, its relevance to how we are "placed" in relation to those around us' (Shotter 1993b, p.32). This allows us to explore those things identified by theorists which are not overt within the everyday social world.

○ helps us, in this post-modern era, to discover each our 'identity' at a time when we are becoming, 'more immersed in communicational activities that expose us more and more to the opinions, values and lifestyles of others' (1993b, p.188). We can, through, 'the verbal processes involved in the practical authorship of oneself' develop an, 'inner dialogue in which one must use words responsively, and that the words one uses are always also another's words; we both shape and are shaped by them' (1993b, p.189). This means we must analyse the wider world, the broader society, in order to understand how it impacts upon the individual.

Yet this is a perspective grounded in language. Let us explore why the single vocabulary of verbal communication is insufficient within social constructionism.

In 1985, following C.W. Mills and Wittgenstein, Shotter could argue that linguistic behaviour has the social function of co-ordinating diverse action. Language in this view is used to achieve concerted action. Much of our talk about how talking works is influenced by the understanding that in talking we transfer already well-formed objects of thought from one location (the 'I') to another (the 'you'). This is a reductionist view of language formation – language has an active formative function, in which something only partly specified is further specified in the act of talking. Less than perfect communication is thus the normal state of affairs, with the possibility of further specification always existing (Coulter 1985). It follows that our knowledge of others has a hermeneutical quality to it: we come to know them not by induction, inference or any other process of a logical kind, but by an imaginative process of interpretation, a process that involves the creation of a conceptual whole from a succession of fragmentary parts (Coulter 1985). This means we may have no more than a partial and perhaps ill-judged understanding of others, and we may also be just as lacking in knowledge about ourselves.

Gergen (1985), too, allows us to move away from language as the building block of the self. Social constructionism, for Gergen, 'begins with radical doubt in the taken-for-granted world', asking one to, 'suspend belief that commonly accepted categories or understandings receive their warrant through observation', for, in challenging both the, 'ontology of mind current in industrialized Western culture', and the ontology of the person, social constructionism examines how we, literally, construct ourselves as people within the social world. An individual's knowledge of the world is contrived not in a straightforward manner where external sources are assumed to be 'there', as uncomplicated, pre-existent entities, but out of endogenic processes which involve thinking and the categorisation of information, and thus interpretation of exogenic (or empirical, external) knowledge. However, we possess, Gergen argues, two 'languages': the 'language of mind' or 'mental language', which is a, 'richly elaborate vocabulary for speaking of emotional conditions, processes of thought, states of consciousness, conditions of memory, intentional ends, motivational urges, and so on' (p.112), and verbal language. The former is constrained by the far narrower linguistic context. Language is, however, but one medium of communication – there are other media such as intuitions which guide actions, and the choice of medium for relating to others can have significant implications for what the world is subsequently understood to be.

It can be seen that Gergen has extended our possible vocabularies. We may therefore use an 'imaginative process' when communicating with others and with ourselves, which may consist of that elusive practice we call 'empathy'. Weiss (in Shotter and Gergen 1989) says:

> Though I never get beyond you, I do get beyond what I confront and beyond what is confrontable... When I confront you, and particularly when I confront you in sympathy, hate, fear, or love I penetrate beyond what is confrontable ... I do not merely encounter you at those times; I move into you. On your side, what I reach is continued into a depth I never fully probe. (p.6)

Social constructionism, then, is based upon symbolic interactionism. The post-modernist influence alerts us to the prospect that if people are formed out of the languages with which they communicate then they must be seen as fragmentary, unstable individuals who, following Foucault, are enmeshed in a web of power relationships. Eisenberg and Shotter allowed us to introduce the role of ideology, of belief systems, of the areas of the world which are closed off to our knowledge, so that we may also focus on what is *not* communicated, what is taken for granted, what is different, the non-overt. We must analyse too the way in which our particular late industrial society helps to shape us. The move away from focusing upon verbal language allows communication of a sensory type, between individuals and between the individual and the wider society, and allows us to relate to the forms of communication used by persons incapable of verbal articulation.

A theory of how the individual absorbs wider societal influences

We have, then, a social constructionism which is symbolic interactionism with a radical bent. What we do not have is a theory of how these external influences pass from society to the individual. Harré (1983) argued that social 'constructivism' does not provide a way of understanding how it is that singular persons can emerge from socially created devices. His attempt to fill this gap through the development of a 'theory of personal being' drawn from the philosophy of psychology, appears apposite. We will discuss it at some length here.

Harré argues that each human being's conception of themselves is more elaborate than could be explained solely by invoking the hypothesis that he or she believes him or herself to be a person amongst an array of persons, each of whom is a publicly observable being. Let us therefore begin by distinguishing between the 'person' and the 'self'. For Harré, the 'person' is the, 'socially defined, publicly visible embodied being' and the 'self' is the, 'personal unity I take myself to be, my singular inner being' which is, 'a theoretical concept acquired in the course of social interactions' (p.26). It is a self which:

- has a personal sense of identity, conceived within a continuous and unique history

- has the capacity for self-reference, that is, knows both what it is experiencing and that it is experiencing it

- is an agent, that is, conceives of itself as being in possession of an ultimate power of decision and action.

The person is the public being, the self the subjective, private being which has no physical referents. The distinctiveness of one's body serves as the basis of the identification of oneself by others, and the basis of one's personal sense of identity has also to be, at least in part, referred to bodily considerations.

The person therefore operates in the social world. Here:

> ...to be psychologically an individual is to be self-conscious and self-activating and controlling. The former includes a knowledge of one's history as well as one's current unique location in the array of persons. The latter includes one's capacities to initiate action upon things and persons other than oneself, as well as to undertake reflexive intervention in oneself. (Harré 1983, p.20)

However, 'neither self-consciousness nor self-activation and intervention is sufficient to establish personal being, since the structures of mind upon which they depend and the forms they take are derived from the social structures and linguistic practices of the communities within which people, to become people, must live' (p.23). It follows that, 'a person is not a natural object, but a cultural artefact' (p.20). So personal beings are 'social productions', and, 'to think, to perceive, to be rational and to experience emotions are cultural endowments not native achievements' (p.20).

Harré likens the concept of the self to that of a gravitational field as it is understood in physics, as a transcendental, non-observable reality. This private, highly subjective 'self' is constructed, he argues, from a theory that individuals develop about themselves, about who they are. The theory that is learned comes from the public, social realm unique to each society, and it includes the lay psychological and social theories found in that society (p.24). We deploy a concept of 'self', 'that functions like the deep theoretical concepts of the natural sciences, which serve to organize our experience and knowledge, whether or not they have observable referents in the real world' (p.145). The self is the organising principle of the psychological unities that confer subjective individuality.

How do we absorb the lessons about ourselves in order to build up a theory about who we are?

The process of theorising about the self begins in infancy, when the mother treats the child as a person rather than a merely animate being. Here, through psychological symbiosis, or 'a permanent interactive relation between two persons, in the course of which one supplements the psychological attributes of the other as they are displayed in social performances, so that the other appears as a complete and competent social and psychological being' (p.105), mothers supply the child with wishes, needs, intentions, wants and the like, and interact with the child as if it had them. We learn here how to receive messages about ourselves, and this process continues throughout our lives: 'Psychological symbiosis is a supplementation by one person of another person's public display in order to satisfy the criteria of personhood with respect to psychological competencies and attributes in day-to-day use in a particular society in this or that specific social milieu' (p.105). So we learn as children how to gain our self-concepts. From then on we rely on:

1. *Language games* involving grammatical models and locally acceptable episode structures (p.256), whereby a 'semantic transformation' 'typified by metaphor' allows us to translate our social inheritance into our sense of personal being. However, the, 'idea that linguistic forms determine psychological structures is now widely agreed to be too simplistic' (p.87), so language is only one part of the construction of the self.

2. *Self-development*, using the self-knowledge garnered from history, and the self-knowledge arrived at from moral assessment. Self-knowledge, 'is coming to see oneself in relation to a moral order' (p.260).

3. *Person history*, which gives one experiences which are synthesised to become a unity (p.144). This sense of continuity, or, 'a life-continuum organized as a trajectory from the past through the present to the future' (p.167), 'offers an experiential trajectory, so to speak, through which a person has at least the wherewithal for presenting himself to himself and others in an organized account of his own history, incorporating perspectives unique to the unified unities of point of view and point of action' (p.144).

The mechanism by which we translate these messages into theories is based on mental processes, including talking to ourselves. Harré suggests that, 'the fundamental human reality is a conversation, effectively without beginning or end, to which, from time to time, individuals may make contributions' (p.20). (The idea of 'interior self-conversations' can also be found in Mead 1934.) This implies that it is this process of internal conversation which allows us to receive and interpret the messages given to us by our environment. The process continues throughout our lives. It is developmental, with each stage dependent upon those which have gone before. The theory of the self as a conscious being is supplemented by a theory of ourselves as agents, capable of undertaking activities. I can come to obey myself.

To summarise, Harré argues that:

° we learn in infancy how to gain ideas about ourselves from the messages others in our environment give to us

° we gather the clues given to us, amalgamate them with information from our personal histories and analyse these using mental processes, most importantly an ongoing internal conversation

° the analysis results in a theory of the self, of that private, subjective being we understand ourselves to be.

The social constructionist model for analysing dementia

If we place this within our model of social constructionism as symbolic constructionism with a radical turn, we can outline our model for analysing dementia. The central question of social constructionism is what is the self or what is the person; in other words, how are identities constructed? We must examine the messages which are received by the individual, so we must examine the wider society, with its ideologies and deep belief systems. Following Harré, we know that the messages are received and the individual incorporates them and builds up a self-identity, suggesting a two-stage process for understanding the world of dementia. The first stage comprises the messages that are given – the construction of dementia as a gerontological illness; and the second stage concerns the recipient – the construction of the person as a dementia sufferer.

Dementia, especially that of the Alzheimer type, is found predominantly amongst older members of a society. The messages given by societies to their older members include:

° medical messages, so we need to look at the messages the medical world gives to older people, and how older people receive and adapt themselves to expectations

° messages about the body, necessary not just to overcome the Cartesian mind–body dualism inherent in medical messages, but also because of the negative connotations which surround the ageing body in Western societies

° if people are constructed through language, we need to explore the language that is used with and about persons with dementia.

These, then, are some of the messages sent to the ageing person. What sort of person, what sort of self-identity, is constructed out of these messages? This is a question to which the social construction of dementia can only tentatively suggest some answers. In this book we will devote the bulk of our attention to the construction of the message, for that is the area which is most amenable to research and which *constructs* the persons we are trying to understand.

CHAPTER 3

What is Dementia?
The Medical Model

There is only one definition of dementia yet there are many meanings. In this chapter we shall deal with the denotative, with the medical description of a bio-medical condition. We will examine definitions of dementia and descriptions of people with dementia, and we will see that they are all based within the medical model. But, as we shall see, there would appear to be an inherent problem in the bio-medical classification of dementia as a disease, since there is no medical consensus on what factor or factors 'cause' the condition. The basing of knowledge of dementia within the medical paradigm is therefore one fraught with problems. The chapter has two parts: the first lays out what we may call the 'classical' model of dementia, that which dominates the literature. The second provides a critique of this model, thus laying the foundations for its total deconstruction in the next section of the book.

The classical model of dementia

A history of dementia could commence with Plato, who recognised senile dementia as a state of madness under the influence of extreme old age. Some millennia later, in 1835, James Cowles Prichard described a syndrome he labelled 'senile dementia' which was characterised by, 'forgetfulness of recent impressions, while the memory retains a comparatively firm hold of ideas laid up in the recesses from times long past' (Henderson 1986). It was, however, in 1907 that Alois Alzheimer published his first report on the type of dementia which now bears his name.

Actual research into the disease, however, gained momentum only in the 1980s, since when it has been dominated by medical research (Bond 1992). Analysis of the empirically based research findings could be summarised as follows:

Cause:	Unknown
Diagnosis:	Very difficult until after death
Pathology:	Some data available, albeit inadequate
Prevalence:	Increasing body of data available, although it is somewhat unsound and inadequate for the planning of services
Effects:	Some descriptive data available
Cure:	Unknown.

Definitions of dementia and Alzheimer's disease (AD) in the classical model

Dementia is the acquired global impairment of higher cortical functions including memory, the capacity to solve the problems of day-to-day living, the performance of learned perceptuo-motor skills, the correct use of social skills, all aspects of language and communication and the control of emotional reactions, in the absence of gross clouding of consciousness. The condition is often progressive though not necessarily irreversible. (Royal College of Physicians 1982, p.139)

Alzheimer's disease is a form of dementia, being, 'a brain disorder characterised by a progressive dementia that occurs in middle or late life. The pathologic characteristics are degeneration of specific nerve cells, presence of neuritic plaques, and neurofibrillary tangles' (McKhann et al. 1984). The result is that the brain shrinks, 'with lessened cortex and white matter, and consequently enlarged lateral ventricles' (Terry 1976, p.2).

Causes of Alzheimer's disease in the classical model

There is much speculation about the cause or causes of dementia. Solving this puzzle would provide, 'the key to developing treatments that are likely to be successful' (Curran and Wattis 1989, p.13). Reviewing research into possible causes, Curran and Wattis list the following possibilities:

- ° a genetically determined susceptibility, for which there is some evidence

- ° infection – there is, however, no evidence that the disease can be transmitted

- ° an autoimmune disease, for which there is no evidence

- ° environmental factors, which may provide a possible cause

- ° head injury, which may perhaps contribute to its development

° neurotransmitter deficits, which have been, and are being, extensively investigated.

The search for a cause, the literature tells us, has met with limited success to date, so that although, 'for prevention and cure, further elucidation of causal mechanisms is essential', such hard data remain elusive (Curran and Wattis 1989, p.14).

Diagnosis of Alzheimer's disease in the classical model

The diagnosis of Alzheimer's disease in a living person has, to date, been very difficult. As Curran and Wattis (1989) have observed, 'definitive diagnosis requires neuropathological confirmation' (p.13), which is, by definition, possible only after death. There is therefore the possibility of misdiagnosis in the living person. McKhann et al. (1984) cite evidence that, 'twenty per cent or more of cases with the clinical diagnosis of Alzheimer's disease are found at autopsy to have other conditions and not Alzheimer's disease' (p.939). Home (cited in Curran and Wattis 1989), found post-mortem examinations revealed that only 6 out of 13 carefully diagnosed cases had the expected characteristics of Alzheimer's disease. Gurland et al. (1982, 1984) have shown that on follow-up many clinically diagnosed cases, 'show outcomes inconsistent with the original diagnosis' (cited in Little, Hemsley and Bergmann 1987, p.808).

The reasons for this difficulty in accurate diagnosis lie both in uncertainty about how dementia actually affects behaviour (for here is a disease the existence of which is diagnosed on the basis of behavioural changes, not pathology), and consequently in developing accurate diagnostic tools for measuring the severity of a pathological state about which such uncertainty exists. Although it is potentially important to identify the disease in its earlier stages, it is not easy to distinguish between what is assumed to be 'normal' ageing and the earlier stages of dementia.

This is because there is disagreement among medical practitioners who take on the responsibility of interpreting behaviours from a bio-medical standpoint.

Hughes (1995), for example, has noted the variations in interpretation of ageing within gerontology as either a 'natural' or 'pathological' phenomenon. Biological theorists, Hughes asserts, have not yet agreed upon a definition of what human ageing is. Bromley (1988) adopts the view that ageing is an intrinsically degenerative process occurring soon after the period of peak functional capacity (around 18–25 years).

Victor (1994), on the other hand, depicts senescence as a normal process, though characterised by impaired organic functioning and capacity to adapt. Ageing as a predictable process of psychological decline is also a prominent paradigm (Stuart-Hamilton 1994). As Hughes argues:

...many older people...expect their recall faculties to begin to fade as they age, attributing minor memory lapses, which in a younger person would go unnoticed, to the process of ageing or even to the onset of dementia...theories of psychological decline are not culturally unbiased, but have emerged within societies which have a view of old people as burdensome and problematic (p.23).[1]

Since researchers have found similar changes in the brains of 'normal' older people as are found in those who had exhibited the supposed symptoms of dementia, Terry (1976) suggests that we should ask what is 'normal' ageing. Henderson and Huppert (1984, p.5) argue that although early dementia is a term now in common usage, 'there are no specific criteria by which its presence can be asserted; it is not itself a diagnosis, but rather a rubric for the early stages of several neuropathologically distinct disorders, and little is known about its natural history'.

Little *et al.* (1987, p.808) point out that:

...the demented patient shows changes in cognition, affect and behaviour which are hard to differentiate from those observed in normal ageing or other age-related conditions. There appears no obvious boundary between normal and abnormal ageing... Furthermore, physical and affective illness and non-progressive organic brain disease can produce changes in the elderly similar to those observed in dementia although very different in outcome.

In his review of dementia, Keen concludes that: 'It is now generally agreed that dementia is distinct from normal ageing, but many signs and symptoms – and also pathological changes – are best conceived as being on a continuum from healthy old age to severe dementia' (Keen 1992, p.9). Furthermore, the aetiology of the disease is unclear and it is not known whether all cases proceed to a moderate or advanced dementia: 'In particular, little is known about features which, at ascertainment, might differentiate a benign course from a more rapid deterioration' (Henderson and Huppert 1984, p.5).

The advanced technological aids available to assist diagnosis of other psychological disorders have proved either inaccurate or extremely costly and are therefore presently unavailable for diagnosing dementia (Henderson 1986). Non-technological methods of diagnosis have therefore been sought. A Work

---

1   This tension between competing interpretations of biological phenomena exists, of course, outside gerontology and may be culturally determined. Freund and McGuire (1991) note that menopause is now indexed in the International Classification of Diseases, even though in many African and Islamic societies, women experienced few of the physiological and psychological symptoms attributed to menopause in Western societies.

Group on the Diagnosis of Alzheimer's Disease could in 1984 suggest criteria for diagnosis, but these were, 'not yet fully operational because of insufficient knowledge about the disease' (McKhann *et al.* 1984, p.939). The lengthy guidelines given by the Work Group for arriving at a diagnosis of Alzheimer's disease are based on ascertaining whether the patient demonstrates symptoms typical of the disease (after eliminating the presence of other systemic or brain diseases), and these, given the difficulties in confirming the presence of Alzheimer's disease, are themselves based on descriptive rather than proven symptoms. The diagnosis is therefore circular in nature: patients will have Alzheimer's disease if they demonstrate symptoms of the disease, although these symptoms are not yet proven to demonstrate the existence of the disease. One study has, however, suggested that the Work Group's criteria resulted in correct diagnoses in between 78 and 88 per cent of cases (Burns cited in Keen 1992).

Apart from diagnosing the existence of any form of dementia, it is necessary to identify its severity in the individual. Reviewing available measurement tools, Morris and Kopelman (1986) point out that there are, 'various instruments...available for assessing the severity of dementia' all of which, 'give a crude estimate of severity, but *none* is sufficient to make a diagnosis in the absence of extensive clinical and neuropsychological investigation' (p.601).

The literature concludes that there is therefore a need for a diagnostic tool which can accurately identify the existence of the disease, its severity and its prognosis. The search for such a measure continues.

Incidence and prevalence of Alzheimer's disease in the classical model

With regard to incidence rates, or the numbers of people becoming demented over a specified period of time, in the relative absence of research, 'our understanding of incidence is poor' (Keen 1992, p.16).

There is no such paucity of data regarding prevalence rates, or the numbers of people who have a condition at any one time. These have allowed a seeming confidence in predictions that senile dementia is probably present in between 5 and 7 per cent of the population aged 65 and over, more specifically occurring in 2 per cent of people aged 65–70 and rising ten fold by the age of 80, 'such that the prevalence in people of this age and over may be as high as 20%' (Wilcock 1988, p.18).

This apparent confidence hides marked variations between surveys. Two examples will suffice. Griffiths *et al.* (1987) found a prevalence rate of 10 per cent, with a significant overall increase over the age of 75 years. Pfeffer, Afifi and Chance (1987), however, estimated the prevalence of early dementia in a predominantly middle-class community to be 15.3% amongst all persons aged 65 and over, rising to 35.8% of those aged 80 and over. In contrast, the, 'combined prevalence of moderate, moderately severe, and severe cases' was 2.2 per cent, a figure which the researchers questioned as being unreasonably low, although they accept their finding of the very high incidence of all dementias.

The variations in findings are undoubtedly a result of both inadequate diagnostic tools and the use of different tools by different researchers. The difficulties in diagnosing dementia have been shown above. It follows that reliable diagnostic tools which are easy to administer are a *sine qua non* for the accurate establishment of the existence of dementia in the population. Problems in using existing tools have been shown by Little *et al.* (1987), who compared three existing measures and found that although the tests revealed similar overall prevalence rates, they had identified different people as suffering from dementia. The authors therefore advise, 'caution when examining epidemiological surveys which use different tools to identify cases. It is incorrect to presume that because studies report similar prevalence rates they are considering equivalent groups' (p.813).

The outcome of these estimates of prevalence, however problematic, is, 'widespread concern aroused by the lengthening human life span' with its attendant increase in incidence of dementia, so much so that there appears to be an 'approaching epidemic' to which the attentions of a variety of separate disciplines have now turned their attention (Shepherd 1984, p.10). An approximation of panic can be noted in such publications as *The Rising Tide*, which commences by noting that:

> This century has seen outstanding success in medical, social and economic progress. The consequences for health care systems will soon be upon us in full flood. Medical advances and the increasing conquest of the disabilities associated with the second half of life mean that more and more people are reaching great old age. Very old people need a lot of care in their final years, much of it because of the greatly increased incidence of mental illness and intellectual failure in old age. *Unless the changes are met, the flood is likely to overwhelm the entire health care system which at present puts most of its energy into the problems of the early and middle years of life.* (NHS Health Advisory Service 1982, p.1, emphasis added)

These worries relate to both health and social care, and to how people with dementia may care for themselves or be adequately cared for in the community.

Effects of dementia in the classical model

Lishman describes the dementia syndrome as, 'an acquired global impairment of intellect, memory and personality...without impairment of consciousness...almost always of long duration, and usually progressive' (cited in Morris and Kopelman 1986, p.49).

According to McKhann *et al.* (1984), the major cognitive processes that are impaired are:

- orientation to place and time

- memory

- language skills

- attention

- visual perception

- problem-solving skills

- social functioning

- activities of daily living.

Given the apparent impact of dementia upon the intellect and powers of communication, it is deemed difficult, if not impossible, to discover how the individual experiences life with dementia. Even where sufferers have cogent periods, the researcher is constrained from being over-intrusive for fear of precipitating anxiety and worry. Descriptions of the subjective experience of dementia are therefore based upon extrapolations from observed behaviour. The following is one example:

> *Memory* worsens. It becomes difficult to hold material in the mind as the fadeout time of current memory becomes faster. Concentration becomes poor and memories of long ago may appear as current events.

> *Orientation* causes increasing problems, as existence becomes dominated by the fight to recall 'where and when it is', with clues as to the identity of other people fading from the memory.

> *Grasp* lessens, so it becomes harder to understand what is going on and what is being said, especially if events are fast moving, with little repetition to aid memory, or when a whole series of concepts are rapidly introduced.

> *Power of Communication* becomes restricted, with difficulties of expressing even those things which are available in the memory.

> *Personality/Emotions* are affected by the stresses caused by the faulty mental mechanisms and difficulties in dealing with a normal environment.

Behaviour is altered as coping strategies, along with the reduced mental mechanisms, fail. Self-neglect is the natural companion of poor decision making mechanisms. Faulty recall, orientation and grasp may result in activities being carried out inappropriately, with these being interpreted by others as 'difficult behaviour'. (Kings Fund 1986, pp. 9–10)

From the point of view of the observer, four phases of changes in activity can be discerned:

Phase 1: there is an insidious onset of the disease, so that relatives may be unsure whether anything is wrong. At this stage, the individual becomes easily upset and angered, and has less drive and energy. Communication, comprehension and word finding abilities deteriorate as memory becomes poorer.

Phase 2: speech becomes slower, and there is increasing incompre- hension and difficulty in holding a conversation. Forgetfulness increases, as does an inability to recognise previously familiar places, people and objects. There may be difficulty in comprehending the time of day, so that day becomes night and night becomes day, and there is also 'perseveration: repetitive action and verbalisation'. At this stage, the person continues to function, but may need supervision.

Phase 3: disability is obvious by this stage. Normal orientation to time and place is lost, as is the ability to identify familiar people or events. Considerable changes in behaviour may occur, and whilst memory of long-ago events may be clear, recent events are often soon forgotten.

Phase 4: by now the individual needs help with all of the activities that encompass daily life and self-care. Powell (1985) places wandering in this phase, but this gives way to feebleness, incontinence, disorientation, and little or no verbal communication.

It should be noted that there appears to be no standard process of movement through these stages. There may be a, 'variability in the course of degenerative dementia, with some patients reaching a certain degree of impairment within a much shorter time course than other patients' (Diesfeldt, van Houte and Moerkens 1986, p.368), and some people may not develop symptoms beyond those of the earlier stages.

Prognosis in the classical model

Does the onset of dementia affect life expectancy? There appears to be a mean age of onset of dementia of the Alzheimer type of between 70 and 75 years, with a mean duration of survival of seven to eight years (Diesfeldt *et al.* 1986). Diesfeldt *et al.* found that dementia which had developed prior to the age of

76, but not that developing after this age, was clearly associated with increased mortality: 'Because of the abridgement of life expectancy, dementia of early onset seems to follow a more malignant course than late onset dementia' (p.369). However, although, 'life expectancy may not be reduced in late onset dementia, the quality of life certainly is' (p.370).

The search for a cure for Alzheimer's disease

To date no cure for Alzheimer's disease has been discovered: 'No drug strategy has so far shown any clinically significant benefit. The most that can be expected from drugs currently under development is that they will temporarily alleviate symptoms' (Curran and Wattis 1989, p.14).

Classical models of care for people suffering from dementia-type illnesses

Only one basic model of dementia care can be discerned in the literature. It is based on the view that the dementia sufferer becomes primarily a body with physical care needs.

Kitwood and Bredin (1992) argue:

> At present there is no coherent theory of the process of care for those who have a dementing illness in old age... In place of theory there is a considerable body of folklore and an abundance of tacit knowledge, the latter embodied often in the work of outstanding practitioners. Also there is a substantial portfolio of practical approaches... Often it is a fairly crude pragmatism that leads to the decision to adopt one of these approaches rather than another.

From this a model of services can be built for the professions charged with providing care for someone with dementia who, the model tells us:

- appears to have difficulty in communicating his/her needs

- will attempt to assure the assessor that he/she is capable of functioning normally

- stands a 50 per cent chance of living alone (Askham 1986)

- demonstrates difficulty in some aspects of self- and home care, but perhaps not in all

- faces irreversible decline

- presents him/herself as someone who is rapidly losing their personality, leaving only a husk behind.

Dementia sufferers therefore:

> ...need people to help them with personal and house care; to safeguard
> them (and others who may be affected) from risks such as gas or road
> traffic, from harming themselves or others, or from being harmed by
> others (for they may become vulnerable to attack, theft and so on); and
> to provide them with companionship and emotional support in their
> frequent loneliness and depression. (Askham 1986, p.2)

In sum, the model of service suggested is one in which the physical needs of
the service user take precedence, with their social needs being secondary and
mental needs assumed not to exist. In practice this model of care is one where
the service user is seen as totally dependent upon others for all their needs, and
where the provider takes over the responsibility for all decisions in their lives.

This is partly due to a deafness to the older person's attempts to articulate
their own preferences or needs. In services provided to all people, and not just
the elderly with a mental illness, there is, 'an ideology where little importance
is attached to the mentally ill person's view, and where the nature and change
in these peoples' problems can be defined only by trained experts – encapsulated
in "cognitive superiority"' (Sheppard 1991, p.168). With relation specifically
to dementing-type illness amongst older people, research findings show that,
having had the label of 'dementia' attached to them, 'even normal behaviour
is interpreted in terms of disease stages' (Bond 1992, p.16).

The result is that elderly people with dementia lose their 'voice', and
'professionals' take over the decision-making process from them. Not only are
elderly people suffering from some form of confusion or dementia, 'less able
to have a realistic knowledge of their own situation', their loss of voice results
in their being, 'less able to convince others that their wishes should be respected.
There is no doubt...that these people are most likely to have all decisions made
for them, even when they retain considerable areas of mental awareness'
(Norman 1987, p.10). The dementia sufferer has to conform to expectations
about how they should behave, based on interventions, 'designed to normalise,
to make subjects conform to the defined norms' (Abbott and Wallace 1991, p.6).

The classical model of dementia is based within a medical paradigm which
states that the syndrome is caused by changes in the brain which result in
behavioural changes that follow a series of stages during which behaviour
progressively worsens. The existence and measurement of the extent of the
syndrome can be ascertained by observing behavioural changes. Care programmes are designed based on the observed behavioural changes.

The medical model of dementia

As we noted in the introduction to this chapter, the bio-medical classification
of dementia as a disease belies the lack of consensus on what causes the

condition. Historically, of course, there are many precedents for this gap between full knowledge of aetiology and attempts to treat or cure an ailment. It is a practice which may crudely be described as 'trial and error':

> Doctors argue that much clinical iatrogenesis is an inevitable consequence of the advancement of medical science. According to this view, the frontiers of knowledge can only be moved forward by attempting new treatments, some of which may prove initially to be harmful to the patient. (Baggott 1994, p.72)

Diagnosis, as we will discuss further in Chapter 5, is not a perfected scientific act. As we have noted, post-mortem examinations have failed to confirm the clinical diagnosis in substantial proportions of former patients. Symptoms can be missed and misinterpreted, perhaps with lethal effect. Even when clusters of symptoms seem to be resolving into a recognisable pattern to the extent that they are indicating a specific syndrome, there is still much room for human error.

What room for error may, therefore, exist when symptoms may only be related secondhand, by a relative for example, and when what is clinically observable is an individual's behaviour rather than physical signs; or when those physical signs are manifest only after death?

It is with these thoughts in mind that we will criticise the classical model about aspects of elderly persons' behaviour which has been categorised as evidence of a disease called 'dementia'.

Criticising medical definitions of dementia

Here we will repeat the authoritative and generic definition of 'dementia' made by the Royal College of Physicians which served to introduce our explication of the classical model:

> Dementia is the acquired global impairment of higher cortical functions including memory, the capacity to solve the problems of day-to-day living, the performance of learned perceptuo-motor skills, the correct use of social skills, all aspects of language and communication and the control of emotional reactions, in the absence of gross clouding of consciousness. The condition is often progressive though not necessarily irreversible. (Royal College of Physicians 1982, p.139)

This definition, however, is not entirely at one with more recent attempts to explain the characteristics of one particular form of dementia included under the generic description just quoted, namely Alzheimer's disease. Alzheimer's disease is now generally defined, even if not always explicitly, as a generalised impairment of intellect, memory and personality with no impairment of consciousness'.

Although purporting to relay a clinical account of Alzheimer's disease, the Royal College of Physicians includes non-clinical and elusive concepts such as intellect and personality in its definition. What, indeed, we might ask the Royal College of Physicians, are the agreed 'problems of daily living', 'the correct use of social skills' and at what point along some spectrum does lack of 'control of emotional reactions' constitute a diseased brain?

It is this deceptively scientific mix of subjectively construed symptoms and clinically observed lesions which makes a definition of 'dementia' only plausible. This problem is compounded by references in the medical literature to such terms as 'moderate or severe forms of dementia', to distinctions between reversible and irreversible forms of dementia, to the 'heterogeneity of Alzheimer's disease' and to senile and pre-senile forms of dementia (Roth and Wischik 1985).

Dementia or Alzheimer's disease?

In the medical literature there has been much debate about whether the term 'dementia' can be acceptably applied to all cases in which individuals manifest similar behaviour. Roth and Wischik point out that the term 'Alzheimer's disease' is considered, particularly in European psychiatry, to refer only to a pre-senile form of dementia. Fraser (1987), on the other hand, asserts that all dementias are premature, therefore Alzheimer's disease should not be labelled pre-senile and others as senile. Alzheimer's disease and 'senile dementia', he states, are morphologically and biochemically similar and probably identical, but some morphological features of Alzheimer's disease are apparent in 'normal' elderly people. Fraser concludes that dementia is, 'acquired brain disease which is both diffuse and chronic' (1987, p.2). This opinion is opposed by Roth and Wischik. Referring to early and late onset dementia, they claim that, 'a growing body of neurobiological evidence has tended to support the existence of a line of demarcation between the two conditions' (1985, p.73).

We shall not attempt to analyse, let alone assess, the relative validity of various bio-medical evidence which has been used to identify an association between neurobiological conditions *post mortem* and dementia, although the subject will be returned to in Chapter 4. There is a proliferation of books and articles written from a medical perspective which provide data derived from post-mortem examinations of persons of various ages who exhibited or did not exhibit signs of dementia, none of which will be listed here for to do so would be invidious. Our interest lies in examining the issue of a dominant medical model of dementia and whether there is scope for alternative models to be considered.

Key issues

The thrust of research into dementia has been almost exclusively bio-medical. This approach, based as it is in the positivist tradition of orthodox medicine, seeks to establish a cause–effect relationship by isolating specific variables which alone could account for an 'abnormal' condition. The idea of a 'cause' is, however, highly problematic. Indeed, in one sense, theories about causality impinge upon the metaphysical. To identify, for example, a virus which 'causes' a particular disease is not necessarily to explain why some people are more or less susceptible to that virus. Medical theories are not immortal; neither are they independent of social and cultural contexts, while medical practice often reflects dissent among contemporary practitioners about what is considered to be the most effective response to particular ailments.

Payer (1990) has drawn attention to the more invasive medicine practised in the USA, where the expectation is for something 'to be done'. Rooted in the dominant ethos of private competitive enterprise, this approach is made explicable – but not necessarily wholly appropriate in terms of effective care or cure – by the social context. Payer also notes the pressure on German general practitioners to deal swiftly with patients by prescribing drugs, because of the criteria set down for doctors' remuneration which is a relatively small fee per medical 'transaction'. We shall be dealing more expansively in Chapter 4 with the contextual relativism of medical practice.

Varying responses among consultant physicians to similar presenting problems have been well documented (Close *et al.* 1993; Coulter, McPherson and Vessey 1988; Eddy 1984; Glover 1938). One example is what has appeared to be fluctuating fashions in treating 'glue ear' among children. Removing the tonsils was virtually *de rigeur* a few decades ago; then grommets fitted into the ear replaced the former, more invasive practice. Now there seems to be a return to tonsillectomies, but what treatment the patient will receive depends also on which consultant is dealing with the case (Martin *et al.* 1991).

Such ambiguities about 'best practice' may stem from professional perplexities around the 'cause' of the problem and from the predominant bio-medical model of disease, issues we will explore in Chapter 5. It is sufficient, perhaps, at this point merely to emphasise the imprecision in some areas of medical theory and practice, both cross-culturally and within cultures. It was for this reason that Cochrane (1972) advocated the wide application of random controlled trials so that efficiency and effectiveness within the medical domain could be improved. The growing appeal of alternative or complementary medicine and the 'watchful waiting' approach in nursing bear witness to some doubt about the exclusiveness of orthodox medicine as effective therapy, and this doubt has arisen because alternative theories about the causes of disease are being seriously considered or reconsidered.

Following this line of thought, the remedy for certain diseases may lie not with the discoveries of ever-advancing medical research, but with greater control over the environment, over individual lifestyle and over social inequalities; and effective means of control may have more to do with personal and political responsibility and awareness than with treatment. In one important aspect of medical practice – the prescribing of drugs – economic pragmatism has intervened to bring about wholesale change. Had there been universal or near universal agreement in medical circles about the efficacy of drugs in controlling and curing disease, there would undoubtedly have been an outcry against this political decision. The muted response must, therefore, indicate acceptance that prescribing drugs was not always essential and that their remedial effect was not always predictable.

Setting out some of the doubts and uncertainties evident in medical theory and practice is not a particularly radical activity. But if the diagnosis and treatment of conditions whose symptoms can be articulated and/or bodily signs materially observed are problematic, what room for error and conflicting opinion might there be in the diagnosis and treatment of diseases whose only indication is behavioural?

Key questions

Certain questions related to the definition of dementia need to be asked if we are to enhance our understanding of what is generally considered to be a socially demanding and economically burdensome disease:

1. If dementia is manifested through abnormal behaviour, why does the bio-medical perspective dominate medical research and practice rather than a psychological or psychiatric approach?

2. What is the current knowledge base on which the bio-medical approach is validated as authentic?

3. What evidence is there that 'reversible dementias' are similar to, or different from, 'non-reversible dementias'?

4. At what point along a spectrum of non-conformist behaviour can the term 'dementia' be acceptably applied and for what reasons?

5. To whom is 'dementia' a problem and in whose interest is a bio-medical approach likely to be applied?

Current theories of the causes of dementia are inadequate in providing answers to these questions.

Theories of the causes of dementia

PSYCHOSOMATIC FACTORS[2]

Fraser (1987) described a psychological examination of dementia as, 'dense and virtually unchartered (sic.) territory' (p.20). There have, however, been some attempts at understanding symptoms such as memory lapses and impaired orientation as responses to traumatic life events and to the onset of old age. In 1922 Ferenczi postulated the theory that the symptoms of dementia were not a manifestation of a damaged organism but a psychotic reaction to the damage itself. Wilson (1955) suggested that dementia had all the hallmarks of a psychosomatic disorder resulting from a restricted life which had become narrow and meaningless. Morgan (1965) interpreted signs of dementia as, 'a defence against personal and inevitable death' wherein individuals selectively remembered past events, excluding the more recent since these would remind them of their impending demise.

In reviewing several such psychosomatic theories, Miller (1977) concluded that though they remained untested in a scientific sense, they provided an interesting proposition that some of the symptoms of dementia might be the result of a patient's reactions to the organic changes which were taking place within the brain.

Fraser (1987) reviewed the literature on possible predisposition to dementia in the wake of critical life events, particularly retirement, bereavement and isolation. His conclusion was that with respect to these variables, 'no compelling evidence exists where dementia is concerned' (p.22). Evidence from his own collaborative research also indicated that an active intellect after retirement is not a safeguard against dementia (Van der Cammen et al. 1987).

What emerges from the fairly limited efforts to interpret dementia as a personal response to either the condition itself or to the concomitant 'disbenefits' of increasing age, is a corpus of hypotheses which remain unconfirmed but not, as yet, refuted.

BIO-MEDICAL EVIDENCE

Medical research has for some time been attempting to discover the cause of dementia.

Efforts have concentrated on the post-mortem analysis of people who have in their lifetime exhibited signs of the disease and, in some research, the results have been compared with the brains of non-sufferers (Lishman 1994). A review of a large number of articles, papers and books reveals the extent to which

---

2   We must here note our indebtedness to Fraser's (1987) literature review, on which much of this
    section is based.

medical research has produced convergent opinion about neuropathological and biochemical factors associated with dementia.

Roth and Wischik (1985) state that:

> The most conspicuous changes which characterise the transition from normal ageing to dementia of late onset (AD), are the proliferation of plaques and tangles in the cortex, and the appearance of the cholinergic deficit in the temporal cortex. (p.81)[3]

Such correlations which have been indicated by medical research do not, however, establish causation. Even if neuropathological factors were incontrovertibly linked with dementia, this would still leave the question unresolved as to why such factors occur. But even such post-mortem data (Roth 1994) reported in the medical literature are still in a very tentative stage.

Price *et al.* (1982) reported that there were no data available to suggest that cholinergic lesioning led to the formation of plaques.

The validity of the hypothesis concerning the formation of tangles has also been questioned. Wisniewski *et al.* (1979) argue that tangles form as a result of viral infections and Selkoe *et al.* (1979) note a connection between tangles and aluminium intoxication. This latter theory is still current, yet it is categorically refuted by Roth and Wischik (1985): 'There is no evidence to suggest that Alzheimer-type neuritic plaques are formed along with tangles in the course of viral infections or aluminium intoxication in experimental animals' (p.85).

They add that, 'solution of the problem of the tangle would advance knowledge of the aetiology and pathogenesis of Alzheimer's disease...unless the view is taken that plaques and tangles are epiphenomena' (p.89). Fraser's wide-ranging analysis of research findings casts doubt on the wisdom of searching for any one causal theory. In his view, the 'choline hypothesis' should not be considered as a theory but as a group of observations that associate Alzheimer's disease with deficiencies in the central cholinergic neurotransmitter system. Other possible 'explanations' also remain highly suspect: these have proposed that virus infection, autoimmune deficiencies or ingested toxins might be the cause of Alzheimer's disease. Multi-causal hypotheses are offered by Crapper, Karlik and Devon (1978) and Wurtman (1985) as starting points for further research rather than carefully formulated empirically derived results.

GENETIC INHERITANCE

Published research has appeared since the 1930s when Sanders, Schenk and Van Veer (1939) detected amongst one family seventeen affected members over

---

3   Plaque: an area in a tissue culture where the cells have been destroyed by infection with a virus; tangle: this refers to a confused mass of nerve fibres; cortex: the outer layer of the brain; cholinergic: refers to the releasing of the chemical acetylcholine by the nerve fibres.

four generations. But, as Fraser points out, there is little agreement about whether a distinction could be drawn between Alzheimer's disease and 'senile dementia'. Much of the current literature still agonises about such a distinction. In their study, Larsson *et al.* (1963) analysed 719 cases diagnosed as senile dementia in Swedish hospitals between 1935 and 1950. Their investigation concluded that there could not be any unitary genetic origin either for Alzheimer's disease or senile dementia.

Breitner and Filstein (1984), referring to the findings of Larsson and colleagues, stated that, if Alzheimer's disease and senile dementia were to be accepted as a single category, the results could point to a dominant pattern of genetic inheritance. The work by Heston *et al.* (1981), Whalley *et al.* (1982), Heyman *et al.* (1983) and by Wright and Whalley (1984) supports the hypothesis about genetic inheritance, although the question of whether such genetic predisposition could be explained on the basis of a single gene or whether a polygenic inheritance is more likely remains unresolved.

A good deal of this research into genetic patterns has addressed the matter of whether senile dementia and Alzheimer's disease are distinctive conditions. The argument in favour of using Alzheimer's disease as a generic term to include both 'pre-senile' and 'senile' dementia has been supported in the literature by data which indicate that loss of memory is almost always accompanied by language disorder (dysphasia) and apraxia (inability)/dyspraxia (impaired ability) to perform purposeful movements of part of the body because of brain lesions.

COMMENT

Although there may be evidence to suggest, or even affirm, that some people may be genetically predisposed towards dementia, there are still no research data on why this phenomenon should be. This caveat is true of all the following hypotheses or theories aired. Indeed this line of enquiry has generated the type of evidence which typifies bio-medical theories about the aetiology of dementia. While still at the stage of trying to isolate a neuropathological syndrome which can explain the cause of dementia, tests to measure the scale and intensity of dementia have been devised and administered, and therapeutic interventions applied. Fraser (1987) has no problem with this apparent illogicality: '...it is axiomatic in medicine that lack of knowledge about the precise cause of a disease is not a bar to effect therapy: diabetes, parkinsonism and hypothyroidism are classic examples' (p.24).

One might argue with equal confidence that the 'trial and error' approach is no guarantee that medical intervention – notably the application of drugs – will not inflict damage. Illich's (1979) thesis relating to iatrogenic diseases can be upheld by citing firm evidence of the harm inflicted on patients by the medical profession. His radical assault upon the hegemony of the bio-medical model of diagnosis and treatment of disease may go too far for some, but his commentary seeks at least to scrutinise the grounds on which orthodox medicine has constructed its social power base.

Florence Nightingale's modest yet powerful dictum that the purpose of nursing and medical care was 'to do the sick no harm' should serve to provide a cautionary brake on ill-informed invasive therapy. 'Watchful waiting' and planned non-intervention may prove as effective as anything else. The key concept which clearly needs to be made explicit in this debate is 'effectiveness'.

DOWN'S SYNDROME AND OTHER DISEASES

Although some research has shown similarities between the brains of Down's syndrome and Alzheimer's disease patients, there is conflicting evidence concerning the accompanying intellectual and cognitive impairment. Deficiencies in acetylcholine synthesis and in aluminium accumulation have been detected, respectively by Yates (1990) and Crapper, Karlik and Devon (1978). So far the attempt to relate both Down's syndrome and Alzheimer's disease to cellular protein abnormalities has not produced any indicative findings.

INFECTIVE MODELS

Other lines of research enquiry have centred on the hypothesis that certain diseases affecting the brain may be transmitted. Relatively rare conditions such as Creutzfeldt-Jakob disease (CJD), kuru (a condition confined to a tribe in New Guinea) and scrapie (an infectious disease found in adult sheep and goats) have been the subject of experiments with animals. Pathological analysis revealed a spongiform change throughout the brain in victims of these diseases. However, the supposition that these diseases could be the result of a virus has been refuted by Rohwer (1984). The transmission theory which sought to establish whether, for example, CJD could be passed from one human to another has, on close scrutiny, served only to establish an iatrogenic origin, since the disease appears to have been contracted as a result of interperson transplants (Corsellis 1979).

Having sifted the evidence from a number of research studies, Fraser (1987) concludes that, 'the infective model of Alzheimer's disease is based on certain resemblances which on present evidence are superficial. There are in fact more differences than similarities between Alzheimer's disease and conditions known to be transmissible' (p.15).

TOXINS

The damage to the brain which can be caused by over-exposure to certain noxious metals has received growing publicity. Current fears, for example, about the possible effect of high levels of lead in the air are causing considerable public anxiety. The poisonous effect of mercury leaching from tooth fillings has also been well documented. Some studies of Alzheimer's disease have suggested that aluminium may contribute at least in part to the onset of dementia. High levels of aluminium intake have been associated with occupational disease (McLaughlin *et al.* 1962) and a form of dementia (Garruto, Yanagihara and Gajdusek 1985).

McDermott *et al.* (1979) carried out a study which matched ten brains from Alzheimer's disease patients with nine controls and found that there was no significant difference in aluminium concentrations between the Alzheimer's disease brains and the control group. Yet the questions remain of whether aluminium merely accumulates in the brain with the ageing process and why it is present in statistically significant levels in the brains of persons who suffered from conditions quite different from Alzheimer's disease (Lapresle *et al.* 1975; Thal 1984).

COMMENT

Research studies which claim to have detected associations between biochemical abnormalities in the brain and various forms of dementia have produced unconvincing evidence. Not only have any empirically derived data from post-mortem examinations failed to provide any predictive value in tracing the possible onset of dementia, such evidence as there is has not managed to isolate physical characteristics which are predominantly or exclusively related to dementia-type conditions. In this respect, hypotheses which focus on toxic impact on the brain remain suspended between cause and effect. Unusually high levels of chemicals within the brain could prove to be the result of other precipitating factors as yet unidentified. To suggest that dementia can be managed or controlled by the ingestion of drugs or by any other avowedly therapeutic intervention is, in our present state of knowledge, logically untenable and ethically questionable.

Social and psychological theories
DEMENTIA AS A DEFENCE MECHANISM

An early proponent of a multi-causal explanation of dementia was Gruenthal (1927). He suggested that senile dementia and cerebral atrophy occurring in certain old people did not constitute a sufficient cause, 'but that unidentified, pathogenic factors had to be present as well'. This was a proposition supported by Rothschild (1937), who described dementia as, 'a long process which has its roots not just in certain impersonal tissue alterations, but in psychological stresses and in special problems which affect the ageing population'. Morgan (1965) extended this speculative discourse with his assertion that senile dementia was a, 'senescent defence against a personal and inevitable death'. According to Morgan, the loss of recent memory which typifies dementia represented a defence mechanism against the constant reminder of the person's age, increasing infirmity and impending death.

Meacher (1972) and Folsom (1967, 1968) also subscribed to the view that old people manifesting signs of disorientation were reacting to a sense of loss of purpose and of identity and, in the case of those in residential homes, to a distressing environment. Miller (1977) reviewed a variety of theories or, perhaps put more accurately, conjectural suppositions, and expressed the regret that there was no experimentally derived evidence to support them. He did, however, draw attention to inferences derived from the literature, notably that, 'some of the signs and symptoms of dementia might be caused primarily by the disease process whilst others could be the consequence of the patient's reactions to these basic changes'. People suffering from depression, for example, may suffer memory loss which could be an effect and/or cause of this defect.

DEMENTIA AS A REACTION TO TRAUMATIC EVENTS

One of the methodological issues in testing for correlation between responses to specific incidents and dementia is that in many studies the data have been generated by questions put to relatives of the sufferer. This approach depends heavily upon retrospective interpretation of behaviour and consequential problems in assigning that behaviour to an identifiable point in time. Amster and Krauss (1974) were unable to discern whether life crises were more prevalent among dementia sufferers and, therefore, a possible cause of such a condition, or whether the onset of dementia detracted from the capacity to cope with stress. Jorm (1990) concluded that the evidence on life stress as a possible cause of Alzheimer's disease is negative.

An extensive review of the evidence for a causal relationship between such life experiences as isolation, bereavement, retirement and mental debility carried out by De Alarcon (1971) revealed no substantial findings which might confirm such an interconnection.

SOCIAL-DEMOGRAPHIC VARIABLES

There is agreement in all studies which have focused on rates of dementia among the population that it is age-related. Although attempts to define 'mild' or 'severe' dementia are fraught with interpretive difficulties, published data strongly suggest that there is a substantial increase in the annual incidence of dementia from 65–69 years of age to 80 and over, with some levelling off when people reach the age of 90 plus (e.g. Gurland *et al.* 1980; Helgason 1977; Pfeffer *et al.* (1987).

Statistics on other possible variables and their links with dementia are much less indicative of a correlation. Several surveys (e.g. Kay and Bergmann 1980; Larsson *et al.* 1963; Torak 1978) have found that the rates of dementia among males and females reflect the ratio of the sexes in the general population. Disentangling cause from effect has been particularly difficult in those studies which examined such factors as socio-economic status, unemployment, area of residence and social isolation (Bergmann 1975; Kay, Beamish and Roth 1964; Torak 1978.) Fraser (1987) concludes from an analysis of findings from social-demographically oriented studies that the evidence for any causal link is unclear and not convincing.

PERSONALITY

Early studies, for example that carried out by Post (1944), concluded that dementing hospital patients tended to be more rigid and obsessional than non-dementing patients controlled for age, and Oakley's (1965) work supported this conclusion. Since, however, these inferences depended for their validity on the retrospective accounts of relatives, the same methodological inhibitions apply as in the case of the 'life events' research mentioned above.

Other studies have sought not to test for a cause–effect model of personality-related factors, but to look for evidence of an association between personality and symptom formation. In particular, Gurland (1981) cited two studies which indicated that personality might influence adaptation to the changes brought about by dementia. Gianotti (1975) described a personality type with a tendency to 'confabulate' (to imagine experiences in order to compensate for loss of memory). This was seen to be a more positive adaptation to impairment and was displayed by individuals who were assessed by the researchers as ambitious, upwardly mobile and independent in nature. Sinnott (1977) – the other study referenced by Gurland – claimed that the ability to become flexible in assuming social roles was a crucial adaptive quality in dementia sufferers.

Diagnostic tests

Older people who exhibit certain behavioural characteristics may be diagnosed as having a dementing-type illness. There is, it is clear, neither consensus nor adequate theorising about the causes of such diseases in older people. However, the disease is diagnosed, so it is apposite here to discuss how this is done.

A large number of tests have been devised in order to quantify the mental and physical states of elderly people. Wilkin and Thompson (1989) have provided a critical analysis of some of the more widely used tests designed to establish the capacity of older people to carry out the daily tasks of living. While their critique is valuable in drawing attention to some of the strengths and limitations of the various tests, the fundamental hypothesis on which such tests are based is tacitly accepted. This relates to the proposition that the tests are actually an objective and accurate means of measuring an abstraction (e.g. 'capacity') by attaching numerical scores to observable behaviour-based indicators. The generic term for these scaled tests is usually a 'dependency measure'. This term suggests that the measures proceed from a negative orientation. Consequently, there is a danger that those who use various rating scales of this kind might be looking for indices of dependency rather than independence. This is, perhaps, an over-statement, a semantic quibble, and yet – as we shall observe later in the book – the language used to depict old age may itself impose a negative stereotype image upon an extremely heterogeneous social 'group'.

One example of such a test is the Crichton Royal Behavioural Rating Scale (CRBRS) which was originally developed by Robinson (1968) for use in the assessment of psychogeriatric patients at the Crichton Royal Hospital in Dumfries, Scotland, but which has also been a medium of assessment in residential and nursing homes and geriatric wards. Part of this scale – the 'confusion sub-scale' – can be used independently of the main scale as a, 'screening instrument to detect individuals likely to be suffering from a dementing illness' (Wilkin and Thompson 1989, p.15).

The headings under which the scored items are arranged are set out in Table 3.1. Those relating to the confusion sub-scale are memory, orientation and communication. A study by Evans *et al.* (1981) appeared to indicate that confusion sub-scale scores of 4 or higher were, in all cases examined, associated with a diagnosis of dementia. In this way, the sub-scale has acquired an accepted degree of validity. Although the CRBRS has had some modifications since it was originally devised, its main components and scoring system remain.

Table 3.1 Crichton Royal Behavioural Scale

Scale Items	Scoring	Confusion sub-scale
Mobility	All items 0–4 except memory and feeding (0–3)	Sum of scores on memory, orientation and communication.
Memory		
Orientation		
Communication		
Cooperation	Items scores are summed to produce total scores. These are grouped into six ranges (0–1, 2–5, 6–10, 11–15, 16–20, 21–38)	Scores are presented in four ranges: 0–1 Lucid
Restlessness		2–3 Intermediate 4–6 Moderately confused 7–11 Severely confused
Dressing		
Feeding		
Bathing		
Continence		

Yet despite its popular acceptance as an instrument of measurement it has, according to Wilkin and Thompson, some marked weaknesses:

> The major weaknesses of the CRBRS are the arbitrary nature of the scaling and the restricted range of items. As in most other scales, the authors have created an additive scale out of what is at best ordinal data. It remains unclear what different scale scores mean. There is no basis for assuming that a score of 10 implies twice as much dependency as a score of 5 or even that two individuals scoring 10 are equally dependent since their scores may be derived from different items. (Wilkin and Thompson 1989, p.18)

Given these fairly stern reservations, some doubt must be cast on the ability of such tests to measure individual attributes. In addition to these technical concerns expressed by Wilkin and Thompson, even well-confirmed inter-rater reliability scores may not eliminate the possibility that tests of this nature are fairly blunt instruments. Results from the CRBRS correspond quite closely with clinical diagnoses of dementia, but this tells us very little about the logic of evidence on which such diagnoses are based. In fact, diagnostic tests and dependency measures are rooted in a medical model of 'normality'.

Allied to this particular orientation in assessing deviation from some arbitrary standard of normal behaviour is an assumption about how people 'ought to behave' in hospital or residential settings. The various dependency measures are at one in positing compliance as the expected behavioural norm. On the 'co-operation' scale for example, residents would gain a low rating if they displayed 'independent ill-directed activity'. This means that they would attempt to perform tasks independently but usually incorrectly, 'for example, will not be dressed but cannot dress self though attempt is made'. On another widely used behaviour rating scale – the Clifton Assessment Procedures for the Elderly (CAPE) – there are a number of items purporting to 'measure' (apparently) socially acceptable behaviour.

These include:

- he/she helps out in the home/ward
- he/she keeps him/herself occupied in a constructive or useful activity (works, reads, plays games, has hobbies, and so on)
- he/she socialises with others
- he/she is willing to do things suggested or asked of (*sic.*) him/her
- he/she hoards apparently meaningless items (wads of paper, string, scraps of food, and so on).

Wilkin and Thompson draw attention to some of the technical strengths and weaknesses in the CAPE battery of items. For example, only 3 of the 18 items deal with mobility and self-care, and some of the wording is imprecise, that is, what do the terms 'sometimes' and 'often' mean in the scoring system? But they appear to accept without question the highly suspect premise on which the whole assessment is based, particularly in relation to what constitutes normal behaviour within an institution (or in any other setting for that matter). What can be inferred from various scores on the items listed above is that elderly persons may or may not at all times behave in a manner that corresponds with norms prescribed by medical and other care practitioners.

The criteria used to define degrees of dementia are contained in one item:

*   he/she is confused (unable to find way around, loses possessions)

0   almost never confused

1   sometimes confused

2   almost always confused.

It might be uncharitable to go further and suggest that an elderly person, in these circumstances, is likely to be construed as confused and socially deviant if he or she fails to meet the expectations of staff regarding what constitutes a well-run hospital or home.

Spurious measures of dependency serve to uphold professionals' control over definitions: 'confused', 'dependent', 'un-cooperative' may be symptoms not of physical or mental incapacity but of a resistance to oppression through an assertion of individuality or, as Kitwood (1990) has termed it, 'personhood'.

It is on such value-laden bases that 'measures' of dementia are often constructed. Their selectivity appears to be justified not by any empirical evidence but by the circular argument that scores produced by the completion of such instruments correspond closely with those judgements made about old people by other professionals. The term 'validated measure' in relation to psychological tests of this kind is highly problematic, since the central construct on which they are based – namely 'dependency' – has been formulated according to criteria that are largely arbitrary and professionally partisan. Like 'intelligence', dependency and dementia are recognisable and capable of being measured only by those who have the power to define them. 'When I use a word,' Humpty Dumpty said in *Through the Looking Glass*, 'it means just what I choose it to mean'. Carroll and his characters contrived to make the surreal appear normal; the bio-medical experts sometimes manage to make the normal appear to be surreal.

Comment

The foregoing narrative depicting the development of professional interest in dementia began with ostensibly 'objective' bio-medical interpretations and attempted explanations of physiological factors associated with behavioural symptoms described in medical terms as evidence of dementia and/or Alzheimer's disease. Other social and psychological 'theories' or, more accurately, propositions, were then set out. All of these propositions were derived initially from observed behaviour. Bio-medical researchers continue seeking to establish confirmatory evidence which would link dementia with neurological lesions in an effort to discover ultimately a means of preventing or delaying the development of this 'disease'. A brief analysis of two dependency measurement scales devised for use primarily, but not exclusively, in psychiatric hospitals, profiled the constricting perception of what amounts to 'normal behaviour', the criterion by which elderly persons as subjects of these measures are deemed to be in need of professional interventions.

The construction of such scales demonstrates in a very concrete way the means by which professionals in various disciplines have tried to mould highly individual characteristics into a uniform syndrome called 'dementia'. The dependency measures illustrate, albeit in a particularly ham-fisted manner, the flimsy edifice on which some scientific theory and practice may be based.

The classical model of dementia provides a description, rather than a theory, where dementia is seen as, 'a medical category defined in social terms as a loss of intellectual power which leads to difficulties in remembering, making decisions, thinking through complex ideas, carrying out practical tasks, retaining information and acquiring new skills' (Bond 1992, p.6). This definition is, according to Bond, a natural concomitant of the epistemological basis of the medical domination of research into dementia to date, whereby health professionals have medicalised the care of people with dementia. The dominance of this medical frame of reference results in dementia being seen as a 'medical problem', with the result that, 'we have mandated the medical profession to define appropriate treatment for the social behaviour and evolved the process of medicalisation. Other professions, having accepted the bio-medical model of dementia, reinforce the medicalisation of dementia through professionalising care' (Bond 1992, p.15).

The construction of much scientific theory, including medical scientific theory, rests initially upon individual perception which, in time to come, may or may not be confirmed as an accurate interpretation of events. Yet, as Hawking (1995) has shown, the development and general acceptance of scientific theory has historically been subject to the political, moral and religious influences of those in positions of power. Proponents of social constructionism would argue that it is currently the scientists themselves who are able to exert a potent influence on what forms of knowledge become socially dominant.

CHAPTER 4

Interpreting Dementia
Psychological and Linguistic Models

The psychological model

So far, the dominant medical approach to understanding the nature of dementia has failed, as it has failed to understand the nature of any illness. As R.D. Laing (1967) asserted 30 years ago, you cannot experience my experience other than through me: 'We can see other people's behaviour, but not their experience' (p.15). This is perhaps an obvious, yet important, statement. It is important because in the context of attempts to define and identify the causes of some human condition labelled by clinicians as 'dementia', the personal dimension of feeling has been largely ignored and the label itself – because it is so prescriptive – has served to exclude other interpretations of what is a multi-dimensional state of being.

What other interpretations are there and what – in the current policy climate of user consultation in matters of health and social care – is the evidence gleaned from communication with those people who are deemed to suffer from dementia?

One under-researched paradigm is the conceptual framework based in *socio-linguistics*. No extended study that we know of has attempted to analyse what so-called 'dements' talk about, how they express themselves and what their conversing means. There is a danger, perhaps, in drawing a false analogy at this point between acceptable and non-acceptable levels of deviant linguistic expression. To unravel the meaning of some poetry or religious or mystical expression is sometimes very difficult. There are some experiences which defy their full articulation in even a copious lexicon such as English. Laing again: 'I cannot say what cannot be said, but sounds can make us listen to the silence' (Laing 1967, p.35). The question is: when does apparent gibberish become exalted to inspiration, to altered consciousness – not drug-induced but prompted by an experience not fettered by 'normality'? Some of the richest insights into the meanings of madness, for example, are to be found not in the theses of psychiatrists but in the works of Shakespeare, Dostoyevsky and Blake. Dementia immediately implies mindlessness; do we assume that people suffering from – or blessed with? – dementia speak only gibberish?

Tom Kitwood is probably the foremost advocate today of alternative approaches to the understanding of dementia. Some key articles in *Ageing and Society* have exposed the flimsiness of medical evidence relating to the aetiology and even definition of dementia. One of his main contentions is that, 'the relation between brain, mind and dementia remains obscure, there is both a logical and empirical problem about the standard paradigm of dementia' (Kitwood 1989, p.4). He argues that the change in brain tissue and the pathology found in the brains of people suffering from senile dementia of the Alzheimer's type (SDAT) after death is not primarily causal but epiphenomenal or consequential. This casts doubt on whether dementia is an organic disease. Kitwood's thesis is that every event, for example, having a desire-feeling, is accompanied by a corresponding biochemical-electrical brain state. Selfhood corresponds to a structural configuration in the brain. Enduring function gradually becomes structure. One of the crucial issues raised by Kitwood is that of causation and restoration: '...there is no sound reason in biology for assuming that functional change is always the consequence of prior cellular pathology' (Kitwood 1989, p.13).

If mental 'state' or 'events' bring about, or are accompanied by, neuropathological changes, the question then is whether these changes can be restored to the former condition; in other words, can the lesions in the brain be repaired? Can there be such a phenomenon as 'rementia'? Kitwood's hypothesis is that one of the key factors is the extent to which the 'experiential self' has or has not been well developed, that is, an integrated centre grounded in feeling and emotion. For this 'experiential self' can remain when the 'adapted self' (derived from role performance and from meeting other people's expectations) declines, as it often does in people of advancing years. According to Kitwood, this would explain how some older people remain intact as a social and communicative being despite the presence – identified *post mortem* – of pathological processes in the brain.

This hypothesis is worth considering, but in our present state of both pathological and psychological knowledge in relation to dementia the associative links between brain and mind and self could lead to other hypothetical constellations. For example, we might postulate a non-impaired experiential self but a damaged brain; or an impaired self but a non-damaged brain. Even if we accept what might amount to an empirically sound hypothesis – that emotional responses trigger chemical processes, so that when we are embarrassed our faces go red or when we are frightened the colour drains from us – such bodily changes may be only transitory, leaving the organism unimpaired.

We know that not everyone's cheeks go red when suffering embarrassment and we can, therefore, logically accept that emotions and life events may affect individuals differently.[1]

What is important about Kitwood's general line of reasoning is that the bio-medical paradigm of cause–effect – that is, some as yet unknown agent brings about chemical changes in the brain which impair certain cognitive processes made manifest in the afflicted individual's capacity to communicate and to behave in a manner which may be described as normally oriented – this model of dementia and its aetiology are reversed. Social experiences in the life of certain individuals prompt them to respond to an external environment in such a way that the conventional adapted self can no longer be sustained. The way of dealing with dementia within a bio-medical framework is to attempt to 'manage' the disease by medication and intensive physical support and tending. Citing evidence of rementia, Kitwood states that we could argue that care-giving involves something far more skilled than, 'attempting to adjust the dementing person to our (cognitive) reality' (p.14). In another paper he adds that, 'a care practice…is relatively ineffective without a coherent theory' (Kitwood and Bredin 1992, p.269).

The typical medical approach to therapy justified by Fraser (see above) is described by Kitwood and Bredin as 'a fairly crude pragmatism' (1992, p.269).

Essentially, Kitwood's attempt at theory-building is situated firmly in a social constructionist paradigm which we shall deal with in much greater detail later. At this point in the discussion, we can say that Kitwood views dementia as a disease designed by the medical profession as part of its perceived special social prerogative to define the human condition in all its manifestations and social contexts. The dominating perspective – Foucault's '*le regard*' – focuses on efforts to maintain the afflicted individual for as long as possible within a socially approved milieu. The problem is the dementing person. Kitwood's riposte to this view is that, 'the dementing illness of one person brings to the surface a much larger problematic which challenges our commonsense and customary ways of being' (Kitwood and Bredin 1992, p.274).

Comment

Is Kitwood's developing thesis any more than fanciful conjecture; a set of rather florid speculative propositions which have, perhaps, even less foundation in empirical evidence than the bio-medical discourse so reviled by the social constructionist and anti-psychiatry schools of thought? Much of Kitwood's argument relies on evidence supplied by carers, and he acknowledges this and

---

1   For an interesting discussion and literature review concerning blushing see Cutlip and Leary (1993).

the fact that almost all the evidence on rementia is anecdotal. He stresses that, 'it is very important for the understanding of dementia that this be put to the test of systematic enquiry' (Kitwood and Bredin 1992, p.278).

One such empirically derived set of data has been offered by Rovner *et al.* (1990). Their study showed that old people manifesting signs of dementia can stabilise when provided with a care environment that fosters activity and co-operation. This raises doubts about the classical medical model of dementia as a progressive disease involving different stages through which the patient ineluctably passes. Following on from this finding, Kitwood and Bredin focus on the potentially therapeutic effect of sensitive care-giving. Their preferred approach to care-giving would be the opposite of the dominant medical and para-medical practice of attempting, 'to adjust the dementing person to our (cognitive) reality; it involves the immensely subtle task of attuning ourselves to his or her emotional reality...it would be far more therapeutic to stimulate the body's own neurochemicals, through means that are fundamentally psychological' (Kitwood 1989, p.14).

Perhaps the most telling criticism levelled at the bio-medical model by Kitwood and Bredin is that it depicts demented people as suffering from different degrees of 'cognitive deficit' and ignores other facets of the whole human being. The tests devised to assess these degrees of deficit reveal this uni-dimensional tendency. One such test, for example, assigns scores of 1 point to each of ten items under the generic heading, Organic Brain Syndrome Scale (the CARE schedule, reprinted in Askham and Thompson 1990).

Amongst these items are:

- doesn't know age
- doesn't know Prime Minister
- doesn't know how long at address
- doesn't know the rater's name.

Exactly what inferences can be drawn from negative – or, for that matter, from positive – scores attached to these items are, at the very least, debatable. The implicit 'normal' cognitive responses are derived from unknown sources. Apart from the possibility that 'normal' individuals across age groups might also 'suffer' from such proclaimed cognitive deficits, tests of this kind are meretricious and self-fulfilling because they are designed to isolate particular stimuli to recall which are least likely to act as stimuli to people already diagnosed as old and in some stage of dementia.

Spurious measures of dependency serve to uphold professionals' control over definitions. 'Confused', 'dependent', 'un-cooperative' may be symptoms not of physical or mental incapacity, but of a resistance to oppression through an assertion of individuality or, as Kitwood (1989) has termed it, 'personhood'.

Part of the Clackmannan Survey Assessment is devoted to a Psychiatric Assessment Schedule. The questions used in order to test the respondent's state of mental order or disorder all focus on the capacity to remember certain facts. These are:

- ° the researcher's last name

- ° the full postal address of the institution or own home

- ° the respondent's full name

- ° their date of birth

- ° their age last birthday

- ° the date today

- ° the current year

- ° the name of the present Prime Minister

- ° the name of the previous Prime Minister.

From some limited empirical evidence amongst persons holding down responsible and challenging jobs, we have discovered that several of them are unable accurately to recall the registration number of their car; are unable to name many of the roads which they travel on each week; have great difficulty in recalling the names of people they have met; and some have problems finding their way out of certain buildings. This, we are fairly confident in assuming, is not because their memories are failing but because they have not seen the need to register such information in the first place. Such paraphernalia has been 'selected out' as of very low significance for the particular day-to-day lifestyle. Yet the compilers of the Clackmannan Scale have devised a list of items which is intended categorically to separate out the dementing from the non-dementing and to accord different gradations of dementia to individuals.

At present the majority of people know their date of birth because they are frequently required to recall that information in order to complete a variety of forms and enquiries. Why should they need to store this information for all time? Further, we can imagine that the experience of living in an institution, with its routine, would probably extinguish the need to know what day or even what year it is. Why should anyone be expected to know the name of the Prime Minister if they have no interest in politics and ignore the media?

This fallacy – of imposing a self-styled expert's perception of normal responses upon the objects of research – illustrates the unwitting arrogance of probably well-intentioned clinicians. These tests, like those devised to gauge dependency levels of elderly people – CAPE and CRBRS, for example (see Wilkin and Thompson 1989) – take no account of individual motivation at a particular time in a particular environment. Longitudinal studies might go some way towards the important contextualising of responses over time but these attempts at equating levels of cognition (externally calibrated) with mental capacity and orientation are crude, demeaning to those being assessed and potentially damaging since the corollary of their results may be a form of therapy wholly, and inadvisedly, structured on an invalid tool of measurement.

Our own experience tells us that we remember what we deem important to us; we recall on a need to know basis and we filter out what we consider to be of secondary or lesser personal significance. The arrogance referred to in our criticism pervades the bio-medical model of dementia. It rates, for example, short-term memory as more worthy than long-term memory; it assumes that strict compliance with social inhibitions is more natural than less compliance; and it depicts the inability to communicate coherently as the fault of the 'patient' and not the more rational observer. It is essentially not an objective diagnosis but an assertion of moral rectitude. The bio-medical model goes beyond the statement: 'Normal people behave in this way; you don't; therefore you are not normal' and implies, almost clamorously, that you *ought* to behave like the rest of us.

This, of course, is old ground:

> Treating someone as 'sick' who is not 'sick' is to confuse what is real with what is imitation; and to confuse literal with metaphorical meaning; medicine with morals. (Szasz 1974, p.x)

It is at this point that we would depart from the emerging model presented by Kitwood and by Kitwood and Bredin, for they, too, rely on a list of attributes which, in their terms, have 'face validity'. It is noticeable that, as psychologists, they too talk about their idea of care-giving as potentially more 'therapeutic' than conventional modes of intervention, formally or informally. It is illogical to reject a bio-medical model as inappropriate but then to accept a need for therapy. While their list of the attributes which may be found among both dementing and non-dementing people deviates from the orthodox 'cognitive deficit' approach, there is little apparent foundation for the items in the list other than a reference to the writers' 'observation' of 12 'indicators of well-being'. These are: affectional warmth, self-respect, humour, initiation of social contact, the assertion of desire or will, social sensitivity, acceptance of other dementia sufferers, helpfulness, relaxation, ability to experience and express a range of emotions, and showing evident pleasure, creativity and self-expression. These characteristics, according to Kitwood and Bredin (1992), provide common ground between dementing and non-dementing.

The list is interesting, not least because of its apparent selectivity and freedom from any stated sampling method. Observation of any other cohort or cohorts of diagnosed demented individuals could well produce much different attributes. Those of Kitwood and Bredin are remarkable for their neutrality or attractiveness. What does 'well-being' mean? We are not told. The predominantly serene nature of the observed could indicate a state of being induced by tranquillising drugs. Non-dementing people can be unpleasant, tactless, solitary, restless, moody, in fact they are capable of being at times the very opposite of each of Kitwood and Bredin's 'sample'. Negative behaviour, in the sense of its being socially undesirable, would be as much a bridge between 'normal' and 'abnormal' old age as positive behaviour. In attempting to make a point that dementia is not a disease but stages along a continuum, Kitwood and Bredin imply: (1) that a curative, that is, medical, approach is appropriate but not at present implemented; (2) that their empirical studies need not have the same rigour as that demanded of the bio-medical approach; and (3) that demented people should be judged not by the degree of cognitive deficit but by attributes which amount almost to a stereotype of the 'dear old lady'.

From these 12 indicators of well-being, Kitwood and Bredin infer four 'global states' which, through sensitive caring, it is necessary to sustain and nurture in dementing old people. These are:

- a sense of personal worth

- a sense of agency – the ability to control life in a meaningful way

- a state of social confidence

- a state of hope – of security about future events.

They maintain that inappropriate, clinically oriented caring tends to work against these states. But that may be true of the mainstream of formal and informal care of elderly people in general. Their hypothesis – that insensitive care serves to inhibit rementia – remains intact because it has neither been proved nor disproved. It may, therefore, take its place alongside the bio-medical 'theories', for in many respects it also adopts a positivist view of dementia as a condition which, in some individuals, may be treated or even cured.

We have seen that bio-medical and psychological domains work within a similar paradigm of disease which is itself regarded as the result of an alien entity 'out there' which has invaded the body. Common parlance speaks volumes in its representation of this dominant medicalisation of human experience. We talk about 'catching a cold or a virus', of an 'attack of flu' or of being 'struck down by a bug'. Much of the imagery of medicine is of a battlefield in which our defence mechanisms ward off or fight would-be pathological aggressors. In Payer's (1990) terms, doctors in the Western world focus on an external 'insult' to the body.

Our research into the care of elderly people diagnosed by clinicians as suffering from dementia has led us to question this aetiological model, not because it has yet to produce persuasive evidence about the cause of dementia, but because it has defined in medical terms a phenomenon that it cannot explain. In this way the medical profession continues to apply its socio-political muscle to an arena of human behaviour which may have quite different meanings to those who are said to be demented (Foucauldian 'discourses'). We need to examine this behaviour within the paradigms of sociological theory because this particular perspective might offer alternative and more hopeful means of enabling so-called dementing people to define themselves rather than be defined by others with professional vested interests (labelling theory). We make this tentative claim because we would prefer to adopt from the outset a moral stance which aims to allow people the freedom and opportunity to define themselves rather than be ascribed a persona by others. Towards this end, we must be wary of imposing upon individuals and making them fit into off-the-shelf sociological theory. To do that would be to arrogate to ourselves the same position of assumed power and expertise that we have found so unattractive in the bio-medical approach.

Our avenue for exploration is eclectic and draws upon the sociology of medicine, the sociology of illness, the sociology of the body, labelling theory, social constructionism, socio-linguistics and post-modernist perspectives. These will be the conceptual frameworks in which we shall be developing our analysis of dementia. Here we can only attempt to map out some salient features of our as yet only partly explored theoretical territory. We need to understand by talking to older people how they see themselves in relation to non-aged others. We know, for example, that Western society extols youth at the expense of age. What does being old and often dependent on others mean in our society? Do many old people depend on others – carers, family, doctors, social workers, nurses – not just for physical and emotional care but for their very identity and self-image? Is dementia partly the result of patient acquiescence?

Language and the construction of dementia: the cultural imperialism of language

It has been hypothesised that older adults have decreased ability to understand language and that this deficit in semantic processing is a cause of age-related differences in memory for new information; conversely, hypotheses have been articulated which propose that memory deficits in old age impair language comprehension and production (Light and Burke 1989). Since 'memory loss' is regarded as a key symptom of dementia, it is important to consider the literature on the inter-relationship between memory, language and cognitive processes.

At one extreme is the hypothesis that the ageing process affects virtually every aspect of the information-processing system. Other psychologists have suggested that the decline in the capacity to store and retrieve data is more selective, with short-term memory being particularly impaired due to deficits in attention-demanding tasks, while those functions dependent on often practised or perceptual tasks are spared (Cohen 1983). Thus 'deeper' levels of processing associated with the encoding of meaning are more likely to be negatively affected by ageing than more 'day-to-day' tasks.

Central to the consideration of any link between ageing, memory and language is the question of the validity of those tests applied in order to attribute correlations between the three variables. Salthouse (1982) records conflicting results, for example, arising out of vocabulary tests for adults across a span of age ranges. While an early study involving nearly 3000 adults found a decrease in vocabulary performance as age increased (Thorndike and Gallup 1944), other research noted the influence of variables other than age upon such performance. For example, Garfield and Blek (1952) and Lachman et al. (1982) noted that older people from occupations which continuously exposed them to new words — such as teachers and college professors — exhibited a significant increase in vocabulary performance with age. It has also been reported that measures of verbal ability increase with age in groups matched for amount of education (Green 1969). This suggests that observed decreases in verbal ability amongst older people may be the result of older generations having had less exposure to education. Salthouse (1982) has confirmed that the differences in verbal ability associated negatively with ageing vary according to the type of verbal ability test used.

While some tests seek to examine adults' ability to retrieve words after having heard sentences read out or to generate a list of words all beginning with the same letter, other tests have set out to be more 'naturalistic'. Burke and Harrold, for example, investigated the capacity of different adult age groups to retrieve tip-of-the-tongue (TOT) words. Bowles and Poon (1985) have described this phenomenon as occurring when semantic information has been accessed but the corresponding information in the lexical domain about the appropriate word is temporarily inaccessible. Burke and Harrold's work indicates that the increase in TOT or spontaneous memory failures in adulthood may be a source of memory problems in old age. They comment that whereas word-finding problems in aphasia or Alzheimer's disease (AD) have been related to deviant or incomplete semantic representations, there is no evidence for such deterioration in 'normal' old age.

Clinical features of language disorder in Alzheimer's disease

In keeping with the orthodox bio-medical depiction of Alzheimer's disease as a progressive, clearly staged disease, Cummings and Benson (1985) identify a disorder of language as consistently present by the middle of the clinical course, ranging from two to ten years after the onset of dementing symptoms. In standardised tests designed to assess aphasia, patients with Alzheimer's disease have been found to be impaired in both expressive and receptive language functions (Appell, Kertesz and Fisman 1982). Indeed Huff (1988) has been able to schematise the progressive linguistic decline in Alzheimer's disease sufferers in this way:

EARLY SYMPTOMS

- ° Circumlocutory discourse[2]
- ° Word-finding pauses
- ° Difficulty in naming objects.

LATE SYMPTOMS

- ° Paraphasias (substituting one word for another)
- ° Simplified syntax
- ° Impaired comprehension.

FINAL SYMPTOMS

- ° Meaningless repetition of words
- ° Repetition of nonsense sounds
- ° Mutism.

In her research into language and memory in persons suffering from senile dementia of the Alzheimer's type (SDAT) Emery (1985) selected three groups of adults: 20 'optimally healthy' elderly adults; 20 healthy 'pre-middle-aged' adults and 20 elderly adults with SDAT. Each sample of 20 consisted of 10 men and 10 women. Variables such as age, age range, educational experience, ethnic type, native language and occupation were controlled. After applying a number of tests, including the Wechsler Memory Scale, Emery concluded that there was a drop in performance from pre-middle-age to old age on most tasks, but that there was proportionately greater impairment in those subjects with SDAT. However, the performance of the SDAT group varied markedly on different tasks, with highest achievement on the least complex tasks.

For example, SDAT elderly were able to repeat phrases and sentences much more successfully than they were able to process them in terms of the logical relationships between components of the phrases or sentences. This suggested

---

2   Circumlocutory discourse refers to the inability of persons diagnosed as having Alzheimer's disease to name an object. Instead they describe its function – for example, a picture of a telescope could evoke the response: 'Something you look out of' or a funnel: 'You pour liquid through that'.

to Emery that deterioration of complex syntactic processing is more severe than, and/or occurs prior to, deterioration of immediate memory, even though memory deficit is more apparent on usual clinical inspection than is decrement in complex syntactical tasks. In general, Emery's data supported the description of primary degenerative dementia as an accelerated ageing of the brain.

Yet why there is a greater capacity for persons with SDAT to perform well on immediate recall rather than on comprehension tests is not clear. Emery acknowledges that these issues are difficult to disentangle because, 'just as the specialist in intelligence testing has difficulty creating a language-free test, it is difficult to devise tasks wherein language, memory, and thought are not confounded'. Further analysis of the medical histories of the subjects in Emery's research prompted the question of whether a model of diathesis/stress – that is, a genetic predisposition in patients to be vulnerable to a variety of viral invasions of tissue – will prove relevant for an understanding of Alzheimer's syndrome.

The central question which has occupied the attention of neuropsychologists and, indeed, researchers across a number of disciplines, is this: are the cognitive changes – disorders of language and memory, in particular – which are associated with Alzheimer's disease a more intense form of deficits found in normal ageing or are they qualitatively different? Light and Burke (1989), drawing on the work of Scheibel and Scheibel (1975) and Squire (1987), note that examination of the brains of normally aged people *post mortem* has discovered a condition of tangles and plaques and loss of neurons in those parts of the brain involved in language similar to that found in the brains of AD-diagnosed individuals.

Research into aphasia (the inability to express thought in words or to understand the meaning of others' spoken or written words) and normal ageing has proved inconclusive. Word-finding problems and difficulties in comprehension may be considered as symptomatic of ageing generally, rather than being indicative among 'demented' persons of a qualitatively different affliction. In cases of amnesia the ability to acquire new information is severely impaired but the ability to recall information acquired in the past is affected less (Zola-Morgan, Cohen and Squire 1983). This would appear also to characterise a differential capacity for memorising in normal old age, probably because of changes in the hippocampus, which is a raised trace on the lateral ventricle of the brain.

DISCUSSION

Attempts to analyse the capacity of normal older adults and those diagnosed as suffering from early or late onset dementia raises the issue which is central to this book. That is: has a dominant bio-medical model of dementia predetermined not only the type of evidence available but also the specific line of questioning? In other words, have professional scientists – including psychologists – imposed on research agendas a limited vocabulary in which to frame answers? Those sociologists of health who support social constructionism as an interpretive framework would claim that defects of language ability and memory amongst many older people have come to be labelled as 'dementia' and thus 'pathologised'. The colonisation by clinicians and medical researchers of such accoutrements of normal experience amongst people of all ages as aphasia, anomia, paraphasia and amnesia has led to a discrete disease classification of such phenomena where such manifestations are construed by others as extended and/or recurring episodes. In order to fit this model, for example, Alzheimer's disease is depicted as progressive, linear and eventually terminal, and the decremental stages of language deficit have been similarly schematised. There are, however, dissenters from the more orthodox bio-medical interpretations of linguistic abnormalities amongst old people diagnosed as suffering from dementia. Laplane (1992) argues that complex cognitive operations are possible without the help of language and that while language is an essential instrument of human thought, thought exists beyond language: 'We cannot', he asserts, 'assess the persisting thought of demented people and for that reason they remain similar to us' (p.38). This proposition challenges the view that apparently impaired capacity to communicate and to interpret verbal messages in itself is indicative of specific cognitive impairment. Shotter (1993) refers to three kinds of knowledge:

1. Practical – how to do.

2. Theoretical – how we explain.

3. 'Sensing' – linked to others' judgements; picking up moral signals about one's self.

Helpful though this might be in structuring our thinking about the cognitive complexity of human beings, it is nonetheless an attempt to impose an artificial order upon a highly elusive interactive process. Physiologically, the brain is an amazingly sophisticated organ. In attempting to diagnose *ex post facto* the presence of dementias in deceased persons, the pathologist makes the fundamental error of reducing 'mind' to biological entity. This fallacy reproduces the bio-medical disaggregation of the person as a holistic being into a visually recognisable array of separate phenomena. It is, in the words of Foss (1994), to confuse the 'organic' with the 'Spiritual'.

If we were to approach the linguistic 'deviancy' of people who are said to be 'demented' from angles other than the clinical, we could infer from their verbal behaviour quite different suppositions. 'Normal' speech is, of course, contextual; one form of socially acceptable language would be quite out of place in certain environments. The stylised language of rhetoric, drama and poetry would come across as profoundly odd in the office situation. 'Speaking in tongues' in the religious context is regarded more as a sign of divine communication than as dementing behaviour symptomatic of a diseased 'mind'. Mime, autism, deafness, Trappism – all reject or have to reject speech as dialogue or conversation, while much artistic endeavour chooses to express itself in media which are neither verbal nor written. Altered states of consciousness seem to require forms of communication beyond the power of ordinary language.

We are not arguing that what appears to be a sign of a degenerative brain condition is really more accurately to be interpreted as a state of 'altered consciousness' in an artistic or spiritual sense. But we are suggesting that the bio-medical interpretation of such manifestations as obscure verbal signals in some old people need have no more credibility than less 'rational' accounts. Who is to say that the prevailing cultural definitions of normal verbal articulation are no more than a social artefact? Language is continually evolving according to the demands of a society's need to communicate new ideas, and each new technology invents its own medium of communication. The ability to perform 'mental arithmetic' – once a sign of 'intelligence' – is almost defunct as electronic calculators have supplanted this particular form of cerebral activity. 'Intelligence' itself is a social construct built, in Western cultures, upon the precept that the scientific mode of logical linked thought typifies the highest form of mental activity. Its written or spoken articulation, therefore, becomes an externalisation of an ordered and well-balanced 'mind'. The education system is then geared towards the propagation of a certain kind of intellectual activity dominated by the core subjects of languages and science. Art, dance, music and drama come to be regarded as peripheral, non-academic time-fillers.

The whole edifice, then, of social normality is founded upon the cultural imperialism of rational language. The two codes of which Bernstein (1974) wrote, identify the disadvantages of lower socio-economic groups in British society since they have to struggle to adapt to the linguistic hegemony of the cultural elite. The classification of individuals into categories prescribed by dominant interest groups provides the fabric for the construction of social order. Deviations from the prescribed social norms may attract intervention by representatives of those dominant interest groups in order to restore order. Those people in such a society whose capacity to communicate in the valued mode appears to be defective may come to be construed as in need of some form of intervention. Once this paradigm of deviance has taken root, it follows that the main agents of restoring social order are likely to assert their diagnoses as appropriate harbingers of action. 'Linguistic diversity' becomes a threat to conventional ideas about the nature of being fully human, and those who express themselves in a 'strange' manner – in the context of day-to-day living – are candidates for the category of 'diseased'/'deranged'.

Elderly people and language

Communication skills and deficits are taken to be indicative of a person's state of mind. Many of the assessment measures – two of which are referred to in Chapter 3 – include 'communication' as a category. Individual elderly people are given scores according to their perceived ability to communicate with others. The degree of linguistic competence is then interpreted as an indication of each elderly person's mental state. 'Confused' expression is therefore construed as the result of a distorted, possibly diseased, intellectual faculty. Ferrer (1992) has referred to this characteristic as 'language impoverishment'.

Yet the interconnection between the mind and articulate thoughts and feelings is open to dispute. Laplane (1992) argues that complex cognitive operations are possible without the help of language. Although language is an essential instrument of human thought, thought itself exists beyond language. 'We cannot,' Laplane asserts, 'assess the persisting thought of demented people and for that reason they remain similar to us' (p.38). The study of language in the form of *discourse analysis* has provided insights into how meaning is constructed by the meanings attached by others to an individual's conversation and narrative (Atkinson and Heritage 1984; Brown and Yule 1983; Gergen and Davis 1985).

Attention has also been given to the linguistic patterns of ageing people (Barbato and Feezel 1987; Bayles and Kaszniak 1987; Gravell 1988). Much of this literature, which has been reviewed by Coupland, Coupland and Giles (1991), identifies a decrement in language facility as people become older. But, once again, the important issue is whether this apparently diminishing capacity to communicate meaningfully with others is a result of the ageing process or the outcome of stereotypical images of elderly people and the type of verbal interaction that is promoted by those who adopt such images. Coupland and colleagues maintain that, 'older conversationalists frequently have their inter-actional roles, and key aspects of their life-span identities, constructed *for* them by younger people...we are drawn to the conclusion that important subjective dimensions of ageing itself are accomplished interactionally' (Coupland *et al.* 1991, p.21).

One example of externally imposed definitions of ageing is baby talk. Kite and Johnson (1988) and Caporel (1981) have documented the tendency, particularly among care staff in institutional settings, to 'talk down' to elderly persons, thus assigning 'second childishness' as an expected attribute of increasing old age. This is not to say that all older people in this kind of setting will either object or accede to such ostensibly demeaning behaviour. Such evidence does, however, serve to substantiate the basic premise of this book, that old age may be both biologically determined and socially constructed.

The recent, albeit limited, study recorded by Ramanathan-Abbott (1994) supports the claim by Kitwood (1990) that the nature of interaction between the informal carer and 'dementing' person can have an effect upon the course of the 'illness'. Ramanathan-Abbott accepts the medical diagnosis of short-term memory loss also as indicative of dementia in a mild or moderate form, but raises some doubt about the assumed correlation between loss of language skills and cognitive skills. Referring to previous research which analysed narratives from Alzheimer's sufferers – (Hunt 1990; Kempler 1991; Ulatowska *et al.* 1988) – he observes that the focus of this research has been almost exclusively on the resultant narrative rather than the interaction involved in eliciting the narrative: 'Neglecting to examine the interactional process is a serious exclusion, since the narrative is dependent on the reciprocal nature of speaking and listening between the interactants' (p. 31).

Ramanathan-Abbott used one case study of a 67-year-old female and analysed the content of verbal interaction between the subject and her husband and between the subject and the researcher–author. Efforts were made by both interlocutors to encourage 'Tina' to recount certain episodes in her past which she considered 'stood out'. Different approaches were used. Tina's husband interrupted the narrative a good deal and attempted to guide and prompt Tina towards certain 'correct' responses. The researcher, on the other hand, was much less intrusive, holding back from prompting or guiding the verbal interchange. Analysis of the data suggested that the two audiences were engaging Tina in different activities: her husband was engaging her more in recognising events of the past, whereas the researcher was more concerned with her recalling them. Discourse analysis showed that Tina was capable of sustaining a logical narrative over time when questioned by the researcher, but appeared to be confused about details and responded only in brief phrases with her husband.

There is the probability that in some of the attempts to stimulate narrative Tina would have been aware that the topic would be familiar to her husband and might, therefore, not consider it necessary to expand in her response. Some of the areas, however, such as life at the day centre which she attended, would not have been familiar to her husband, yet the nature of her abbreviated narrative corresponded closely in these episodes with all other occasions.

From this case study and ongoing research into AD-diagnosed persons, Ramanathan-Abbott drew some significant conclusions. They are:

1. The patient's ability to produce extended and meaningful speech is, in part, interactionally produced.

2. There are parallels between the patient's weakening sense of self and a non-facilitative social context.

3. The recipient's prompt is crucial in generating particular kinds of narrative.

4. Alzheimer's disease talk is likely to be developed if the patient is engaged in recall rather than recognition, and this can emerge only from a facilitative interaction.

Sabat (1991) had drawn attention in earlier studies to the ways in which an interlocutor could adjust his/her mode of interaction so as to allow the respondent to be an effective interactor. By pausing rather than intervening in the course of a patient's narrative, Sabat allowed the other person more time in which to express their ideas. By accommodating their interactional needs, Sabat enabled them to present a strong sense of self rather than collude in the representation of a confused and inarticulate person.

The findings of Sabat and of Ramanathan-Abbott confirm the general proposition enunciated by Polkingthorne (1988), Radley (1990) and several other socio-linguists: that the act of speech, and of narrative in particular, affords an opportunity for individuals to achieve their, 'personal identities and self concept' (Polkingthorne 1988, p.150). Who listens and how the listening and interaction are performed by various audiences can – according to these socio-linguistic theories – play a crucial part in sustaining positive or negative images of elderly people.

The presentation of 'self'

The seminal work by Goffman (1969) depicted the individual need to present a self that was socially acceptable. The 'self', in this sense, was not therefore an immutable entity, but a persona which could adapt to the exigencies of differing social demands. More recently Sabat and Harré (1992) have drawn on this constructionist theory of the 'self' and used its key principle within the field of psycholinguistics which, in turn, has been influenced by the work of Wittgenstein (1980) and Vygotsky (1971). Writing about the construction and deconstruction of self in persons with Alzheimer's disease, Sabat and Harré argue that the individual self can manifest any one of its repertoire of personae in clusters of behaviour displayed in the appropriate social context, but that it is important that the persona should be the 'right one', that is, that it should be socially acceptable. They dispute the notion embedded in the work of Cohen and Eisdorfer (1986) that declining mental abilities can ultimately lead to a 'loss of self': '...in Alzheimer's disease self, or personal identity, remains intact far beyond the disintegration of many cognitive and motor functions' (Sabat and Harré 1992, p.452).

Their interpretation of the possible 'meanings' of behaviour recalls the basic tenets of labelling theory:

Once an Alzheimer's Disease sufferer has been positioned as helpless and confused, it is rare for his or her behaviour to be seen in a way different from that which conforms to the original positioning (p.454).

Thus if there is a loss of the capacity to present an appropriate self, in many cases the fundamental cause is to be found not in the neurofibrillary tangles and senile plaques in the brains of the sufferers, but in the character of the social interactions and their interpretation that follow in the wake of the symptoms (p.460).

COMMENT

The thesis on which the discussion of Sabat and Harré is based derives from empirical data gained from a small sample of Alzheimer's disease sufferers whose behaviour was either directly observed by the writers or reported to them after observation by others. The logic of such a theoretical foundation may, therefore, appear to be frail in view of the relatively small number of observed 'cases'. There are arguments for and against such an inference. First of all, we may say that the main core of the bio-medical interpretation of behaviour which has come to be identified as the result of physiological lesions is also – and unashamedly – built upon an assumption that the 'cause' of 'dementia' of the Alzheimer's disease type must be somatic. Empirical evidence to sustain such a presumption – as Chapter 1 established – is still being pursued. Tests *post mortem* have so far proved inconclusive.

On the other hand, we could argue that those writers schooled in psycho-linguistics and socio-linguistics are themselves 'constructing' an anti-dementia model which – similar to the bio-medical model of dementia – seeks to present its case deductively from a given epistemological starting point. In this sense, its discourse may be as tendentious as any other.

The work of Gubrium

Gubrium notes that there is controversy in the neuropathological literature as to whether there is a quantitative or qualitative distinction to be made between the processes of ageing and Alzheimer's disease. Symptoms described in various texts are numerous; from confusion, disorientation and forgetfulness to irritability, restlessness, agitation and sleepwalking. While ageing itself is asserted as a possible cause (Reisberg 1981), others strenuously oppose this view (Alzheimer's Disease and Related Disorders Association (ADRDA) 1982). While acknowledging the general dissonance among those who have tried to ascribe a definitive syndrome to the disorder, Gubrium focuses in one important paper (Gubrium 1987) on the conventionally described chronology of Alzheimer's disease and to what is referred to as the 'three stages' relating to a patient's cognitive and motor activities.

The account by Hayter (1974) has been particularly influential in assigning a time period and its characteristic symptoms from a nurse's point of view. Memory loss is the first symptom and this stage is said to last between two and four years. The second stage, which may extend over several years, involves poorly controlled motor activity, progressive memory loss, aphasia, a tendency to wander and various types of repetitive action. The third, or 'terminal' stage is relatively short, about one year, and is characterised by general physical decline and eventual death. This account of the onset and development of the disease has provided a guide for care-givers as to what symptoms to expect, in what sequence and how to manage the course of the disease. Consequently, the informal carer's emotional adjustment to the situation is said to progress in a similarly serial pattern, proceeding from a denial that anything is wrong with their spouse, partner or relative to eventual acceptance of progressive decline and inevitable death.

Gubrium's participant observation of meetings organised by the American ADRDA confirmed the apparent need among sufferers' kin, and in much of the professional literature intended to assist carers, to establish a sense of order to help them cope. This observation is corroborated by an analysis of the literature produced by the British Alzheimer's disease Associations. Yet a good deal of literature also suggests that symptoms may not follow some ordered sequential mode; that there is 'disarray' (Gubrium 1987). However, commentators such as Berger (1980) have attempted to explain such deviations in the pattern of the disease as 'variations on a general code'. The need for informal carers in particular to perceive an orderliness in the career of the disorder lies in their concern to respond appropriately to predictable symptoms of the defined stages.

Gubrium presents data from his observations of carers' conversations, from experience as a researcher in day hospitals and from a review of related literature. He concludes that those concerned in dealing with Alzheimer's disease, 'do not as much encounter general developmental regularity in the course of illness, as they use it and its destructured opposite to both express and guide their actions and related frustrations' (p.22). Thus developmentalism, 'enters into experience more as culture than as regulating structure, revealing developmentalism's symbolic and practical functions' (p.22), a reading supported by Bury (1982).

ORDERING DISORDERS

Gubrium's gloss of the sequential 'fallacy' with regard to Alzheimer's disease sits within his broader critique of developmentalism as a descriptor of human conduct generally. The human need to discern order amongst our experience has favoured a positivist system of discoverable 'facts'. Yet it is argued that this scientific endeavour may act in order to limit the possibility of alternative explanations. Hawking (1995), for example, having described a scientific theory in these terms ('...a scientific theory is just a mathematical model we make to describe our observations; it exists only in our minds' (p.155)) explains that many scientists have refused to contemplate the possibility of there having been no beginning to the universe. Hawking's own postulate that space and time may be without boundary and that the universe would, therefore, have neither a beginning nor an end runs counter to more orthodox dimensions of scientific thinking.

Conclusion

We have shown in Chapter 3 that medicine and psychiatry attempt to make sense of the world of dementia through bringing an orderly, explanatory theory to bear upon the holders of the disease. We will, in the next chapter, deconstruct the way in which these models have emerged, by examining the way in which neuroscientific evidence allies with the overwhelming practical problems of medical diagnosis and the needs of society to have a medicalised model of dementia. It will be seen that the medical model of dementia exists 'only in our minds', just as dementia is deemed to do.

CHAPTER 5

The Scientific Construction
of the 'Disease' of Dementia

Introduction: the cultural location of medical knowledge

In Britain, which is perhaps in this regard typical of other Western, industrial-ised countries, 'health' is seen as a largely medical construct. The medical definition of health provides us with the dominant ideology about health.

Western medicine is based on Cartesian (from the French philosopher Descartes) logic, that is, the concept of the body as a biological organism, totally separate from the mind of the individual. Cartesian dualism, Turner argues:

> ...is based on the principal assumption that there is no interaction, or at least no significant interaction, between mind and body, and therefore that these two realms or topics can be addressed by separate and distinctive disciplines. The body became the subject of the natural sciences including medicine, whereas the mind...was the topic of the humanities, or the cultural sciences. (Turner 1984, p.32)

With regard specifically to medicine: 'The cartesian division in the medical sciences allowed medicine to treat the problems of the body with minimal reference to social or psychological causes' (Turner 1992, p.3).

The result is the 'dominant metaphor of biomedicine', that is, 'the body is a biochemical machine. The patient is the owner of the body-machine which is brought to the physician for repairs' (Kirmayer 1988, p.57).

However, this is a peculiarly Western approach. Other cultures see the mind/body interaction, and indeed the whole concept of illness and disease, differently. We have, in the West, tended to assume that the Western approach is 'correct', whilst those of other cultures are seen as interesting but of little utility. This is now changing, as social scientists in the West come to realise the value of perspectives from other cultures. Take, for example, the answer to the question, 'what is disease?'. There is no one answer to this question, but what is fascinating about it, Turner argues, is that, 'medical sociology (and perhaps more specifically medical anthropology) constantly points to the fact that many of the categories, both of professional and everyday use, which refer to illness, sickness or disease are variable across time and space' (1992, p.161).

If this is so, then it is just as possible for sociologists and anthropologists to examine Western medicine as a concept arising out of, and hence redolent of, a particular culture as it is for them to examine the medical beliefs of other cultures.

If medical culture is understood as, 'the meanings and values implicit in bio-medical knowledge and practice and the social processes through which they are produced', then it can be seen that Western medicine of the 20th century is, 'pervaded by a value system characteristic of an industrial-capitalistic view of the world in which the idea that science represents an objective and value free body of knowledge is dominant' (Lock and Gordon 1988, p.3). Gordon argues that, 'bio-medical theory and ideology...claim neutrality and universality. Mirroring this ideology, social and historical studies traditionally have considered western medicine as a "constant", the universal against which other medical systems were mapped' (Lock and Gordon 1988, p.19). The result is that social scientists have until recently left unquestioned the dominant ideology of their time; scientific 'facts' have been reified and assumed to be beyond the realm of social analysis (Lock and Gordon 1988, p.3). Now Western social scientists have started to question the foundations of their own culturally ingrained beliefs. Western medicine – bio-medicine – is increasingly being understood as 'culturally and historically specific and far from universal'.

Thus the content of modern Western medical knowledge, previously seen as grounded in reified science and beyond the scope of sociological enquiry, has only recently itself become a subject of analysis. Once medical science is opened to the world of social scientific enquiry, the options for theory and practice are quite breathtaking: 'The very idea of a bounded medical system, reasonably autonomous and clearly distinct from other social institutions, is a cultural construct, as is the "belief" (superstition?) that diseases are "real" entities and that their elimination crystallizes the essence of what medicine is all about' (Lock and Gordon 1988, p.4).

We can go so far, Lock argues, as to see Western medical tradition, dominated by the concept of Cartesian dualism and dependent upon supposedly rational methodologies, in fact as a form of religion: 'Medicine, in presenting an image of life beyond time and space through rituals that dramatize the dominance of humans over nature, occupies similar religious space as the medical practices in more traditional societies' (p.41). This type of religion sees the person as:

> ...independent of society and culture, owner of his or her own symptoms, increasingly able now to detach from self and body to observe,

cultivate, and even contractually join the physician in rationally treating his or her own case. In general, medicine offers a strong sense that *humans can overcome nature, no longer a victim, but in the omnipotent driver's seat.* (p.41, emphasis added)

In sum, Western systems of health care are based upon a particular ideology which has grown out of the history, culture, religions and belief systems of the West. They have become, in the West, 'taken for granted' assumptions which few people question.

That is the background to this chapter, in which we will show that dementia as it is seen in older people was deliberately (although not self-interestedly) made into a disease entity. It commences with Fox's (1989) thesis that until the 1970s Alzheimer's disease was a rare illness which affected middle-aged people, while senility was one way of growing older. According to Fox, senility became classified as Alzheimer's disease so as to attract research monies. We will use arguments drawn from the sociology of science to show how, once researchers have found a clue which appears plausible in the light of that which they are seeking, that clue becomes sedimented under a weight of further 'evidence' which gives the appearance of irrefutable proof. This allows us to move, in Chapter 6, to an exploration of how this 'knowledge' becomes common medical currency, and finally we will move from the 'science' to the 'art' of medicine, that is, we will examine the processes of medical decision-making which allow diagnosis of a constructed disease.

The science of medicine

It is Patrick Fox's (1989) thesis that in the space of 12 years Alzheimer's disease rose from being, an obscure, rarely applied medical diagnosis to the fourth or fifth leading cause of death in the USA. This was not, he argues, the result of an epidemic, but of the reclassification of senility from a normal life event into a disease with the name of Alzheimer's. Historically, he points out, Alzheimer's disease had been regarded as a form of dementia afflicting those aged between 40 and 60, and senile dementia had been regarded as a routine part of the ageing process. This change was, Fox argues, the result of political pressures whereby a coalition comprising the National Institute on Aging, medical scientists and care-givers required a 'categorical disease focus' in order to attract funds for research. Diseases which afflict large numbers of people are the primary beneficiaries of funds for research, hence those who wished to undertake research in this area required a shift in the bio-medical conceptualisation of Alzheimer's disease away from that of a disease of younger people towards one which allowed 'senility' to become a specific disease with distinctive pathological characteristics and symptoms. This was now included under the label 'Alzheimer's disease', thus ensuring it could be categorised as synonymous with Alzheimer's disease, and at one fell swoop increase enormously the number of sufferers.

Is it this easy to change the identification of a physiological process so that it becomes a disease with specific pathological characteristics and symptoms? Surely medical diagnosis is based upon a science which ensures that it is physiological and not political processes which determine what are and are not diseases? In the next chapter we will explore whether the answers to these questions support or refute Fox's hypothesis.

Let us first examine in more depth Fox's description of how Alzheimer's disease came to be recognisable as a disease caused by deterioration in the brain cells. He traces the inspiration for the change to Robert Terry, a neuropathologist who in 1976 applied electron microscopy to samples of brain tissue, the result of which allowed the development of a perceptibly different understanding of the biological structure of Alzheimer's disease, after which biomedical research interest increased. One of the most notable advocates for such research, Dr Robert Katzman, linked two incidents together. First, he used epidemiological information to calculate that 'senile dementia' was the fourth leading cause of death in the USA. Second he argued that the research findings of neuropathologists meant that senile dementia and Alzheimer's disease should be seen as synonymous. These two supposed facts, when brought together, provided the touchpaper which led to an explosion in political activity. However, these projections were, as acknowledged by Katzman, relatively simple. The neuropathological evidence was based on very limited research evidence, and it is unclear how Katzman could use epidemiological evidence about the existence of changes in the chemistry of the ageing brain when very little was known about such changes. (Convincing proof would require at the very least empirical study of the brains of deceased persons.) Furthermore, and perhaps crucially, the identity between senile dementia and Alzheimer's disease was at this stage a *suggestion*, but a suggestion which 'tied' senility 'to a specific disease' thus dissociating it from the commonly held belief that growing old itself caused dementia.

The Alzheimer's Association of the USA was formed and, from its inception, to the chagrin of relatives of people with dementia who saw such a focus as narrow, was strongly influenced by those interested in promoting bio-medical research.

It now became possible, following lobbying and persuasion, to interest public bodies in providing funds for research. Between 1976 and 1989 funds devoted by the USA's National Institute on Aging to bio-medical research into Alzheimer's disease rose approximately 800-fold, allowing the development of a veritable research industry with many neuroscientists now dependent for the development of their careers upon the existence of Alzheimer's disease as a disease caused by degeneration of the brain structure with age. Research evidence began to accumulate. The discovery of neurochemical changes associated with the disease meant Alzheimer's disease as it affected older people was now a 'specific neurological disease' and not 'general aging' leading to an 'age-related deterioration of the brain'. This must be emphasised. Senility became not a natural process of ageing, it became a disease, with a name and a specific chemistry. This broadened its field of interest to the wider scientific field.

The organisers of the Alzheimer's disease movement used social as well as political tactics to raise awareness. An important part of the research process was ensuring that results were published not only in the scientific but also in the popular press, where they were relayed in the form of interesting stories which aimed to counter popular beliefs about ageing. The result was that the research findings of 1976 created a snowballing effect. Similar findings published in 1964 had roused no such interest, demonstrating, Fox argues, the link between political and bio-medical activity in the creation of a disease concept.

In sum, Fox argues that Alzheimer's disease as a disease which affected millions of people was 'discovered' in the mid 1970s in the USA. Assumptions based on early and very limited neuropathological research and unsupported epidemiological calculations formed the basis of a process of concentrated and skilful political endeavour by a scientific community interested in developing its own field of interest. Public perceptions of ageing were challenged. A phenomenal growth in research into the structures of the ageing brain followed. 'Senility', a normal if unwelcome process of growing old, was relabelled as a disease.

Fox's (1989) essentially descriptive paper has traced the history of Alzheimer's disease as we know it today to its origin in a politically informed research process. It challenges the popular understanding of science, that is, that it involves the discovery of pre-existing truths which lie waiting to be discovered, given the appropriate wisdom and technology. If this is so, then the discovery of neurofibrillary tangles and their relationship to dementia cannot be dismissed – there is a real process at work here which, regardless of how its discovery led to the formation of a research industry, must have implications for our understanding of dementia. This hegemonic view of science has been undermined by work in the sociologies of science and scientific knowledge which show how work in the laboratory is itself highly selective, 'non-scientific' and socially constructed. This is achieved through an examination of the *social* nature of science, that is, how scientific work is carried out by human agents working in groups and who relate to other groups. We will now draw upon the sociology of science, as it will enhance Fox's thesis by showing how, once scientists receive funding and equipment to search for something, they can often find it. Its insights will allow us to extend Fox's thesis so that we can understand how very limited research into Alzheimer's disease has created not only a research bandwagon, but the medical profession's perspective of Alzheimer's disease.

The sociology of science perspective

Science is generally understood, amongst the public and many members of the scientific community, as a quest for truth where, as noted above, objectively situated facts wait to be captured through the perseverance of a systematic enquiry carried out under conditions of a rigorous rationality. Since the 1970s, however, there has been an 'outpouring' of studies which challenge this perspective through, 'forc[ing] the recognition that all scientific knowledge is always, in every respect, socially situated. Neither knowers nor the knowledge they produce are or could be impartial, disinterested, value-neutral, Archimedean' (Harding 1991, p.11).

This conclusion arises as a result of the vigorous and systematic subjection of natural and technological scientific knowledge (since the 1970s) to the type of scrutiny long used in understanding other systems of belief. This phrase, 'other systems of belief', which we have borrowed from Knorr-Cetina and Mulkay (1983), encapsulates in four words the conclusions of researchers within the field of the sociology of science: that science itself is no more and no less than one system of belief, albeit a dominant and markedly authoritative one. Influenced by the works of Kuhn and Feyerabend, the sociology of science moves beyond their ideas by informing itself through intensive and in-depth empirical studies of scientists at work. There has been an emphasis on *how* scientists, as participants in a process of collective social action, do their work and thus produce scientific knowledge. The methodologies of sociologists of science include ethnography, ethnomethodology and discourse analysis, and they suggest that, rather than being a technical process, scientific work is social, with the social integral to the cognitive and technical. The technical, rather than being objective and 'out there', displays characteristics which mark it as a social phenomenon (Knorr-Cetina and Mulkay 1983). However, sociologists of science/scientific knowledge seek to discern what counts as true and false belief, but they do not seek to assess or evaluate the claimed truth statuses of science (Woolgar 1988). They tend to be critical of 'essentialists', who assume there exists an, 'actual (transcendental) object called "science"', according to Woolgar (1988, p. 21). His position is that of the 'nominalist', which, 'suggests that features proposed as characteristic of science stem from the definitional practices of the participants' (*ibid.*). The social study of science extends beyond the study of the social arrangements and organisation of science – it examines science as a, 'belief system which extends far beyond the formal social organization of science, and far outside the walls of the laboratory' (Woolgar

1988, p.12). But it is a belief system which is a form of knowledge which has 'no essential difference' between itself and other forms of knowledge. There is, Woolgar argues, 'nothing intrinsically special about "the scientific method"; indeed, even if there is such a thing as the "scientific method", much scientific practice proceeds in spite of the canons of scientific method rather than because of them' (*ibid*.).

A large corpus of knowledge now exists within the sociology of science, or the sociology of scientific knowledge as some adherents prefer to call it. It is not our intention here to provide a full analysis of the issues and debates within the discipline. Our discussion can draw only upon some of the more cogent theories which have emerged from it. It is our intention to draw selectively from the discipline so as to show how, once the suggestion has been implanted that senility equals Alzheimer's disease, a veritable scientific industry could grow upon such foundations, rendering factual the proposition that senility and Alzheimer's disease are one and the same thing. The areas touched upon so as to help us extend Fox's thesis are the work and the writings of scientists. These areas together challenge the hegemony of scientific thought.

The work of scientists

Mendelsohn's (1977) 'simple' thesis, that 'science is an activity of human beings acting and interacting, thus a social activity', is an early and accessible example of the arguments contained within the sociology of science. The whole of science, Mendelsohn argues – its knowledge, its statements, its techniques – has been created by human beings and developed, nurtured and shared among groups of human beings:

> Scientific knowledge is therefore fundamentally social knowledge. As a social activity, science is clearly a product of a history and of processes which occurred in time and in places and involved human actors. These actors had lives not only in science, but in the wider societies of which they were members (1977, pp.3–4).

Scientists bring these worlds with them into the laboratory. Furthermore, Mendelsohn continues, our (and by 'our' is meant society in general, including those members of a society who have become scientists) ways of understanding, explaining and interacting with nature vary over time and across cultures. To understand how the scientific world functions it is therefore necessary to 'delve deeply' and, 'to recognize the historical processes which lay behind the explanations of the social group itself' (p.7), that is, out of all the theories which could emerge at any one time, those which develop and become influential are dependent upon the wider context within and from which they emerge, including the wider world in which the scientific community lives.

Woolgar (1988), writing from the standpoint of the sociology of scientific knowledge, develops these ideas. It has been axiomatic that science is a form of knowledge which is unaffected by differences in space, culture or time, so that it (uniquely in terms of forms of knowledge) can escape its social context, that is, it is a universal phenomenon without variation. This principle has been challenged by the social study of science which argues that:

> ...the universalism of scientific truths is a myth, that the appearance of universalism is the *upshot of* (that is, the consensual response to) a complex social process whereby variations in the form and legitimacy of scientific knowledge claims are gradually eliminated. The apparent lack of social variation in scientific knowledge is the accomplishment of, not the condition for, science. (Woolgar 1988, p.22)

In other words, science ensures for itself its place as sole arbiter of what is 'knowledge' by eliminating all other claimants.

Furthermore, Woolgar argues that 'scientific knowledge' may itself constitute (construct, define, accomplish) the natural world, through *discovery*. 'The metaphor of scientific discovery, the idea of dis-covering, is precisely that of uncovering and revealing something which had been there all along. One removes the covers and thereby exposes the thing for what it is; one pulls back the curtains on the facts' (Woolgar 1988, p.55): so the discovered object has a prior existence. However, as Woolgar demonstrates with regard to the discovery of America, that which is revealed will have no predetermined identity (that which we know as America existed before its discovery by Columbus or whoever, but at that time had no identity to people in Europe) and thus has to be given an identity (America or the Indies?). The giving of an identity which allows all of us to apprehend that discovery in a single way is a complex social process by which several identities may compete with each other until one becomes dominant. The identity is then the end result or accomplishment of work done by participants, work which involves defining that which has been discovered and persuading the wider population to accept this version. In sum, objects may have an existence in the natural world, but *how we come to understand them* is the result of a social process by which their identity is socially constructed through mobilisation of resources and arguments. This inverts the traditional assumption that an object gives rise to its own representation: now the representation gives rise to the object.

Woolgar's arguments, first that science maintains its status by imposing on all forms of knowledge its own criteria for accepting what is knowledge, and second that science takes naturally occurring phenomena and dictates how we shall perceive them, have important implications for our arguments about dementia, but they are still at a highly theoretical level. The sociology of science, as exemplified in Knorr-Cetina's work, demonstrates the reality of how scientists work. We need to understand this reality if we are to trace the mechanisms implicit in Fox's analysis.

In Knorr-Cetina's words (Knorr-Cetina and Mulkay 1983, p.14 *et passim*) observations of scientific laboratories led her to see science as a 'process of production' of 'selectively carved out facts'. These 'facts', rather than having the status of pre-existing entities, are the result of a process of construction. The, 'products of science are contextually specific constructions which bear the mark of the situational contingency and interest structure of the process by which they are generated, and which cannot be adequately understood without an analysis of their construction' (p.5). They are constructed in laboratories by scientists whose concern is primarily that of making things *work*.

A specific process is at work, involving a chain of decisions, of selections made at one time which are themselves based on previous selections. Understanding can be made through deconstruction. If we take the scientific fact X, we can trace the inspiration for the research which produced X to a previous piece of research which concluded that W existed, and that the next steps to further understanding involved a choice of paths a, b, c, d, or e. If c has been chosen (leading to the discovery of X), then what may have been discovered if any of the other four choices had been decided upon? Similarly W was itself arrived at by a process of selection from choices i, ii, iii, iv or v. If W was arrived at by following choice iv, then what would have happened if choices i, ii, iii or v had been followed? And the process can be taken back through yet further stages. In sum, the selections of previous research become a resource for continuing scientific operations, but they determine that certain options are closed off.

Furthermore, those selections which become such a resource become 'solidified', made factual, through their incorporation into ongoing research. An innovation becomes accepted and becomes a 'fact', which becomes the basis for further 'facts', which then result in the development of more and more, until a river is flowing, the source of which is rarely traced. This results in 'laboratory manipulations' where individual scientists work with, 'the crystallised products of previous scientific and non-scientific work' which become the 'scriptures (the authoritative writings)' of an area.

These crystallised products are also constituted by, 'the exegeses and symbolic manipulations of the laboratory' manifested through communication in (a very broadly defined) writing. These communications are 'directed at and sustained by' interactions by others, through *discursive interaction*, in other words through the persuasive techniques by which scientists persuade other scientists of the validity of their arguments. There is thus a, 'bargaining which marks the highly selective construction and deconstruction of scientific findings and leads to the continuous reconstruction of knowledge' (Knorr-Cetina and Mulkay 1983, p.14). The process is thus one familiar to all researchers, where a hypothesis is put forward, criticised, amended, represented and possibly accepted by the scientist's peer group. It is thus a *social process*, where, 'innovation and acceptance are temporary stabilisations within a process of reconstruction of knowledge' (*ibid.*).

The scientific endeavour revolves around the production of *new* information which emerges out of a bed of crystallised information. For, influenced by the work of Bourdieu, Knorr-Cetina argues that scientific strategies are also political strategies, where scientific choices are investments designed to maximise social authority and recognition.

Myers's (1990) exploration of the social processes of the construction of scientific knowledge (in this case from biology), reveals, following Knorr-Cetina, how alternative choices arise at various times. He quotes Ernst Mayr's remark that advances in biology involve conceptual shifts rather than discoveries, so that the same facts come to be seen from a radically different perspective. So a natterjack toad has always been a natterjack toad, but the way we humans understand the reality of the natterjack toad has evolved. Further, in any field of science we see only the successes: 'That we do not see the armies of the other interpretative options – the losing views of phenomena – is only because...the losing army is immediately buried. We see only the shining armour of the facts that remain' (Myers 1990, p.259). This may be because, once a choice has been made, scientists select (construct) evidence that supports that choice (Nelson 1994). These become the basic tenets of the discipline, complexes of theories and assumptions which are rarely questioned but any one of which may be 'fiddled with' in order to save the theory (Proctor 1991). It is only when anomalies become too great, and when an alternative is sufficiently elaborated, that Kuhn's famous 'paradigm shift' will take place, and a, 'new stage of "revolutionary science" begins to unfold in which facts change their meaning' (Proctor 1991, p.211).

The above studies of the social process through which scientific knowledge can be interpreted are part of the *programme of constructivism* (Knorr-Cetina and Mulkay 1983) which states, first (as we have seen), that scientific investigation is not a descriptive exercise involving some external nature, but is a productive process which produces artefactual knowledge as a result of a 'process of (reflexive) fabrication' (p.119). That a process of production is involved means, second, that products are 'highly internally structured' as a result of the selections which have been made at different times and passed down through the research community. Scientific products are therefore, 'not only *decision-impregnated*, they are also [third] *decision-impregnating*' (p.122). Science, therefore, is a process of, 'selections designed to transform the subjective into the objective, the unbelievable into the believed, the fabricated into the finding, and the painstakingly constructed into the objective scientific fact' (p.122).

This process leads to the question: 'How do scientists rule out and bring in alternative possibilities, how do they reach and break up closure in ongoing work?' (p.123). There is no one answer to this question, but because of the consistency of findings that laboratory work has a 'locally situated, occasioned character', then, 'notions of indexicality, of opportunism and of contingency and idiosyncrasy' provide at least part of the answer. In other words, through luck, through careful planning, through fitting with the spirit of the age, all these determine which theories achieve universal factuality. These factors are assisted by the day-to-day messiness of laboratory work which limits the possibilities of replication, the contingencies within which scientific work is undertaken (such as availability of resources), the choice of which resources to utilise and the necessity of veering away from one consistently applied criterion in order to 'go along with' the research procedures and thus away from the rules. In sum, 'scientists adjust their research goals to suit the selections made, and they adjust their selections to suit new circumstances created by their research' (p.126). The logic of research is therefore an opportunistic logic in which self-referential efforts are made at consistency-making, and in which scientific products emerge from a form of discursive interaction which is directed at, and sustained by, the arguments of other scientists within the scientific community. A similar logic, Knorr-Cetina argues, applies when answering the question which commenced this paragraph, that is, how do scientists rule out and bring in alternative possibilities, how do they reach and break up closure in ongoing work? This leads to her conclusion that, rather than science tackling a 'decreasing stock of problems' about the world, science works with a, 'potentially increasing stock of problems created by science in the process of secreting an unending stream of entities and relations that make up "the world"' (p.135). The known world which emerges out of scientific work is a cultural object which constructs our world, what it is and what it consists of, for us through language and practices.

Discussion

THE SEDIMENTATION OF IDEAS WITHIN DEMENTIA AND ALZHEIMER'S DISEASE

Scientific advances appear to be made by conceptual leaps, such leaps often being enhanced by metaphors which allow phenomena or concepts which seem to have little connection with each other to be, often suddenly, seen as related or analogous in some way. 'This is the source of creative extension of knowledge' (Knorr et al. 1980, p.27). It is also what appears to have happened in the transmogrification of senility into Alzheimer's disease, when Katzman combined (unrelated) epidemiological data with his existing data on Alzheimer's disease in the form of the disease which was then recognised, that is, pre-senile. Having made the intuitive leap, and 'proven' it with the aid of scientific experiments, the idea has to become entrenched in the practices of the community of scientists working in that field. But why should one piece of work rather than another become what Kuhn labelled 'an exemplar' or shared example, become indeed (again from Kuhn) a community-wide paradigm, where, 'scientists speak unproblematically in terms of real objects' (Pickering 1992, p.110)?

Latour (1983) answers these inter-related questions by arguing that it is possible to follow how sciences are used to transform society and redefine what it is made of and what are its aims. The process involves, first, scientists capturing others' interests and second showing that, if others wish their problems to be solved, then they must formulate them in such a way as to conform with the possibilities offered by science. In other words, problems are defined in the language of science and, in being so defined, can alter the nature of the problems which affect society.

The study of dementia shows that this is very similar to what has happened with that condition which scientists 'revealed' as a disease. It also reveals which knowledge is used by those involved with people with dementia in order to inform their understanding (Gubrium 1986). Dementia reveals a further layer in the process of the embedding of scientific discovery into factuality. Gubrium provides transcript data from part of the proceedings of a 1977 workshop and conference at which Dr Katzman was present. In addition to Gubrium's analysis, it can be seen that, in the context of discussions in which participants were trying to establish whether Alzheimer's disease was actually a disease, those with expertise in the field such as Drs Katzman and Terry could elude parts of questions which contradicted their perspectives. This suggests that scientists may not hear, may become deaf to and therefore cannot comprehend, questions from a paradigm different from the one they individually and personally hold, and acting from within this security of total expertise they can convince others by literally not 'hearing' and therefore not answering the questions from people who do not conform to their own world view. This would suggest that once an idea has become dominant, its dominance is perpetuated by this process of selective deafness where those who disagree are robbed of the ability to be heard. This selective deafness is indeed demanded within, and is a necessity for, the maintenance of a scientific community which is held together by claims-to-truth.

Harré's (1990) discussion of the social world of scientists, how it is constructed and maintained by its practitioners through speech-acts, illustrates this. In a paper imbued with irony, he argues that scientists belong to an, 'esoteric order, a "community of saints"' (p.82). This 'esoteric order' maintains its coherence through the reciprocals of trust and belief, where, 'the illocutionary force of a scientific utterance is "trust me" and its reciprocal, its perlocutionary effect, is belief' (*ibid.*). Within this 'moral order', when scientists cite evidence they ask members of their community to trust their claims to truth and other members, through the belief systems of that community, do so. Scientific papers therefore often commence with a review of relevant research in that field. For the current finding to be relevant, all the works cited must be trusted for their accuracy and truth, an accuracy and truth which rests within a perceived level of expertise. Therefore, 'trust is built up upon a basis of faith in the reliability of those who are trusted – and derivatively in what they write or say' (p.83).

This sense of community is maintained, according to Harré, by the use of the academic 'we' in scientific papers, which draws the listener into complicity, to participation as something more than an audience, for they participate in the process of thought and thereby commit themselves to the proceedings. New members are drawn into the moral order of the community in a very deep way. They learn the rules they must follow, including how to carry out experiments, how to turn out finely polished presentations of their research which disguise the 'incoherent chaos of nascent research programmes' (p.90), and how to use 'the narrative of objectivity, of human indifference' (p.99).

The community thus continues, reliant upon what Harré calls an official rhetoric, in which trust and belief are tacit and which is so successful that it, 'represents the most perfect and generally sustained moral order ever created by mankind. Alongside the history of the moral force of the order within the scientific community the minimal success of "Love thy neighbour" makes a regrettably ironic contrast' (p.98).

Scientific writing is thus necessary for the development and maintenance of an idea within the scientific community and for the maintenance of the community itself. Scientific work has to be translated into written language which, in the form of papers in journals and at conferences, allows the dissemination of ideas throughout the scientific community.

The writings of scientists

Latour (1979) shows that even the, 'dullest, most mechanical, most systematic and most straightforward' of laboratory processes is, 'chaotic, illogical, opportunistic, contextual and constantly reconstructed' (p. 69), and is so far from the world of 'order, logic and rationality' that disorder is the very substance of science. It is the task of scientific writing to change this disorder into the appearance of order, of scientific logic. Furthermore, the existence of scientific writings allows, 'facts', however arrived at, to take on a life of their own, distinct from the circumstances of their production. Every time the phenomenon is referred to as a fact its factuality becomes more firmly established, its 'out there-ness' becomes more concrete (Woolgar 1988).

Sociologists of science use discourse analysis to reveal how scientists' accounts of action and belief are socially generated. Scientific writings reveal the ways in which scientists specify and contextualise their world through the written word, a world which appears far different from the one they reveal through the informal, spoken word (Mulkay, Potter and Yearley 1983). Scientific writings have been shown to: (1) use rhetorical devices to construct a world based solely on logic; and (2) sediment previous findings.

Scientific writing as the rhetoric of logic and sedimentation process

Science, Myers (1990) argues, is, 'like other discourses in relying on rhetoric; it just uses a different kind of rhetoric' (p.4). This rhetoric is highly impersonal and imbued at its essence with *logic*. All pronouns are deleted and the passive voice is used, so that something was done, rather than somebody doing something. This 'empiricist repertoire' (Mulkay *et al.* 1983) seems to allow the natural world to speak and act for itself. Science in the guise of impersonal engine of methodology and logic rather than fallible human beings, achieves its findings (Harré 1990). Indeed scientists who break the rules by revealing the real-life world of the laboratory in their findings, may find their work dismissed as non-scientific. A close reading of scientific texts which discuss experiments can thus reveal the social reality behind a text – in other words the strategies used by scientists to persuade us of the truth of their claims (Myers 1990).

Woolgar (1988) and Gilbert and Mulkay (1980) provide an accessible model for understanding the construction of scientific writings. Scientists:

1.   Incorporate a claim to be taken seriously through their very position, in a 'serious' journal.

2.   Guide the reader through the arguments in the way desired by the author, through the careful use of openings and headings. The opening sentence of a scientific paper will typically contain, 'not a statement about the physical world', although ostensibly that is the claim that is made, but 'about the customary nature of certain beliefs' amongst that section of the scientific community (Gilbert and Mulkay 1980, p.273). Where authors wish to denigrate the work of other scientists, they will describe the work of those others as mere assumptions, and will fail to provide supporting literature, thus making it appear as if the impugned scientists had themselves broken the rules of scientific discovery. This isomorphism between text and presumed reality is continued with further social accounting devices which claim a collective belief among the scientific community, seen

in such devices as failure to cite negative experimental findings or criticisms.

3. Use externalising devices to suggest that the phenomenon has an existence of its own, beyond the realm of human agency, so it does not appear as the product of actions but as something which is come across, perhaps almost by accident. Externalising devices include use of the passive or semi-passive (e.g. it could be seen; I was able to) voice, so that the scientist appears as 'fortunate bystander' or 'lucky witness' to the discovery of an objectively occurring phenomenon. Use of the active voice would reveal the scientist's role in the creation of the phenomenon, something which is revealed in informal accounts, such as discussions, but which is rigorously suppressed in print.

4. Use pathing devices which establish relationships between current and past work so that experiments appear as the latest stage of an extended process of linear-cumulative development. A picture is presented of a sequentially connected series of events, with metaphors underpinning a text which supports this idea of following a path, for example the use of 'coming upon'. Any opposing scientific perspectives are excluded or maligned. The resulting text contains systematic and meaningful differences between the informal and formal accounts of the process of experimentation. The 'unique, specific actions' of each individual experiment are rendered so as to appear as if they are highly routinised activities which do not differ from 'invariant' and legitimate scientific procedures.

5. Use sequencing devices to connect described events and activities, constructing the objectivity of the fact while eliminating any other potential paths, and giving the appearance of an uninterrupted linear process (e.g. by citing evidence accruing over a number of years, in date order).

6. Claim logic as the basis for valid inference, thus cutting out alternative ways of reading the text. In doing this they subsume that large part of their knowledge and skill which is tacit, for scientific experimentation is dependent upon 'artful accomplishments' incorporating interpretive processes.

In sum, the reader is engaged within a traditional version of rationality in which genuine scientific knowledge is seen as being built up unproblematically by means of accurate, reproducible observations of the natural world and in which personal or social factors are, 'deemed to be separable from and irrelevant to the depersonalised propositions and practices of science' (Gilbert and Mulkay 1980, p.289). The reader:

> ...is asked to concur with the authority of presentation, to interpret textual events and actions both as being about some external phenomenon and as giving rise to the phenomenon. In addition, the externality of this phenomenon is to be approached by way of a process of path following, in which the relevance of individual items is seen not for themselves, but as steps on the way towards the phenomenon. The intrusion of the author in this process is minimised by various externalising devices. The sequential nature of the procedure is further provided for by a variety of features which demonstrate connectedness...
> In this manner, alternative ways of *reading* are cut-out or background[ed]. But such is the congruence between the reader's means of understanding the path-like nature of the report and the means of understanding the path-like nature of the discovery process, that alternative ways of *proceeding* in the investigation are also cut-out or backgrounded. (Woolgar 1980, pp.261–2)

APPLYING THE ANALYSIS

Let us now examine, in the light of the above discussion, the paper by Katzman which both he and Fox identify as the catalyst which led to the merging of Alzheimer's disease and senility into one disease. Until that date (April 1976), Alzheimer's disease was regarded as a disease which affected people under the age of 60. The Editorial in *Archives of Neurology* was entitled: 'The Prevalence and Malignancy of Alzheimer Disease'. The dropping of the possessive apostrophe is interesting, for in the very title of the piece the 'indexical reference' is removed so that, in Latour and Woolgar's formulation, the disease can cease to be the property of the one person who discovered it and can now become the property of the scientific community which will guarantee its factual status.

Katzman's Editorial opens by stating that Alzheimer disease is, 'a phenomenon well known to neurologists' and that he and Karasu had estimated, in a publication the previous year, that it, 'may rank as the fourth or fifth most common cause of death in the United States' yet that it is unlisted in the US vital statistics tables as a cause of death.

This opening paragraph achieves three things. First, it locates Alzheimer's disease as the territory of neurologists (it is 'a phenomenon well known to neurologists'). Second, it builds up a community of neurologists interested in the disease, a community which possesses greater knowledge than those not privileged to join its ranks (the 'outsiders' who compile the vital statistics tables are not privileged with such knowledge as is possessed by the 'insiders'). Finally, this opening paragraph embeds, in the process of sedimentation, a previous finding, that Alzheimer's disease, 'may rank as the fourth or fifth most common cause of death in the United States'.

It is only in the opening sentence of the second paragraph that the actuality of the singular status of the disease is questioned, that is: 'The argument that Alzheimer disease is a major killer rests on the assumption that Alzheimer disease and senile dementia are a single process and should, therefore, be considered a single disease'.

Any doubts are immediately removed by a sequence of arguments referring to previous research – the 'process' originally referred to in the previous sentence thus unequivocally becomes the 'disease' with which the sentence ends. One piece of research is found which could challenge the assumption, but this is dismissed as follows: In Larsson *et al.*'s genetic, 'analysis of the kindred of patients with senile dementia, numerous relatives were found with senile dementia, but none with a diagnosis of Alzheimer disease. However the incidence of the *Alzheimer senile dementia complex* is strongly age-related, even among the elderly' (emphasis added), so that, 'the absence of any relative with "Alzheimer disease" might be related to its relative infrequency in patients under 65'. A second genetic study is then cited, which, 'encountered the two diseases in the same family'. The labelling is interesting here, for opposition is dismissed by first elevating senile dementia into a disease, or complex, and second by referring to *two* diseases, so that senility itself has now had its status surreptitiously altered. The use of the quotation marks around 'Alzheimer disease' dismisses Larsson *et al.*'s work with irony. Senility and Alzheimer's disease then become 'two disorders' which can be distinguished by, 'neither the clinician, the neuropathologist, nor the electron microscopist'. The community of neuroscientists is thus called to close ranks around the factuality of the argument, as they are again urged to by the final two sentences of this second paragraph: 'Today, the majority of workers in the field accept the identity of the two disease [*sic*]. We believe that it is time to drop the arbitrary age distinction and adopt the single designation, Alzheimer disease.'

Here we see: (1) a grammatical or typographical error which, in losing an 's', contributed, albeit unintentionally, to the overall argument, that two 'diseases' are actually one; (2) the 'we' being related to 'the majority of workers in the field' so that the two become one; and (3) the dismissal of a long-standing distinction by the word 'arbitrary'.

The third paragraph extrapolates from European research in order to establish the prevalence of 'Alzheimer disease' in the United States. By the opening sentence of this third paragraph, the factual status of 'Alzheimer disease' as a disease of all age groups is now presupposed, as shown by its use in the first sentence of this paragraph. The European surveys are described as 'excellent'. They estimated the prevalence of, to quote Katzman, '"severe dementia" or organic "psychosis"' at 4.1 per cent, and of '"mild dementia" and "mild mental deterioration" or "chronic brain syndrome without psychosis" at an average of 10.8 per cent. Furthermore: 'Estimates of the incidence of Alzheimer disease (senile dementia) among patients over age 65 with organic dementia vary between 40 per cent and 58 per cent'. All surveys are thus assumed to show the existence of 'Alzheimer disease', whether or not they had used that label, thus ignoring the difficulties in extrapolating data from one population to another. 'Severe dementia','organic psychosis', 'mild dementia', 'mild mental deterioration', 'chronic brain syndrome without psychosis' and 'senile dementia' all become 'Alzheimer disease', and the figures for this disease – which had not been diagnosed as such in the European surveys – are then extrapolated for the United States.

Katzman goes on, in the fourth and fifth paragraphs, to calculate the malignancy of this newly established disease. Studies of life expectancy amongst people who are classified as 'demented', as having 'senile dementia' or 'arteriosclerotic brain disorders' and even 'the presenile form of Alzheimer disease' provide the basis for the calculations, but there is another lexical sleight of hand, 'Alzheimer disease' is now re-labelled 'senile dementia', thus reinforcing the argued equivalence between the two. Katzman then assumes that life expectancy and cause of death are the exact equivalent, so that severe 'senile dementia' now becomes the main cause of death of between 60,000 and 90,000 American people each year, rather than the, 'bronchopneumonia, myocardial infarct, pulmonary embolus, cerebrovascular accident, or other acute event occurring at death'. In sum, his calculations are based not on the empirical evidence deemed so necessary in order to qualify as scientific research, but on assumptions which conflate: (1) various 'dementias' with a disease; and (2) reduced life expectancy with actual cause of death.

This conflation is necessary if 'our goal' (which we must now read as the goal of the community of neurologists) is, 'not to find a way to prolong the life of severely demented persons, but rather to call attention to our belief that senile as well as presenile forms of Alzheimer are a single disease, a disease whose etiology must be determined, whose course must be aborted, and ultimately a disease to be prevented'. These are the closing words of Katzman's Editorial (and its being an Editorial is itself a signifier of expertise). Were senility *not* to be labelled a disease but a normal process which happens to the body, then this last sentence would mean a call to research into the aetiology of ageing, 'whose course must be aborted' and ageing would be seen as 'ultimately a disease to be prevented'.

The writings of scientists provide layers of sediment over earlier findings, thus rendering them seemingly factual. Latour and Woolgar (cited by Harré 1990) show that the results of research programmes at first include the date of discovery, and the person and the methodology used. These 'indexical references' disappear from later writings, as the findings achieve a factual status within the body of scientific knowledge which the scientific community itself guarantees. In dementia it is the writings of scientists *and others* which have provided the sedimentary layers over Katzman's calculations. Gubrium's thesis (1986) is littered with quotes from authors citing Katzman's calculations. In the second paragraph of the very first page of a weighty tome entitled *The Biological Substrates of Alzheimer's Disease*, Benson writes that: 'utilizing the best data available from the world's literature, Katzman (1976) described Alzheimer's disease as a malignant disorder that ranked as the fourth or fifth most common cause of death in the United States' (Benson 1986). The Alzheimer's Disease Association of the United States meanwhile constantly repeats Katzman's calculations, as can be seen in the extracts from their newsletters in Gubrium's (1986) analysis, but they repeat them without assigning authorship which, as the above writers show, renders something factual. By 1994 British writers were eliding Alzheimer's disease and dementia, as if the two were proven to be identical, without recourse to proof. Roth (1994, p.57) refers to, 'Alzheimer's disease, the commonest form of dementia in later life', as do several other writers in the same volume (two of whose work we discuss below). Benson (1994), for instance, notes that the earlier discussion about whether, 'Alzheimer's disease was a separate disorder or merely represented an earlier onset of senile dementia of the Alzheimer type has been resolved in favor of the latter hypothesis', suggesting a neat inversion, that the term 'Alzheimer's' should really have been applied to the senile type all along, with younger sufferers now added in. He continues: 'The view is now so completely accepted that the term Alzheimer's disease now stands for the diagnosis of the entire spectrum of individuals with progressive degenerative dementia, not just those with a presenile onset'. Other writers in the same volume refer to Alzheimer's disease as one of a group of dementias, but the one which is most common amongst the elderly (Huppert, Brayne and O'Connor 1994).

APPLICATION: THE CONSTRUCTION OF OBJECTS AND OF DEMENTIA AS A DISEASE THROUGH SCIENCE

Woolgar suggests a five-stage model of the way in which scientific discourse constitutes its objects:

> *Stage One*: scientists have documents, including publications, papers, previous results, research apparatus, received opinion, and so on.

> *Stage Two*: some of these are used to project the existence of a particular object.

> *Stage Three*: splitting occurs – the object is now perceived as an entity separate and distinct from the documents used in Stage Two.

Stage Four: inversion. The relationship between documents and objects is inverted, and the documents are used to explain the existence of the object.

Stage Five: the crucial phase. Here the rewriting of history so as to give the discovered object its ontological foundations, that is, the first three steps are pushed into the background, forgotten or denied.

We have seen that just such a process has occurred in our understanding of dementia. We can now show how scientific discourse has constituted its objects, in this case dementia as a disease, and we can locate Katzman's paper in the model.

In Stage One scientists have documents, including publications, papers, previous results, research apparatus, received opinion, and so on, which in Stage Two are used to project the existence of a particular object. We can see here that Katzman took two types of document, those analysing neuropathological changes in the brains of older people and epidemiological evidence of the ageing process, and used these to produce one document which fulfilled the requirements of the second stage. He has projected the existence of a particular object, that is, a disease with its own label and aetiology. Fox has shown how successful he was in this objective, leading to the third stage, in which splitting has occurred and the object, dementia as a disease, is now perceived as an entity separate and distinct from the documents used in Stage Two. The fourth stage, inversion, where the relationship between documents and objects is inverted and the documents are used to explain the existence of the object, has already been explored (but only by implication) in Chapters 3 and 4, where we explored the accepted definitions of dementia as a disease. Here we will explore the stages in a little more depth, to show how history is rewritten so as to give the discovered object its ontological foundations as a disease, that is, the first three steps are pushed into the background, forgotten or denied. In doing this we will return to Britain, and show that a similar process to that outlined by Fox in America has occurred in the United Kingdom.

Two papers by historians of dementia will be used to explore the process of how documents are now used to project the existence of the object, in this case a disease labelled Alzheimer's disease. They are taken from a book containing 23 papers, entitled *Dementia and Normal Aging* (Huppert *et al.* 1994) which is, 'based on the premise that the challenge of dementia lies in establishing the true relationship between dementia and normal aging' (Preface). Others might argue that the use of the singular for the noun 'challenge' denotes authors who see their own work as at the centre of the dementing universe, with all other participants, carers, sufferers, and so on, unchallenged. However, in its exploring of the 'continuity model', which sees most of the variables associated with dementia falling along a continuum with normal ageing, it provides an important balance to the medical/scientific model. The selection of these two papers is of interest because they are found within a book which, overall, supports the idea that dementia is *not* a separate disease, but is a part of the 'normal' ageing process. This is because, as Huppert *et al.* observe in their introductory overview, many of the, 'numerous biopathological and cognitive-behavioural changes' associated with 'normal' ageing are the same as changes attributed to the dementias; researchers have, 'either yet not identified those changes which are unique to the dementias, because the changes observed are confounded with age-related changes. The other is that normal aging and dementia form a continuum, the changes differing in degree but not in kind' (p.3). They conclude that, on the evidence of the 23 papers in *Dementia and Normal Aging*, the continuum model is best supported. Here, 'chronological age, intrinsic variables and environmental factors combine to determine when disability becomes manifested. *It is a convenience to apply a diagnostic label when a threshold of disability has been reached*' (p.10, emphasis added).

Let us commence with the arguments found in the second chapter of that long and interesting collection of papers, that of Berrios, from whom we obtain a picture of dementia as an historically accepted concept, with 'normal' ageing and dementia distinguished at least since the beginning of the nineteenth century, a time when ageing was seen as the result of the body wearing out through 'wear and tear', but when dementia then referred to a global term for many apparent disorders of the mind. In eighteenth century France dementia, 'was reversible and affected individuals of any age' (p.22); in nineteenth century Europe an 'anatomoclinical model' emerged, under whose rubric many disorders of the mind were included. There was, however, a 'gradual attrition', Berrios writes – using a metaphor which mimics our understanding of dementia – in the numbers of conditions included under the term 'dementia' and by the 1900s it had come to be seen as an irreversible disorder of intellectual functions. This latter period, we must note, is that in which Cartesian dualism was already dominant in Western medical thought, and the illustrations Berrios offers show the ubiquitous nature of dualist thought. Alzheimer, from whom the 'disease' has its name, undertook his famous project in 1907. Alzheimer, in reporting the case of a 51-year-old woman, was able to refer to neurofibrils, the existence of which had been known for some time, and to plaques, which had been associated with dementia since the 1880s. Alzheimer argued in favour of the continuity model, but his highly influential contemporary, Kraepelin, 'was keen for such cases to be a new disease' (p.21) and his influence held sway into the 1950s at least. It was indeed Kraepelin who allotted Alzheimer's name to the disease.

It is in Berrios's discussion of Alzheimer's work that we see the imprint of the present imposed on the past, for he moves easily from reporting Alzheimer's study of a 51-year-old woman to reporting early instances of knowledge of the physiology of the brain. In so doing he conflates Alzheimer's study with senile dementia, as the following quote shows:

> [I]n Prague, Fischer gave an important paper in June 1907 pointing out that miliary necrosis could be considered to be a marker of senile dementia. Nor was it a new syndrome that was described by Alzheimer: states of persistent cognitive impairment affecting the elderly, accompanied by delusions and hallucinations, were well known. (pp. 32–33)

From Berrios's perspective, Alzheimer had intended only to show that, 'such a syndrome could occur in younger people' (p.33). Do we then have a neat reversal, where in the late twentieth century the disease had to be reinterpreted, remade into one where a disease which affected younger people became a disease of older age groups, in contrast with the early twentieth century when efforts were made to show that a syndrome suffered by the elderly also affected younger people?

Berrios's chapter is followed by that of another historian, Lishman (1978), who straight away demonstrates that he is writing about the past with the words of the present, for he observes, in noting the relative absence of research into dementia for most of the twentieth century, that, 'neurobiological research has provided us with not one, but several, models which may explain the aetiopathogenesis of Alzheimer's disease, *the commonest of all dementing disorders*' (p.41, emphasis added).

For, as we know, Alzheimer's disease is so common only if its name is allocated to behavioural processes which affect the elderly. Lishman, like Berrios, shows that the analysis of dementia has taken place within a context where ageing was long seen as a process of deterioration, of wearing out. Lishman, too, follows Berrios in seeing the early twentieth century as a period when a disease of older people was, it was argued, also one suffered by younger persons.

The mid-twentieth century is, for Lishman, the 'dark ages' of research into dementia, for in this period medical and psychiatric texts virtually ignored the topic. During this period, it is clear from Lishman's discussion, dementia was seen not as a disease but as a part of ageing. Medical texts treated Alzheimer's disease as essentially premature senility, psychiatric texts used simple senile deterioration as the paradigm for senile dementia and contained no hint that Alzheimer's disease could affect the elderly (p.44). It was not until 1958 that McMenemey 'fully document[ed]' Alzheimer's disease, seeing it as a disease signified by abundant tangles and plaques in the brain and independent of age. Now, 'things at last became clearer in the neuropathological laboratory' and in the United Kingdom a start was made to clarify the nosological status of dementia in the elderly (p.45). This resulted in 'a new tidiness' as the, 'amorphous conception of senile mental illness' was refined so that many categories were excluded. In this statement we again see our understanding of dementia reflected in the ways in which people write about it, for here in this one sentence, of the 'tidying' of the concept, we see that which has occurred in studies of dementia in the last three decades, in which it has been 'tidied up' into a disease which explains, or seeks to explain, the amorphous symptomatology of dementia in older people, all of which is now seen to signify Alzheimer's disease. This metaphor, of tidiness, implies order is made out of disorder, by the mere effort of categorising people. It allowed senile dementia to be compared properly with pre-senile Alzheimer's disease (pp.45–6). The result of neuroscientific research which undertook these comparisons was that, 'opinion grew steadily that they were virtually identical except for the matter of age of onset' (ibid.).

In the 1950s and 1960s, according to Lishman, 'the dementias began at last to be placed on a firm scientific footing'. In the 1970s, 'we came gradually to the concept of dementia as a problem worthy of being tackled in the light of the "medical model"'. In a discussion of results of experiments in the 1970s, Lishman conflates Alzheimer's disease with senile dementia: experimental results led to 'new-found confidence' which, 'opened not one but several openings for research into the commonest of all dementing conditions, viz. Alzheimer's senile dementia' (p.47). Here we see echoes in Britain of Fox's analysis of what happened in the USA. Three groups of neuroscientists led the field. Based in Edinburgh, Newcastle-upon-Tyne and London, they produced papers which are widely quoted in British and American texts as showing the various changes in the structures of the brains of people with dementia. In an echo of what happened in the USA, attention to Alzheimer's disease was spurred on by realisation of the numbers of elderly persons afflicted with the condition and threatening to overwhelm the caring services, so that the Medical Research Council nominated research into the dementias as a priority area in 1977 (p.47). Publications on dementia, in Britain and the United States, rose from an annual 100 publications per year throughout the 1960s and 1970s to 1500 in 1990, as shown in the Cumulated Index Medicus, with the vast majority of these papers dealing with senile dementia of the Alzheimer type.

In this research of the last two decades, Lishman writes that Alzheimer's dementia is conceptualised in terms of the medical model of illness. It is this medical model which guides research methods. Having such a disease process behind it, research is dominated by the searches for mechanisms based on such a conception. In other words, neuroscientists have looked long and hard, over many years and in quite large numbers, for evidence of a disease. Lishman states that the developments of the past two decades have operated in the main as a vigorous opposition to the idea that Alzheimer's changes are analogous to old age. He argues that it seems to have been important to discard what he calls 'this prejudice' in order to open up research on a widespread front. This is very interesting in terms of this discussion for three reasons: first, there is the use of the pejorative word 'prejudice'. As applied to the idea that dementia and ageing are analogous, it shows that Lishman has achieved that which Woolgar says happens: the original documents are lost, and now documents are put forward which build the new consensus. Lishman, as a historian, makes an important contribution to rewriting the past. People seeking to know the history of dementia in the 20th century are likely to turn to his work, and that of others like him, and will ignore the original documents. Here he propounds the view that the idea of dementia as not-a-disease is prejudicial, is biased, is out-dated. Second, there is the explicit meaning of the sentence. It means, simply, that research could not be opened up on what he calls a wide front until dementia was seen as a disease and not a natural process of ageing. This, of course, echoes what Fox says about the USA. Finally, the military metaphor of the 'wide front' of research, signifying that researchers are involved in a battle against dementia, is actually very narrow – it refers to laboratory research into dementia as-a-disease. However, by describing such research as a 'wide front' Lishman erases the possibility that any other methods of research could perhaps have proved worthwhile.

The closing paragraphs of Lishman's paper, however, adopt an entirely different tone. The breathless excitement of the previous paragraphs, listing discoveries made and progress achieved, gives way to a considered thoughtful-ness. He warns, 'ageing and Alzheimer's dementias are interlinked closely'. Indeed, 'in the very elderly there may be little in the brain to distinguish Alzheimer patients from non-dements of equivalent age', so that, 'it would seem that when Alzheimer's dementia affects the elderly it becomes progressively harder to draw firm demarcations between neural ageing and the Alzheimer process – to see where the one has ended and the other has begun' (p.51). 'Alzheimer's disease' may be 'brain ageing after all' and, 'it is possible that we have seized on the medical model of Alzheimer's disease too readily', for, 'in Alzheimer's dementia...the brain picture seems to point towards that of aging itself'. The distinction between 'ageing process' and 'disease', he feels, 'may melt away – an artificial dichotomy drawn from older concepts'. For neurobi-ology may now have reached the stature where, 'we may *no longer have need of the shelter of a formal disease model to provide an impetus to scientific effort*' (p.52, emphasis added).

Lishman here not only acknowledges, but carefully cites, the confused conclusions from neuroscientific research into aged brains. What does he mean by that concluding sentence, which we have here emphasised? If we examine the metaphors used, we see that neurobiology was in its infancy (had not yet reached sufficient stature) and too little to fend for itself (it needed 'shelter'), indeed may have wandered off in aimless directions (it needed impetus), without 'a formal disease model'. The 'formal disease model' provided it with a means of support (research funds) until it was big enough to fend for itself. Here we have the very same process in Britain as Fox argues occurred in the USA, of a necessity to see dementia as a disease in order to secure research funding for neuroscientific endeavours. Now, Lishman implies, neuroscience has reached adult status – it has so much stature that it is ensured of a livelihood without needing to perpetuate the disease model of dementia. Is this why research papers are now increasingly showing the similarities rather than the differences between the brains of people diagnosed as having dementia and those diagnosed as 'normal'?

Analysis of these two recent papers on the history of knowledge about dementia thus reveals the essential reductionism of dementia to that of a single perspective – a neurophysiological explorative journey. We see in these papers the perspective of history as a linear progress from chaos and ignorance towards understanding, the very opposite of that which is seen in dementia, so dementia becomes 'tidied up', becomes controllable through its reduction to the status of disease, a process achieved by science.

We see here Woolgar's final two stages in action. Stage Four is inversion, where the relationship between documents and objects is inverted, and the documents are used to explain the existence of the object. Here two historians have used documents to explore the history of dementia up to the present day, and have, for all save the earliest period, focused solely on the documents produced by neuroscientists, projecting the idea of what is knowledge from those documents back into the past and reading the past only as if it were concerned with gaining an understanding of what dementia is. The fifth stage, Woolgar's crucial phase, sees the rewriting of history so as to give the discovered object its ontological foundations, that is, the first three steps are pushed into the background, forgotten or denied. The documents used therefore explain the object, dementia, as a disease. Any contrary perspective is 'prejudice'.

Conclusion

Let us now summarise the implications of these arguments. If Fox's thesis is correct, then in dementia we have a process whereby medical scientists (and we have seen similar processes occurring in Britain and the USA) did not seek a cause for a pre-existing disease. Instead we have a process where neuroscientists needed a disease, so they identified something as that disease and then sought the cause of that which they had labelled a disease. They have 'constructed' the evidence in the sense that they have assumed a causal relationship between changes in brain cells and behavioural changes which are now seen as symptoms of a disease. Once this hypothesis became accepted then all subsequent research grew out of that original conclusion. All other possible solutions were rejected out of hand.

This conclusion is supported and illuminated by the work of Ludwik Fleck, as discussed by Löwy (1988), a Polish-Jewish physician, bacteriologist and immunologist whose work, dating from the 1920s and 1930s, is now influential in the sociology of health. Fleck, basing his arguments upon his own clinical laboratory practice, contended that scientific knowledge is constructed by distinct 'thought collectives' composed of individuals who share specific 'thought styles' and who have difficulty in communicating with members of other thought collectives. The training required in order to become a member of a particular thought collective develops in the novice the relevant thought style and ability to 'see' what is seen by other members of that collective, but hinders the ability to look at an object from any other point of view. Individual medical specialists can observe pathological phenomena within one framework only. Furthermore, modern 'scientific' medicine is as dependent upon social and cultural factors as were other forms of medicines in the past, and indeed, Fleck argued that popular beliefs about illness contribute to the formation of expert medical knowledge. Popular knowledge is taken up by experts who translate it into scientifically acceptable terms through searching for scientific support for that which they are seeking. In other words, what they 'see', what they discover, is determined by what they are seeking (Löwy 1988). This illuminates our above arguments, that once neuroscientists had concurred in the hypothesis that changes in brain cells were the cause of dementia, they would undertake ever more refined studies of deterioration in brain cells which would 'prove' their hypothesis. They had been alerted to look for and to see such deterioration and thus would find it. They would become blind to other explanations.

CHAPTER 6

Medical Diagnosis
and the Construction of Dementia

Introduction: the translation of science into practice

Neuroscientists researching in the field of dementia publish details of their work in scientific journals. We could here suggest a model whereby doctors read the journals, learn the results of neuroscientific research into dementia, and proceed to diagnose it in patients. To assume such a straightforward relationship between doctors reading about and then identifying senile dementia of the Alzheimer's type through diagnosis would be to develop an intuitively attractive model but one based solely in the cognitive domain and therefore full of gaps. We have argued that scientists 'invented' the disease in older people, but there is a long distance between this and doctors' diagnosis, for surely the doctor will not diagnose a non-existent disease?

This chapter explores the process of diagnostic decision-making with the aim of answering the question, 'how did the "knowledge" garnered from the scientific model of dementia become transferred to general practice?'. To answer this question we must delve deeply into the art of diagnosis, for medicine is traditionally divided into science and art: the 'science' is the body of medical research which informs medicine; the 'art' the process of diagnosis. This chapter tries to fill in the large gap between these two aspects of medicine by analysing how, once specific patterns of deterioration in brain cells had been 'proved' to be the 'cause' of a 'disease' in older people, that knowledge was made available to doctors so that they could then diagnose the existence or otherwise of this disease in people displaying relevant symptoms.

The chapter is laid out as follows. First, a definition of the 'official' model of medical diagnosis is given. We break it down into its constituent parts: taxonomy, reasoning process, and diagnosis, and discuss each in turn, examining how the medical model treats each stage and criticising each one through the alternative prism offered by sociologists. In this reading Leder's (1990) hypothesis of 'the flight from interpretation' will prove influential. He argues that modern medicine has been 'bewitched' by the ideal of 'achieving a purified objectivity', an ideal which is impossible given the subjective nature of diagnosis, a subjectivity from which physicians flee.

The diagnostic art

Diagnosis is regarded as the *art* of medicine. In medical texts it is seen as the process of converting observed evidence into the names of diseases, where the evidence consists of data obtained from examining a patient, and diseases are conceptual medical entities that identify or explain abnormalities in the observed evidence. This presupposes a logical, systems model of diagnosis, that is, a healthy host becomes diseased and, through the doctor's reasoning based on aetiology, diagnosis and prognosis, becomes an evolved host (Feinstein 1967). Diagnosis involves deductive and inductive logic in order to 'map' symptoms (and other patient data) on to a disease (Schaffner 1985). It requires: (1) an adequate set of disease definitions and classifications (a taxonomy); (2) a reasoning process that will allow the doctor to use the signs exhibited and symptoms expressed by the patient so as to; (3) make a diagnosis. We will explore each of these in turn.

Taxonomy

We will begin this discussion of taxonomy by using Wulff's (1981) introductory text to clinical decision-making, a delightfully irascible book whose author is at pains to point out what he sees as the shortcomings of the medical profession. Taxonomy is, for Wulff, the 'concept of a disease entity', with the word 'taxonomy' derived from two Greek words meaning 'arrangement' and 'law' so as to give the meaning of a classification system. But, he emphasises, we are not talking of a classification of *diseases*, although that is what is usually assumed, but of *patients*, so taxonomies are nominalist in the sense that they name given classes of patient. They furthermore are a *predictive system* in that they allow decisions about diagnosis and treatment to be made.

A variety of criteria are used in such a classification, he continues, including anatomical criteria, symptoms, metabolic disturbances and aetiological factors. Wulff's history of taxonomy is a classical study of the modernist assumption that humanity is engaged in a process of moving from ignorance towards enlightenment, where ideas from the eighteenth century are 'ludicrous in retrospect', and those of the nineteenth are major steps forward, even if hindered by the primitiveness of contemporary technology. He suggests that the ingredients of today's taxonomy reflect the history of medicine from the seventeenth century to the end of the nineteenth century and thus illustrate what is regarded as the growing rationalisation of medicine.

Today's taxonomies comprise the following:

1. *Name of the Disease.* These are of historical interest, in Wulff's schema, for their origin is often to be found in history. Sometimes they represent early assumptions about causes, sometimes they carry the name of the man (nearly always a man) who 'discovered' them.

2. *Definitions.* This is a man-made system, so, 'it is up to the members of the medical profession to define exactly what they mean by the disease names, which they have invented' (p.53). As taxonomy is a classification of patients: 'In order to define a disease entity, they must fix a set of criteria *which are fulfilled by all patients said to be suffering from the disease and by no patients not said to be suffering from the disease*' (p.53). There is a problem here, he says, for most textbooks do not provide a logically satisfactory definition but an ultra-short description, and this dearth of explicit, logically satisfactory definitions reflects the attitude of doctors to the concept of disease. This attitude is one which leads to a failure to identify patients with the same disease, he argues, for different diagnostic criteria are used.

3. *Causes of Disease.* These are elicited by aetiological (or causative) factors which cause a series of changes in the organism which comprises the pathogenesis of the disease. The causative factors may be *necessary* (where the disease always occurs when this factor is present), *sufficient* (where the cause always leads to the disease, but sometimes the disease is not preceded by this particular cause), or *contributory* (where the presence of a factor leads to an increased probability of the disease). Diseases are, Wulff argues, caused by multiple determining factors, but there is a time-honoured concept within medicine of 'one cause – one disease', leading to treatments being based on the assumed aetiology or pathogenesis of the disease. Here, he says, 'one is reminded of Lasegue's statement that doctors explain everything and pass quickly from hypothesis to practice' (p.59).

Wulff ignores what Engelhardt (1985, p.63) says is an ancient dispute in the theory of medicine, a dispute between physiologists and ontologists. Ontologists hold that diseases are enduring clusters of signs and symptoms which await discovery and become constellations of pathological findings. This, we must note, is a highly positivist ontology, or pursuit of understanding of what exists. Physiologists, on the other hand, hold that nosologies and disease phenomena have their boundaries invented, not discovered. For physiologists all that is real are the laws of physiology. The certainties of classifications of disease, such as the International Classification of Diseases (ICD) and the Diagnostic Statistical Manual (DSM) devised by the American Psychiatric

Association, disguise under the mask of confidence a debate within medicine itself, and impose upon that debate, 'an ongoing attempt to standardise medical diagnoses and information gathering' (op cit, p.63). From this ontological perspective, dementia would always have existed, but it would require the developments in medical science which have occurred in the late twentieth century to prove its location within a deteriorating brain. For physiologists, perhaps, the brain would be seen to change with age, but these changes would be subject to different labels at different periods of time.

Taxonomies are somewhat limited in their use, for the assignment of a patient to a disease class, as Wulff shows, is fraught with difficulties. Many diseases remain enigmas to the medical profession, so quite arbitrary definitions of diseases are made and used by different researchers, and in most, Wulff argues, the disease process as a whole is only poorly understood. Feinstein (1967), writing as a medical scientist, argues that the identification of a disease by its name depends upon criteria which are subject to observer variability, (in today's medical world diverse groups of diagnosticians, from radiologists to laboratory technicians); thus the numbers of observers have multiplied and the opportunities for confusion have multiplied. Verbal morphological descriptions may be subjective so that, even though a common vocabulary is used, different connotations may be applied to the same name and different observers may use the same 'disease' name for diverse abnormalities. Tests expressed numerically may be subject to error or variation, and the same entity may be tested by different methods or expressed in different units. Performance of measurement tests may not be standardised between laboratories. Often the 'diseases' detected in tests do not conform with the patient's symptoms, and the tests available are now so many and so varied that similar problems as exist in diagnosis exist in the choice of test to undertake.

The idea of a taxonomy thus begins to be seen as more and more elusive. Its elusiveness becomes understandable if we analyse a taxonomy through semiotics. From Saussure comes the idea of language as a system of signs, where signs have two components: the signifier or mark or sound of a word, and the signified, or the *idea* or *concept* to which the word refers (Sarap 1993). The signifier here is the name of a disease, the signified the concept of the disease entity itself. Sarap traces this concept to Derrida's argument that reality is so difficult to grasp that the signified is just another signifier, and so complex does the web of signifiers become that reality becomes indeterminate. In this perspective, the taxonomy of diseases can be understood as an attempt to place labels upon various physiological changes which are sensed by patients but which can only be apprehended by diagnosticians through external signs. That which the patient senses subjectively is rendered external through a taxonomy of internal physiological sensations which diagnosticians have to 'know'.

This leads us to ask how particular disease labels are attributed. 'They are certainly not determined by naturally occurring categories and phenomena' (Atkinson 1995, p.47), for diseases or syndromes are historically and culturally specific (Herzlich and Peirret 1985). Sickness is symbolically, 'one of the major ways in which individual and group misfortune is "embodied"' (p.145), so that the individual sufferer's experiences and expectations, 'cannot be fully understood without being placed within the macrostructure of society', a macrostructure which has 'conceptions' about sick people, which the sick internalise and sustain, which, 'orient, organize and legitimate social relationships and, to a certain degree, "produce" the 'reality' of sick people' (p.146). But just as patients are constructed so too, we must suggest, are members of the health care professions, groups of people charged with responsibility for producing the 'reality' of a cure for illness.

We can here borrow Chia's (1994) analysis of the role of decision-making in management texts, for his analysis may suggest the reality behind the process of labelling of diseases. Decision-making has been a central concept in management and organisation theory for at least 50 years but, Chia argues, it is:

> ...better understood as an *explanatory principle* created by decision theorists and researchers to help them make sense by providing plausible connections between different aspects of observed behaviour. Such explanatory principles serve as ideational 'linkages' that enable us to create a plausible and coherent pattern from what we apprehend. They *are not* attempts to describe reality as it is in itself. As such, the principal characteristic of the 'explanatory principle' is not so much 'truth' in any strong sense but 'coherence'. (p.794, emphasis in original)

Decision-making therefore should be seen as, 'the product of a *post-hoc* rationalization process in which the cause/effect relationship established has been abstracted, reified and chronologically reversed' (p.794).

Decision-making thus becomes a 'conceptual invention'. The reification of concepts is, he argues, a common tendency, for it helps us understand our lives. In Chia's words, we need to make an '"incision" in the flow of our lived experiences' in order to 'punctuate' our lived experiences 'for the purpose of ordering and responding to such experiences'. This is because reality is so complex that we have to limit it in order to make it cognitively manageable; in other words we must, 'delimit the scope of our attention by punctuating our

phenomenal experiences, removing equivocality and thereby helping to con-
figure a version of reality to which we then subsequently respond' (pp.795–6).[1]
'Decisions therefore are primary ontological acts of carving out a plausible
reality', for, 'things, events and social entities arise from ontological acts of
decision. What we apprehend as significant and worthy of investigation is
always already constituted by our very decision to engage in the investigative
activity itself' (p.796). We make decisions in order to carve out a reality which
we later claim to have discovered, for, Chia argues, we are engaged in an
inescapable and active participation in bringing about that which we experience: we bring forth reality.

Even such basic categories of time and space, he says, are not 'out there' but
are inherent constituents of the mind, which we conceive of and then deploy
in order to apprehend the phenomenal world. In doing this, we use linguistic
structures which are our necessary conceptual apparatus for thinking of the
world in discrete, static and hence describable terms, for we can only apprehend
through the facility of language, and without language reality is, in Chia's
perspective, but a meaningless moving mass. As reality is so complex we cut
out a part from the whole of our phenomenal experiences and make that part
stand for the whole.

Foss (1994) has argued in a similar fashion, saying that:

> Medicine, in a sense, gives definition to our humanness. Its research
> strategies, disease and health concepts, therapeutic options, virtually
> every nuance of its theory and practice secrete assumptions about the
> human self. Today's practice of medicine, reflecting the 'modern' or
> Enlightenment scientific and meta-scientific thought world, provides us
> with one compelling version of who we think we are as we leave the
> twentieth century. (p.291)

Foss's argument develops in such a way as to support Chia's analysis. He cites
the results of studies into how the brain works. Brains, he writes, resist
explanation by the analytical tools of classical, steady-state dynamics. They are
complex. 'Not possessing filters designed…to distinguish in advance signal
from noise, brains have to accomplish this task on their own in the face of an
endless barrage of incident stimuli' (1994, p.308). The manner in which they
do this is explained by physiologists, who have identified a self-organised
chaotic generator that responds to environmental input by replacing it with an
internally generated chaotic activity pattern. This pattern is transmitted further

---

1   Here again we have the metaphor of dementia: reality is so complex we cannot make sense of it
     but we somehow do so by limiting it; in dementia that ability of making sense somehow
     disintegrates.

into the brain to provide a basis for future selectivity. These self-organising brain dynamics furthermore entail relative independence from the properties of their substrate, indicating the existence of a hierarchy of developmentally related but mutually irreducible self-organising structures. The result is that the person-who-thinks is 'isomorphic with' but, 'irreducible to the unself-conscious living animal body' (p.309).

Summary: taxonomies as arbitrary, historically and culturally bound classification systems

This analysis can be applied with equal force to the labelling of diseases, which can now be seen as a process of carving out a reality which helps both patients and members of the health care professions to understand the world around and within them. Disease labels can be seen, using Chia's argument, as necessary conceptual apparatus for thinking of the world in discrete, static and hence describable terms. Where Feinstein (1967) saw the classification of diseases as an, 'intellectual mechanism for organizing and remembering his [the clinician's] observations' (p.13), it can rather be seen as an intellectual mechanism for organising and remembering the clinician's sense of his or her own reality. Taxonomies are, following Wulff, ways of categorising patients. Rather, we have said, they are ways of configuring reality. Diagnosticians therefore use taxonomies to carve order out of the chaotic world of illness and death which they meet every work day. They make sense of the chaos, and cope with the reality of their own fragility, through categorising people into groups designated as having a certain physiological malfunction.

Furthermore, those who work *with* the body have a greater investment, in the sense of understanding the world, in the body than the rest of society. They depend for their existence upon certain perceptions about the reality of the body. As we will show when we discuss the sociology of the body, our apprehension of the body is one of our prior experiences of the carving out of reality. Those who work primarily with a corporeal body have the importance of the body magnified for them, for the body for them takes on greater meaning. It comprises their world of work and a major part of their lives.

Taxonomies are therefore quite arbitrary, historically and culturally bound classification systems, which will vary according to how the body is understood and how reality is carved out. They do not merely classify diseases, or patients, but reality.

The reasoning process

The second stage of diagnosis is a reasoning process, which is described in medical texts as an orderly process which proceeds from the general (the gathering of initial information) to the specific (the diagnosis). This is where the 'art' of medicine is seen to be located, for much of the reasoning process is assumed to be based on the physician's capacity for inductive logic. Here the doctor and patient meet, and the process starts with the doctor attempting to identify the cause of the patient's illness and ends with him or her applying their clinical judgement in order to identify a disease label and arrive at a prescription. The process of medical decision-making, an inherent part of the reasoning process, is now subject to much research, notably by psychologists who attempt to identify the cognitive processes brought into play during medical decision-making, and to make these available so that they can be improved upon, thus blending art with science. Dowie and Elstein (1993) argue that clinical judgement can be successful only if it is not only an art, a 'fundamentally non-logical, qualitative activity which is emotionally concerned with the unique individual' (p.5), but also, 'implicitly if not explicitly – logical, quantitative, detached and statistical' (*ibid.*).

We have, in the introduction to this section, encapsulated a continuing debate in medical writings: is the physician drawing upon art or science when making a decision? Current books whose titles imply a full exploration of medical decision-making, such as that of Dowie and Elstein (1993), already refer to and contain papers and chapters which attempt first to describe physicians as involved in rational models of medical decision-making and second to educate them about how to be more rational, more scientific. The idea that medical processes of reasoning are cognitive and scientifically based is seen in the results of research into decision-making processes, and didactic treatises on clinical decision-making. One typical, and popular, normative decision-making process is Bayesian inference, based upon Bayes's theorem, which states that the decision-making process should proceed as follows:

1. Information-gathering, or cue acquisition. Here the physician gathers information from the patient.

2. Generation of several hypotheses based on an identification of the cardinal clues offered and a clustering of items according to their importance.

3. Selection of the most appropriate hypothesis, and a search for confirmatory evidence to support the hypothesis.

4. Diagnosis.

Bayesian theory (presented highly simplistically here) presents statements in terms of hypotheses and levels of confidence as to their probability (one may hypothesise that it will rain tomorrow and, having heard the weather forecast, be 50 per cent confident of its doing so). These statements are subjective, so individuals may legitimately assess quite differently.[2] The metaphor of the computer and the way it arrives at results is implicit in this model.

This theorem, presented here in the simplest form possible, is inherently attractive to a generation brought up with computers and their methods of analysis, where the metaphor of computing informs much of our daily lives. It may indeed have resonance for the non-medical public, who may intuit, indeed may need to believe, that this is the way the medical mind works when developing a diagnosis. Indeed the working hypothesis of this chapter, developed after considering the arguments of the previous one, is that physicians, when diagnosing someone as having dementia, gather clues about the person's behaviour in a process which can be modelled as $(1 + 2 + 3)$, and arrive at a conclusion given to them by science, so that the equation becomes $1 + 2 + 3 = 75$.

However, a further reading of texts on medical decision-making raises some problematic questions, for the texts seek to argue both that medicine is *really* an art which is mistakenly apprehended as a science, and that medicine is a science which suffers the shortcomings of not being scientific enough.

Feinstein, for example, in 1967 published a method of medical reasoning based on mathematical formulae which was designed to allow physicians to classify their knowledge and then to categorise patients according to certain criteria. Feinstein's method will not be explored here; what we wish to show is that Feinstein was attempting to rationalise a process seen as inductive and inherently non-scientific, and trying to prove to clinicians that *they could be scientific*. This contrasts with much of the literature from the social studies of medicine, which attempts to prove the opposite, that medical decision-making is not based on science but on some other processes which can be included under the rubric of 'art'.

Feinstein, for example, describes the act of clinical decision-making as an experiment, where the purpose is to 'repeat a success of the past' (p.23). However, when a laboratory investigator makes decisions in conducting an experiment, we require that the ingredients of his reasoning be explicitly defined. We insist that he be able to specify his methods, his data, and his interpretations of the data, and that the specifications be precise and reproducible. When a clinician makes decisions in the experiments of therapy, we generally assume that the procedure is too complex for scientific documentation. The reasoning process used is quite different from deductive logic, for it, 'depends not on a knowledge of causes, mechanisms, or names for disease, but on a knowledge of patients' (p.12). Clinical judgement is therefore an 'art', 'a

---

2   Fischoff and Beyth-Marom (1993) provide a more technical discussion of Bayesian decision-making, while Clouser (1985) provides an intuitive understanding of the theorem.

humanistic application of established modes of therapy', but as an art it is unreproducible in the sense in which experiments are or should be reproducible, and clinical judgement, clinicians were taught, contained some mystic realm of intuition. The clinician is usually permitted to justify his work, Feinstein argues, on the basis of 'hunch', intuition, or a nebulously defined clinical experience. Clinical decisions are allowed a rationale that need not be overtly rational, and reasons that need not be particularly reasonable. If the clinician seems knowledgeable and authoritative, and if his reputation and results seem good, he can be forgiven the most flagrant imprecisions, vagueness and inconsistency in conduct of therapy. In one of his more damning judgements, Feinstein accuses the clinician of not bothering to use a scientific name for his method of designing, executing and appraising therapeutic experiments: 'He calls it *clinical judgment*' (1967, pp.26–7).

Five traditional clinical axioms, Feinstein argued, led remorselessly to the belief that clinical judgement could not be scientific. The five axioms were(are) that science is concerned with the discovery of cause; that clinical reasoning is so intricate and unquantified that it cannot be expressed through scientific analysis; that the description of symptoms and signs can only be made using non-scientific language; that the clinician, 'believes he finds a constant association between the abnormal structures and abnormal functions that occur in human illness' thus rendering science unnecessary; and that the diagnostic names clinicians use adequately represent the, 'morphologic and laboratory abnormalities of disease' (p.55). Each of these, Feinstein argued, was wrong, and he set about establishing a method of diagnosis designed to overturn each one, for he argued that physicians, in making diagnoses, are involved in the translation of science into practice. However, this is not an easy process, for, 'ever since Kelvin stated the doctrine that measurement was a prerequisite to science, biologists have been trying to measure, and clinicians have felt lost' (p.61). They have felt lost because many of the symptoms presented to clinicians are subjective, and are by definition difficult to measure.

Contrast this now with Malterud's (1994) arguments, written a quarter of a century after Feinstein. Medicine, she writes, claims to be a discipline founded on scientific knowledge, with scientific knowledge being a paradigmatic monopoly which continually extends its territory, claiming legitimacy as the one and only valid epistemic voice of medicine (p.183). However, she argues, this traditional medical epistemology does not accurately represent medical knowledge. At medical school, she writes, she was taught that medical knowledge consisted of great quantities of universal, ever-lasting facts and truths, but she found when practising as a doctor that the scientific bases of the bio-medical paradigm contradicted that clinical epistemology encountered in the 'interpretative human interactions of clinical medicine'. It is necessary, she writes, for clinical epistemoloy to be acknowledged within the medical culture, but this is still not the case.

In sum, we have a debate in which one group of contributors (medical scientists) are critical of the art or intuition within medical reasoning processes, and another group (located within the social studies of science) which attempts to prove that medical reasoning is based not on science but on art. The debate is located within analyses of power and the legitimacy-making role of science, with medical writers seeking to entrench physicians' power base through grounding of their actions within science, and students of the social sciences seeking to remove the 'science' from medicine so as to show its social base.

Berg (1995), basing his arguments upon experience in the USA, has traced the arguments from the medical side to an evolutionary process which has been occurring in medicine in the post-war years. He shows that the dominant discourse in medicine is now one in which medicine is seen as a science which is seriously flawed by its practitioners' shortcomings. This is a process which has developed in the post-war years, when there has been a project involving, 'the gradual and unswerving process of turning an art into a science' (p.438). However, this has not been a, 'single, unilinear process in which a previously "unscientific" practice became "scientific"' (p.438). In the early post-war years medical practice was seen as an artful application of scientific knowledge. In the decade of the 1960s, medical practice was seen to have inherent weaknesses, such as a lack of uniform procedures and terminology, which had to be addressed in order to allow medicine to become more 'scientific'. By the 1970s, influenced very much by the work of Feinstein and others, medicine came to be seen not as primarily the *application* of a science located elsewhere, but a scientific activity *itself*. The late 1970s and the 1980s saw the emergence of a new discourse: that of the scientific status of medical practice as a feature of the physician's mind. Informed by cognitive psychology, medical decision-making was seen as a hypothetico-deductive process where the physician's brain worked in much the same way as does a computer or indeed that, supposedly, of a scientist: generating hypotheses, testing and verification. Here intuitive, inspirational leaps were to be eliminated. Medical practice continued to be seen *itself* as a form of science, but a form of science located in the mind of the physician, a mind equivalent to that of a computer. All these models, though dominant in a particular period, continue to co-exist.

Medical practice has since 1945, in short, been rephrased in a cognitivist discourse, resulting in the development of a normative framework which (ostensibly) allows scrutiny and judgement of physicians' decision-making processes. According to Berg, it has come to be seen as an enterprise of reasoning or calculating minds where the, '*description* of medical action as a scientific activity functions as an explicit yardstick which allows one to evaluate (and criticize) what physicians do' (1995, p.461). Berg goes on to argue that it was the existence of the tools (computers) which shaped the cognitive perspective of medical practice. In other words, it was only the advent of computers which allowed medical scientists to think of the medical brain as such a rational, logical processor. He concludes that there has been no gradual transformation of a practice into a science, but rather a set of discontinuous images in which the notions of 'science' and 'medical practice' themselves changed shape, and which has resulted in the 'quality of care' now being interpreted as accuracy in diagnosis.

While the development of computers may in part have stimulated perspectives of the medical reasoning process, this post-war concept is one that conforms fully with the mechanistic concept of the human body which originated with Descartes's excision of the connection between mind and body. Here the body belongs to the external world which can be subjected to quantitative analysis; it is one made of atomic fundamentals. The mind belongs to an internal world of subjectivity, and has no effect upon the physical world of the body. There is thus a discontinuity between these worlds (Foss 1994). Cartesian dualism sees the body as akin to a machine, and disease as the failure of various mechanical functions (Hewa and Hetherington 1994). Medical research and medical practice are each based on a subscription to the mechanistic model, where the body can be repaired through the replacement or repair of parts, for disease is nothing but 'physiology gone astray' (Zucker quoted in Foss 1994, p.295). It is a difficult body, for physicians, Baron (1992) argues, are trained to regard the body as an impediment to diagnosis. The living body of the patient is, 'a translucent screen on which the silhouette of disease is projected' (p.38) and the physician must, 'render the patient's body...transparent so that the true disease can be directly apprehended' (ibid.). Given the impossibility of this, and the reality of dealing with warm, unique, living bodies, 'diagnosis becomes an act of struggle with the body'. Here the metaphor of the body-as-machine becomes reified: the body becomes a machine and disease is, 'mechanical breakdown of the body-machine'.

As the patient's body is a machine, then, we must argue, so is the doctor's, a machine whose control centre is located within the brain which, being mechanistic, must itself use mechanical processes of reasoning, but which, processing information as does a computer, is so much faster and more accurate than the average human brain. The doctor–machine is therefore perhaps more akin to a cybernaut. The analogy is made more apt by the process of training of doctors, which seeks to eradicate the expression of emotions, to encourage detachment and to suppress signs of humanity.

The metaphor of the medical encounter thus becomes one where one machine is assessed by another, superior, model of machine.

This, however, is a metaphor against which some doctors continue to fight, as can be seen in Malterud's (1994) paper, referred to above. The reason for this tendency is to be found in the act of diagnosis which, rather than being the definitive process we might expect, is a mapless search for the name of the disease. It is to this next stage, diagnosis, which we will now turn.

Diagnosis

The reasoning process and diagnosis, although conceptually distinguished by analysts of the decision process, intertwine and overlap.

Diagnosis, for Feinstein (1967), is the act which:

> ...gives a name to the patient's ailment, the thinking goes chronologically backward to decide about pathogenesis and etiology of the ailment. From diagnosis also, the thinking goes chronologically forward to predict prognosis and to choose therapy. As the main language of clinical communication, diagnostic labels transmit a rapid understanding of the contents of the package; diagnostic categories provide names for the intellectual locations in which clinicians store the observations of clinical experience. The taxonomy used for diagnosis will thus inevitably establish the patterns in which clinicians observe, think, remember and act (p.73).

To repeat what was said above, diagnosis is based largely on inference and proceeds as follows Feinstein (1967):

1. Direct observations of a patient's illness, as manifested in the patient's 'story' of his/her illness, result in first-order classifications.

2. The results of certain tests are, on the basis of the initial assessment, ordered.

3. Intellectual processes comprising sequential series of deductions are undertaken. This step includes at least three distinct acts of classificational decision, that is, decisions as to how many symptoms and signs are needed for identifying a disorder, the identification of the number of disorders present, and inference about the structural abnormality responsible for the disorder.

4. Achieving the anatomic diagnosis.

The 'art', which is perhaps 'intuition, or just good sense', is located specifically in the first of these stages, information-gathering, when the clinician gains, 'understanding and clues from a patient's choice of words, his [sic] facial expressions, his gestures, his movements, and his subliminal messages. The clinician can empathize with the patient's emotional state and come to see how the patient is interpreting his illness' (Clouser 1985, p.52). Diagnosis thus becomes a socio-psychological process (McMullin 1985).

For many or most of these stages, standard criteria may be unavailable or criticised, so that, 'every clinician has his own criteria for clinical diagnosis', and possesses his/her own techniques. The result is that, 'the same diagnostic name may represent different clinical entities to different clinicians; conversely, different diagnostic names may be used for the same disease' (Feinstein 1967, p.84).

Under pressure to provide a disease label in a situation of imperfect knowledge, a clinician may make an often thoughtful, educated and accurate anatomical guess, but it is just that: a guess (Feinstein 1967). Physicians are, furthermore, 'prone to overdiagnose...[or] to make a diagnosis of "non-disease" which then forms the basis of the therapeutic decision' (Wulff 1981, p.117), for they follow the maxim, 'when in doubt make a diagnosis' (p.118).

The logic and certainty of the process of diagnosis, which appeared so inherent in the stages just outlined, suddenly appears to wobble. Is the act of diagnosis as definitive as we are led to believe? We will here interpose a case study, of another illness which affects older people, which illustrates how uncertain is the process of diagnosis.

A CASE STUDY OF DIAGNOSTIC PROCEDURES

Thirty per cent of men may ultimately undergo a prostatectomy, making this one of the most common elective surgical procedures in men (Boyle 1994). It is undertaken primarily to remove obstruction of the urethra arising from benign prostatic hyperplasia (BPH) and cancer of the prostate, one of the most common cancers in men. Surgeons regard it as a major procedure: American urologists state transurethral prostatectomy accounts for 38 per cent of the major surgical procedures they perform. They regard the operation as complex and believe achievement of proficiency requires that during residency training more prostatectomies than any other urological operation should be performed (Holtgrewe et al. 1989). However, prostatectomy is a surgical procedure with a very high geographical variation, with rates ranging from 60 to 368 per 100,000 of the population, those in the USA being more than double those of Europe (Blais 1993; Keskimaki et al. 1994; Roos et al. 1988). In the USA one study found variations between districts of equal to or below 60 per 100,000 male Medicare beneficiaries to equal to or above 130 per 100,000 (Lu et al. 1993). Rates have been found to vary between the English health regions from 77 to 144 (McPherson 1990); variations correlate positively with income (Mulholland, Harding and Bradley 1995). Overall, prostatectomy rates increased throughout the 1980s. In Columbia, for example, radical prostatectomy rates in men aged 65 and over were 5.75 times higher in 1990 than in 1984. The relative increase was similar in all age groups (Lu et al. 1993). In Denmark the total annual number of prostatectomies increased by 43 per cent between 1977 and 1985, when the transurethral procedure (TURP) gradually replaced traditional open surgery. Incidence rises with age: in 1990 the rates of TURP among Medicare patients in the USA (including all indications) were approximately 25, 19 and 13 per 1000 for men over the age of 75, 70–74 and 65–69, respectively (Lu *et al.* 1994).

Prostatectomies therefore show a high incidence with marked geographical variations. The variations may be due to prostatism remaining a difficult clinical problem to diagnose, since many of the symptoms and diagnostic tests are non-specific, especially in the elderly (DuBeau and Resnick 1992). Eighty-eight per cent of autopsy specimens from men aged over 80 years have been shown to have histological BPH, which is an indication for prostatectomy. Despite its being such a common occurrence, little is known with any certainty about either the epidemiology or aetiology of BPH. Incidence increases with age (Boyle 1994), which has implications at a time when the population is ageing. However, the incidence, even the population prevalence, is difficult to determine for a variety of reasons. Knowledge of risk factors is sparse and surgeons disagree about them. Norwegian urological units consider urinary retention occurring more than once or residual urine greater than 500 ml an absolute indication for surgery. However, agreement on how to classify different symptoms into categories according to severity is not good (Hanssen and Wold 1994).

In the midst of such confusion, and in the absence of a scientific basis for decision-making, a consensus panel was established in the UK with the remit of deciding upon a basis for population-based surveys of the need for prostatectomy (Hunter *et al.* 1994). Some, but only a limited, measure of agreement was arrived at. However, Hunter *et al.* warn of the problems of decisions arising from panels of this type, in that they may, 'arrive at collective ignorance rather than wisdom' (p.64).

Prostatectomy is illustrative of, but by no means unique in, the confusion and uncertainty surrounding diagnosis and decision-making. To this case study of prostatectomies we could add similar stories for three-quarters of the most common surgical procedures (Mulholland *et al.* 1995).

We will now explore Feinstein's model of the diagnostic procedure to explore how diagnosis is difficult, tends towards inaccuracy and error, but gives the appearance of certitude.

EXPLORING FEINSTEIN'S MODEL OF DIAGNOSTIC PROCEDURES

The first of Feinstein's stages was direct observation of a patient's illness, as manifested in the patient's 'story' of his/her illness, resulting in first-order classifications. This is the stage where doctor and patient meet and the doctor attempts to elicit from the patient information which will lead to the diagnosis. This process has been analysed within the emerging field of medical hermeneutics. Hermeneutics refers to the study of theories of the interpretation of meaning (Daniel 1990) and is concerned with the relationship between language and understanding ourselves (Lock 1990).

Lock (1990) commences this analysis by arguing that medicine is, 'subject to the same kinds of limits that other human knowledge and activities are subject to – namely, that understanding, describing, and carrying out the activities of medicine are mediated by language' (p.42), so that the body of medicine (the somatic body, disease entities and physiologies) can be understood as a kind of text. Medicine can therefore be understood as a narrative plot which patterns events through a sequential chronicling, for stories can only be understood through such patterns or else they remain disjointed statements. These narratives form the basis, 'of relating immediate understanding to causal connections' (p.47). Lock identifies one narrative plot, that between doctor and patient, but to this we must add medical science itself as a narrative plot. However, Lock introduces the concept of a dialectic of explanation and understanding, where medical science and the doctor/patient encounter include a dialectical relationship. He describes the procedure as follows. The case:

> ...begins with the biographical particulars of the individual and is developed and expanded to a more general frame by the available scientific configurations. This scientific assessment must then be brought into relationship with how a life is changed by the disease and treatment processes. In this way *a medical case can be thought of as a struggle between an explanation of the real events of the disease process and the significance and meaning of these events in the broader context of the patient's life.* (1990, pp.47–8, emphasis added)

The patient offers a story at the point where his/her subjective explanatory attempts have failed, at which point the physician can initiate the healing process through the use of the reductive pole offered by medical science (p.48). Scientific explanations, Lock argues, serve a clarifying and de-mystifying purpose, allowing an episode in a patient's life to garner a sub-plot of its own. In other words, the scientific foundations of medicine are necessary in late 20th century society for an understanding of one's life and thus how one constructs the story of the self. The patient therefore approaches the doctor in order to achieve an understanding of how to construct the self which has changed with illness.

Leder (1990) takes us further into the actual meeting between doctor and patient. The patient is a kind of text to be interpreted through the doctor's reading, and, 'where there is interpretation there is subjectivity, ambiguity, room for disagreement. The personal and provisional character of clinical judgment cannot be expunged' (p.10). The patient, the ill person, constitutes for Leder the *primary* text to be interpreted, but this primary text has four sub-texts:

1. *The experiential text*, or the 'elaborative interpretive process' by which the patient has come to understand him/herself as ill.

2. *The narrative text*, which consists of the physician's taking of the patient's history, and which is written by three different authors: body, patient and doctor.

3. *The physical text*, which arises when history-taking gives way to physical examination. The body has its own words, but these are available only partially and in fragmentary form to the doctor. Other methods of communication have to be substituted, and these come from within the 'physician's lived-body', for the physician, 'while objectifying the patient, does not simultaneously objectify her own organs but lives them out as interpretive tools. Through clinical training, the doctor's senses have been shaped into acute and knowledgeable instruments' (p.14). This interpretive process, Leder argues, is not dependent upon intellectual heuristics, for the physician's knowledge, 'resides right in the body. The physician's hands have come to know the feel of a tumour, though she may have difficulty formulating this corporeal wisdom into the logic of principles and rules' (*ibid.*). Physicians therefore gain knowledge which they cannot put into words. They gain them through 'the senses', for 'their well-documented regard for personal, even visceral, experience reflects the role of the senses as a physician accumulates medical knowledge' (Tanenbaum 1993, p.1270). Tanenbaum, writing not as a social scientist, supports Leder's interpretation in arguing that the physician's encounter with the patient is based on a, 'subjective process of unspoken inference and intuition' where the process is, 'a gestalt or story rather than an algorithm' (*ibid.*).

4. *The instrumental text*, which comprises the results of diagnostic testing. The text now achieves, 'the status of a separable artifact, detached from the body of the doctor and patient alike'. Technological diagnostic equipment, as it becomes more complex, moves away from, 'an image-based text to a set of symbols which demand decoding' and 'the disembodiment of the clinical text reaches its limit: the person-as-ill translated into a series of numbers' (Leder 1990 pp.15–16).

Diagnosis therefore comprises, for Leder, a variety of symbolic forms – linguistic, perceptual, mathematical – and thus is complicated beyond measure. From Heidegger, Leder notes:

Any confrontation with meaning presupposes a certain 'fore-structure' of understanding: one's reading of a text is chanelled [*sic*] from the start by interpretive assumptions and hypotheses, even if these later prove insufficient. So it is for the doctor. Almost from the moment the patient walks in, the physician is generating provisional diagnoses which determine which questions will be asked, what tests ordered. (p.16)

The patient must and does participate in this, through a, 'groundwork for collaboration [which] rests in structures held in common by the hermeneutic participants...within a life-world [of both doctor and patient] saturated with medical meanings' (p.17).

This is where medicine meets hermeneutics, for Baron (1991), responding as a physician to Leder's theory, argues that although Leder makes explicit many aspects of clinical practice that doctors would like to ignore in seeing the patient as a text, the patient is reduced to the status of a fixed thing which can be subject to interpretation, rather than a text which moves, as it 'is the mutual creation of the participants in the clinical encounter' (p.28). Thus:

> Clinical practice occurs at the intersection of a patient's need and a doctor's power and impotence. We, my patients and I, do the best we can. We should not distract ourselves looking for the text; we *are* the text, such as it is, ineluctably subject to our own existential situations and limitations. As we bungle along, understanding and misunderstanding, applying incomplete knowledge as well as we can manage, we require above all a recognition that we have only each other to work with. Making sense of *that* in a positivist, secular culture seems to me to be the major task confronting medicine today. (p.28)

This is important – what we have is one text but comprising two actors: the physician and the patient. Leder's hermeneutic had in many ways ignored the contribution of the physician to diagnosis, save in the role of active interpreter to the patient's passive interpretee. In this Leder has ignored one half of the human interaction of the doctor and patient relationship.

Let us explore the physician-as-text, commencing with Gordon's (1988) analysis of 'clinical science and clinical expertise'. She argues that the claim that medicine is scientific serves almost as a 'covering law', symbolising a universal, 'objective' truth and legitimising the authority of the medical profession, but in practice both medical science and medical practice are often found to be neither very scientific nor very artful. Medical practice, or more precisely clinical judgement is, she says, not grounded in intellectual, cognitive and analytic forms of knowledge, but in 'embodied' knowledge, knowledge 'sensed through and with the body' (p.270). Basing her analysis on Dreyfus and Dreyfus's (1986) paean to the role of intuition in skill, she argues that the diagnosis undertaken by a skilled and experienced clinician is not based on science but on, 'concrete experiences which seem to be remembered through pattern recognition and seem to be organized as whole, real situations like gestalts, paradigms, exemplars, images, or prototypes rather than as intellectual categories, decontextualized elements or rules' (p.270). The skilled diagnostician, in short, through long experience has learned to recognise certain 'patterns', perhaps hundreds of thousands of them, and can recognise them in a patient within a very short time of the commencement of the diagnostic encounter. An expectation is thus built into diagnosis, and a gestalt is quickly formed, with evidence subsequently gathered by the clinician to justify this original decision.

In reply to Gordon we must argue that the Dreyfus and Dreyfus model (1986) presupposes the existence of a solid, objective knowledge base. Their division of knowledge acquisition into five stages, from beginner to expert, has an intuitive appeal, reinforced by their use of such examples as riding a bike or driving a car. Those skills are, however, capable, save within the worst excesses of solipsism, of being objectively verified. Should we not balance our bikes very well, we will tumble into the roadside verge. Should we fail as drivers, we will crash our cars and cause damage both to ourselves and others. The knowledge base of medicine is, we are arguing, to a large extent socially constructed. Taxonomies of diseases place somewhat arbitrary names on collections of signs and symptoms which, in other cultures and at other times, have or had different names and different (albeit often less successful) remedies.

Nevertheless, Gordon's (1988) conclusion accords with the general tenor of our argument. Although she warns that 'real clinical expertise' is based not on 'arbitrary subjectivity, guessing, mystical intuition, instinct, routine or habit' but on 'sound, concrete, situational understanding' (p.278), she qualifies this somewhat by arguing that successful physicians demonstrate 'an intuitive sense of patients'. The knowledge they embody, she says, may be found in what Foucault has described as 'subjugated knowledges', that is, those deemed not scientific and therefore non-legitimate. Implicit in Gordon's analysis is the poverty of language of Western societies which does not allow us to articulate much that is 'non-scientific' and, moreover, an acknowledgement that we acquire knowledge about others in our Western societies, even among those trained to abandon all but scientific modes of thought, in ways which are not amenable to rational analysis. Let us now explore Berg's analysis of diagnosis, for it explains much that Gordon was exploring – the 'gestalt' of diagnosis.

Berg (1992) sees the physician's role in diagnosis as one of transforming patient problems into solvable problems. Traditionally the doctor is seen as uncovering data about the patient during the interaction with the patient. What happens, he shows, is that the data are *(re)constructed*, for, 'the type of questions a physician asks, the way she asks them and her interpretation of the answers shape the symptoms of the patient' (p.157). The physician asks questions which select the 'information which corresponds with the transformation she has in mind' (*ibid.*), thus leading the patient down a predetermined path of the doctor's

choosing. The examination procedures selected or ignored similarly prestruc-
ture the 'pathological reality' he or she will want to counteract, and the patient's
symptoms are then directively interpreted. Data, medical criteria and disposal
options which are obtained but do not conform to a proposed transformation
are, typically, reinterpreted or reconstructed. The result is that there is a 'logical
gap' between diagnosis and treatment, which become independent entities:

> Physicians do not first search for a diagnosis and then, subsequently,
> decide upon a therapy. This phased, two-step motion does not
> characterize medical problem solving. On the contrary, from the outset,
> the transformation process is unidirectionally geared towards the
> construction of a disposal. (p.169)

Thus the useage of the terms 'diagnosis' and 'therapy', as if they are two separate
entities, results in an 'artefactual distinction'.

Berg argues that it is necessary for the doctor to behave in this way in order
to undertake 'routines' which are essential in two ways: they facilitate medical
action and they provide safety through *doing what everyone else is doing*. Routines,
Berg argues, are, 'frame[s] of reference, and…stepping out of the routine implies
a deviation from the "safety of the norm", psychologically necessitating an
explicit legitimation for doing so' (p.172).

The physician is therefore engaged in defensive manoeuvring. In Gordon's
model physicians were involved in quickly forming a diagnosis based on their
experience of thousands of similar encounters. The very speed of diagnosis may
itself be a defensive posture.

But why should physicians need to defend themselves, and from what? From
Kirmayer (1988) we may note that bio-medicine has set aside the emotional
and moral dimension of distress, which leads to the question of how the
physician is affected by emotion and distress. Does he or she construct the self
as a bio-medical machine free of emotion? This may be so. Physicians, 'launder
bodily language to reduce the affectivity of medical discourse'. They use,
'acronyms whose convenience disguises the reality of sickness' and substitute
'arbitrary signs' for, 'words that would reveal the body's disorder and bring the
physician into a more intense emotion-laden relationship with the suffering
patient' (Kirmayer 1988, p.61). The doctor is thus engaged 'all day long' in a
process of 'cognitive distancing from suffering'.

This is a process which commences during medical training, where, 'medical
students are treated as disembodied intellects who can absorb endless amounts
of detail with little attention to their own emotional and physical needs'
(Kirmayer 1988, p.81). Medical training involves some very subtle processes
of change in the way students perceive themselves and others. The, 'training of
students to be "competent" physicians entails a reconstruction of commonsense

views of the patient, sickness, *and the personal boundaries of the medical student*' (Good and Good 1994, p.91, emphasis added).

Medical students reconstruct the patient. We know from anthropology, Good and Good say, that, 'the person is a cultural construct, a complex and culturally shaped way of experiencing self and other, a "common sense" that richly combines culture and ideology, interpersonal relations and development'. Therefore, 'cultural "work" is required to reconstitute the person who is the object of medical attention. This person is a special abstraction, requiring a reorganization of experience from commonsense reality, and this reconstruction of the person is essential to a student becoming a competent physician' (p.97). Medical students learn to reconstruct the person-as-patient so that they become more machine-like, so that the, 'appropriate response to the medicalized body is an active one: "Let's figure out how it works and let's fix it"' (p.97). They learn a new language, the language of bio-medicine (cf. Kirmayer), but this language contains a sub-text, for, 'the language of medicine consists not of learning new words for the commonsense world, but the construction of a new world altogether' (Good and Good 1994, p.98). They learn a form of reasoning based on physiology and pathophysiology.

Medical students thus reconstruct themselves. They learn to, 'redefine their personal boundaries in several ways' (Good and Good 1994, p.100). 'As students gain clinical experience, they begin to question what constitutes appropriate personal boundaries in relation to patients, what aspects of the private lives and bodies of patients they should seek or accept access to, and what aspects of themselves they should reveal to patients and to colleagues and faculty' (*ibid.*). They, 'express concerns about opening themselves to the pain associated with the suffering of patients, about how they can remain available to that pain without being overwhelmed' (pp.100–101), but they learn defence mechanisms which they take with them as they become experienced clinicians. Menzies Lyth (1988) showed that workers in health develop defence mechanisms which allow them to distance themselves from the more traumatic aspects of their work.

Cartesian dualism, so dominant in Western bio-medicine, can thus be seen as a defence mechanism which is called to the aid of physicians. They must separate *their* minds from *their* bodies in order to cope with the emotional assault presented by the diseased bodies and anguished minds with which they are emotionally bombarded every day.

Diagnosis can now be seen not as a rational, logical process but as a struggle. The patient approaches the doctor for explanation, the doctor seeks to provide understanding but in a way which contradicts his/her training. Taught that diagnosis is a process of hypothetico-rational deduction, that evidence is garnered through objective, scientific means and that they must remove all emotions from the encounter, the doctor must now resort to patterns which contradict that training, patterns where the essence of the non-Cartesian self comes into play, where the physician's mind and body must become one in order for the physician to understand and interpret the reality of the patient. The physician must bring into play the skills of psychotherapy and counselling, but within a discipline which abhors the scientific vacuum of those interactive encounters. Where earlier we saw the diagnostic encounter as a meeting of body/machines, now it is seen as an encounter of body/minds.

There is thus a large gap between what Friedson (1986) calls formal knowledge – that found in academia and taught to members of the professions – and the knowledge which is used in practice. Formal knowledge is transformed and modified by the activities of those participating in its use. Members of the professions *represent* formal knowledge, but, 'exactly what knowledge is employed is problematic: it cannot be predicted from the formal knowledge ascribed to them' (p.210). Physicians' formal knowledge, that gained during training, evolves in practice into something considerably more individual and idiosyncratic.

To the physician, the most powerful person in the meeting of body/minds that is the diagnostic encounter, is accorded the power of apportioning a disease label. The patient appears to concur in this, for patients *expect* their doctors to be omnipotent and wish certainty in the diagnosis (Lupton 1995). The act of faith which allowed bio-medicine to become *the* dominant form of healing system despite the absence of proof of its superiority over other forms (Stacey 1988) is, it seems, replicated in the individual medical encounter.

DISCUSSION

The process of diagnosis can be seen not as the rational, scientific process generally assumed, but as an interpretive process where the patient seeks to describe his/her symptoms in a language which may only inadequately describe them, and the doctor attempts to achieve access to inchoate and inaccessible signs and symptoms and to transcribe them into a medical terminology which itself is marked by imprecision. This is doubly so in the case of an older person diagnosed as having Alzheimer's disease as, first, the individual's symptoms are relayed through a third party who can observe only the outer manifestations of this seeming illness, and second, the causes of the disease, even within the traditional medical definition, are not amenable to testing.

Both carers and doctors can thus be seen in the diagnostic encounter as constructing the diagnosis of Alzheimer's Disease. Ineichen (1987) has noted that physicians often do not wish to accord the label of Alzheimer's disease, and often are ignorant of the disease. They are, however, under some pressure to do so. The doctors' knowledge will be influenced by that of the public, and carers may bring pressure upon the physician to provide the label of Alzheimer's disease. Fox (1989) argues that the Alzheimer's disease movement in the USA used the media very cleverly in order to build up a picture of Alzheimer's disease which reflected the interests of the dominant actors: the neuroscientists. The public was alerted about the research, and was taught to regard senility not only as a particular disease, but one for which a cure could be sought. Fleck, we have seen, saw medical knowledge as based upon popular knowledge, taken up, rearranged and reflected back upon the populace (Löwy 1988). There is a sense here in which general practitioners are members of the public, albeit a cohesive and select group of members. General practitioners, too, along with other members of the health professions, are likely to blend their common-sense knowledge with scientific knowledge of disease (Hughes 1977).

Carers *need* a disease label to be applied (Gubrium 1988), for it helps them to understand what is taking place in their world. Physicians need a disease label which they can apply. The neuroscientific world has provided them with the disease label which appears to be required of all save the sufferers themselves.

CHAPTER 7

Society and the Construction of Dementia

The Sociology of the Dementing Body

The previous chapters have explored how 'senility' was, in the interests of neuroscientific research, recategorised as a disease rather than a natural process of ageing. We showed how it is possible, once a 'disease' has been identified, for physicians to diagnose it in patients. This chapter has two aims. First, it seeks to explore the reasons why society has seemed keen to adopt so speedily this category of disease. We will use the sociology of the body to illustrate the endemic fear of ageing and, ultimately, death in Western societies, and the reasons behind this fear. We will argue that, in an era of the 'medicalisation of everything' the search for a 'cure' for dementia is, in effect, a search for the cure for ageing and, ultimately, death. In an equation which lacks correlational adequacy but signifies the triumph of hope over reason, then if (dementia) = (ageing and death) then (a cure for dementia) = (a cure for ageing and death). Second, we will attempt to reflect these arguments back upon the ageing person.

The sociology of the body

To grow old in late twentieth century Western societies is to retreat into something akin to the sick role, a sick role defined by others and reflected in the patterns of action displayed by the claimant to the role. To grow old is to become dependent, but this dependency is created by a society which restricts life chances and opportunities at older ages (Townsend 1981). It is the sociology of the body which can inform understanding of both the structured dependency of the elderly (Townsend 1981) and the construction of the person with dementia in modern societies. Our understanding of the sociology of the ageing body is hindered by that reluctance to deal with the elderly which pervades the social sciences. There is as yet only the seed corn of a sociology of the ageing body. Here we must explore what we may call the general sociology of the body, tentatively explore what a theory of the sociology of the ageing body would contain within itself, and apply this to our understanding of dementia.

The most basic statement in the emerging sub-discipline of the sociology of the body is that the body is inextricably bound up with identity: physical presence is necessary in order to establish a dialogue with other individuals and groups (Moore 1994), with the body acting as the basis for the use of language (Johnson 1987) and therefore for communication. Human bodily existence provides the 'model' for the psycho-somatic entity called the self (Falk 1994) constructed primarily through consumption (Falk 1994) or through interaction with others (Harré 1991). This may seem obvious, but the body has been notable in its absence from social scientific theories.

The sociology of the body comprises a critique of that Cartesian logic which has informed Western medicine, of a dichotomy between mind and body, resulting in the dominance of the body and the invisibility of the mind. Modernism was and is concerned with rationalism and with reason, and so was averse to the highly irrational *desiring* body. Sociology, including the sociology of health, has complied with this tradition, concerning itself largely with the question of the conditions for stability and change in social systems which, studied at the level of society rather than at the level of the individual members of society, presumes that the individuals who make up society are body-less decision-making agents (Turner 1991). Sociologists indeed have been scared by the implications of regarding humankind as possessing bodies: 'Any reference to the corporeal nature of human existence raises in the mind of the sociologist the spectre of social Darwinism, biological reductionism or sociobiology', argued Turner (1984, p.1), thus warranting to a certain extent the sociological hostility. Bodies, in this perspective, remain the machines which allow individual locomotion, and no more. This body is merely a physiological product which has a biological reality, and which has use within sociology merely as a metaphor for a stable society. To see the body as a seat of desire, a source of emotions and of sexual passion is to see it as non-rational, as the opposite of capitalist rationality and bureaucratic regulation, the very essence of that contradiction between nature and culture which forms a broad theme in social theory (Turner 1984).

Feminist perspectives on the body

As an introduction to the diametrically opposite view to this one, let us first explore feminist analyses of how gender is socially constructed, for if gender arises not as a result of certain biological imperatives then the whole nature of embodiment must be opened to examination. Turner (1984) argues that societies have four inescapable tasks: the reproduction of populations; the regulation of bodies; the restraint of the 'interior' body through disciplines, and the representation of the 'exterior' body in social space. Turner's sociology of the body becomes a sociology which examines social control and a consideration of women's bodies as they are controlled within a system of patriarchy. A sociology of the ageing body resonates with this argument, given the demographic distribution of the sexes in the older age groups. How the body is constructed as a gendered being has been explored by feminist writers, some of whom see gender as central to feminist theorising. Calas and Smircich (1992), for example, state that despite the variety in feminist theorising it is all addressed to the issue of gender.

What is gender? The *OED*'s definition is that gender is a, 'grammatical classification…of objects roughly according to the two sexes…' and sex is, 'being male or female or hermaphrodite' and 'males or females collectively'. These definitions are reflected in a dominant Western discourse which stresses the essential and embodied nature of gender identity: we come to be men or women purely as a result of our biology. From anthropology, however, comes the knowledge of how ethnocentric is this view, as gender identity is given as much by the performance of appropriate activities as it is by the possession of the appropriate genitalia and internal organs. Psychoanalysis, too, stresses that feminine and masculine identities are not natural or given in biology, but must be constructed and should be understood therefore as cultural achievements (Moore 1994). So, 'on the basis of genetalia (*sic.*), we assign children a gender' and thus, 'a framework of master rules – through which they make sense of a whole series of other rules' (Mills and Murgatroyd 1991, p.69). (Mills and Murgatroyd use the term 'master' in relation to rules to capture the cultural dominance of men over women.)

Thus gender is something we learn. We learn how to be women and how to be men, we learn how to be masculine and how to be feminine. This is a process which starts in babyhood (see the discussion in Mills and Murgatroyd 1991), through patterns of body training given us by our parents and others (Haug cited in Shilling 1993). By the age of three, research has shown, children recognise that jobs are sex-typed. Mackie (1987) has examined gender social-isation in adolescence, and argues that male and female identities are shaped differently, with females being educated to 'be' (that is, to exist as feeling creatures in their roles as wives and mothers) and males educated to 'do' (strive, fight, initiate, stress strength and toughness). The result is that, 'by and large, young women are prepared throughout the school system to be "feminine", and when they come to search for their femininity – to clarify their identities – they are overwhelmed with images of domesticity; of love, marriage, moth-erhood, and so on.' (Mills and Murgatroyd 1991, p.74). Young men, on the other hand, 'leave school as "men"'. As these young men search for their identities through the lens of masculinity, they will often find that they are expected to be life-long workers, to be anti-feminine (e.g. not to show emotion, to be successful and outdo others in countless ways), to be aggressive, to be sexually active and forceful (e.g. to be the initiator of sexual activity) and to be self-reliant (e.g. 'tough, cool, in control'). This, 'creates a web of rules (of masculinity) that influence the way male activity is constrained and male identity constructed' (*ibid.*).

It is therefore, 'through the "doing" of gender that gender is reproduced' (Mills 1993, p.142). Gender:

> ...is both something we do and something we think with, both a set of social practices and a system of cultural meanings. The social practices – the "doing" of gender – and the cultural meanings – "thinking the world" using the categories and experiences of gender – constitute us as women and men, organized into a particular configuration of social relations. (Rakow quoted by Mills 1993, p.142)

The focus in recent feminist theorising has been on gender relations, where 'men' and 'women', two categories of persons, are created and their bodies connected to culture. In this perspective, both men and women are prisoners of gender, although in different ways (Calas and Smircich 1992).

Informed by feminist theorists, let us now explore developments in the sociology of the body.

Post-modernism and the sociology of the body

Post-modernism, in its critique of rationality and certainty, allows through the sociology of the body, a critique of the view of the body as merely a biological machine. The body is often seen within this sub-discipline as a social construct which has no reality outside social relations and which is thus amenable to transformation. Rather than the seemingly obvious route of reconciling the Cartesian dualist dichotomy, the body is seen as a surface, without depth, in which the mind and the body are one, where there is, no longer a prior, inner 'identity' so that that which is done to the body affects the integrity of the person (Fox 1993). This is, following Deleuze and Guatarri (1977), a body-without-organs in which the body is experienced as a non-organic concept, not in terms of its biological organisation but rather as a surface (Lash 1991). In other words (and very simplistically), when we look in the mirror or at other people we do not see a mass of organs covered by skin, we do not even envisage the reality of what is going on beneath that mantle, we identify and recognise only the surface. Here in the body-without-organs 'the ego is no longer prior'. Identity is constructed through inscription which gives the self, gives subjectivity. The 'body of inscription' is not the organic, anatomical body of medicine but the 'non-organic, political surface'. It is a social body, the one which we present to others when acting out our roles. This is the body one sees when one looks in the mirror: a body with skin, and features, and textures, a thing to be beautified and cared for, which provides the satisfaction of the tactile senses. It is that body which one 'does', as distinct from the body one 'has' or 'is' (Turner 1992). It is the visage one presents to the outer world, and which one uses to augment verbal communication (Freund 1990).

The sociology of the body owes much to the work of Foucault and his analyses of how bodies are controlled within societies. Medicine, for Foucault, is one of the modes of control over bodies. The metaphor of (wo)man-the-machine has dominated medical thought since the 17th century. In this perspective, the medical body was viewed not, 'primarily as purposive and ensouled; nor as the scene of moral dramas; nor as a place wherein cosmological and social forces gather; but simply as an intricate machine' which can be repaired, if it breaks, by a physician, 'drawing upon a reservoir of scientific knowledge concerning how the machine works, and employing the technologies of repair' (Leder 1992, p.3). From Foucault (1973) comes famously and now ubiquitously the idea that the body is the ground upon which the medical profession achieves its power, thus disempowering the person who 'owns' the body in question, so that the patient becomes 'inauthentic'. Through its regard of the body, the medical profession comes to know the body in a way that is complex and technical and which allows of no other way of knowing the body. The medical profession 'inscribes' the body, the process of inscribing resulting in a description which makes it a strange and alien territory to the lay possessor of the body: 'The inscription of the body which medicine deciphers in its examinations, is not straightforward, it cannot be "read" "correctly" by just anyone: the reader must be an *expert*. And consequently, this expertise is achieved at the expense of those who must be subjected to the power of the gaze' (Fox 1993, p.29). It determines that selfhood and subjectivity are constructed within the domain of externally imposed power and knowledge. Bodies thus become governable, through the process of governmentality. This is a dual process of power in action, involving the objective imprimature of government dictates over conduct, and the subjective, 'sense of personal responsibility, rights, freedoms and dependencies' (Fox 1993, pp.32–3). Furthermore, 'self-surveillance' or the 'care of the self', involves a person's continually reflecting upon and regulating his/her conduct within the strait-jacket of self-imposed moral goals. The person thus becomes disciplined. This perspective of the body is not confined to the medical world – it has entered the world of politics, for where people are conceived through their bodies as machines they can, in the way of machines, be manipulated and trained for precise social functions (Leder 1992, p.3, citing Foucault's *Discipline and Punish* (1977)).

The twentieth century has seen the rise of the metaphor of the individual body as a cell in the larger body, the body politic (Armstrong 1983). Armstrong uses Foucault's insights to analyse developments in the twentieth century. In a situation of universal literacy it behoves societies to ensure conformance to their norms by more subtle means than force or overt power. The metaphor of the biological system supersedes the metaphor of the machine, for the biological system has autonomic control mechanisms which operate without conscious imperative. These are akin to Foucault's 'micro-physics' of power, where power is spread throughout a society, ensuring unthinking conformance to the rules of that society. Now it is the duty of all members of a society to maintain themselves as healthy, lest their ill-health contribute to the illness and destruction of the societal-body. The medical profession and others involved in the provision of health services organise themselves in such a way as to monitor every citizen's participation in the political body (Armstrong 1983). A myriad of other institutions – the state, the family, the school, the media, commodity culture, and so on, – participate in the regulation of this 'moral imperative' to be 'healthy' (Lupton 1995). Health promotion is part of this process, Lupton argues. It is, she says, a discourse which is taken up and integrated into self-identity, its logic directed at, 'allowing individuals to uncover their true state of health, to reveal their moral standing and indeed shape their true selves by strategies of bodily management' (1995, p.138). The result is that health is now, 'what one does, as well as the condition one is in' (*ibid.*). There is now a 'health ethic', similar to the work ethic, within which moral judgements are made about the ill and in which the body has become an outward sign of inward moral standing (Lupton 1995). Illness becomes seen as failure (Baron 1992). However, the manner in which this discourse is taken up is contingent, in whole or in part, upon individuals' status at work, position in the life cycle and relationship to other interacting institutions, allowing resistance in whole or in part, consciously or at the unconscious or non-discursive level, by the individual. Resistance to this dominant discourse in the form of an espousal of a fatalistic notion of health as largely a matter of luck, is shown by older age groups, working-class rather than middle-class people, and men rather than women.

Control of the body is also achieved through consumption and commodification. In late twentieth century society the representation of bodies has achieved over-riding importance: we have become obsessed with our bodies, especially with their appearance. The body, Shilling (1993) argues, has replaced the existential and ontological certainties of religion, which were external to the individual, and has become within consumer culture 'a bearer of symbolic value', with a tendency to, 'place ever more importance on the body as constitutive of the self'. The body, for Shilling, is becoming increasingly central to people's self-identity, increasingly representative of the self. People are now relating to their bodies in increasingly reflexive ways, identifying themselves with their bodies but relating to only the exterior territories or surfaces, 'at a time when unprecedented value is placed on the youthful, trim and sensual body' (Shilling 1993, p.3). The body has become a project to be worked on, to be constructed.

The body which is desired often contradicts the lived experience of the body.

Patriarchal culture, for example, fetishises breasts, judging women by these, 'daily visible and tangible signifiers of...womanliness' which are an important aspect of their identity for most women (Young 1992, p.216). Yet patriarchal culture demands breasts which conform to, 'one perfect shape and proportion', that is, 'round, sitting high on the chest, large but not bulbous, with the look of firmness', solid objects which contradict 'the fleshy materiality of breasts' (p.218).

The body, furthermore, is the seat of consumption, and consumption is, in Falk's (1994) thesis, profoundly connected with the sense of self: 'I consume therefore I am'. Falk's analysis is usefully based in a historical perspective, thus allowing us to understand how society has evolved in the way it has. He summarises the long histories of philosophy and economics to argue (p.105) that for centuries human beings have been seen as 'desiring creatures' who desire more than their natural needs, and who desire to compare themselves, competitively, with others. The development of mass production in the nineteenth century allowed people to become consumers of goods similar to those of persons whom they wished to emulate: the goods took on the character of the aspired-to, and through absorption into the self (but not in the cannibalistic sense) allowed the consumer to identify him/herself with the status, lifestyle or social identity the object stood for. It became possible for the individual to be, '"like" the other, to identify him/herself with the other and even gain the same status the other occupied without actually taking the place of the other' (p.121). The 'other' is of course the aspired-to other. The goods are not aspired to for themselves, but because of what they symbolise. Their utility value, to borrow a term from economics, is not in what the goods can *do*, but in what they allow to happen, for it is through consumption that the individual socially constructs him/herself, using the goods as the 'building bricks' of the self. These building bricks have two 'sides': they allow the person to construct him/herself as a member of society, and they allow the individual to construct him/herself as a being separate and distinct from that society.

In Falk's thesis the 'other' are the aspired-to. In this formulation there must be people whom one wishes to distance oneself from. Foremost among these are the aged, for the aged provide evidence of the remorselessness of decline and the inescapable reality of death (Shilling 1993). The sociology of the body therefore alerts us to the place of the older members of our society.

The sociology of the ageing body

The sociology of the body becomes in many respects the polar opposite of that which has previously been held, for where previously the body was nothing but a physiological instrument it now in analytical discourse loses its biological status. It is something that one has, from which one gathers perceptions of self-identity, but from which all acknowledgement of the reality of corporality is absent. This presents problems for a sociology of the ageing body, for the biological status of the body becomes more and more visible with age. We must therefore turn to the middle ground as articulated by Lupton (1995), who argues for a dialectical approach to the body, whereby bodies are located in nature but are shaped and experienced through discourses which limit individuals' control of their bodies. Here we have the lived body of phenomenology, a body which is both an expression of individuality and the centre of the world of experience, and which is intimately linked to the essence of the person. This body of the middle ground is one which has a biological basis which can be stigmatised and/or affected by disease, but the way in which it is affected and/or stigmatised will be the result of discourses of the body. Here illness, disability or growing old are biological processes mediated through discourse. Shilling, too (1993), argues that the biological foundation of the body must be incorporated into analyses, so that the body can best be envisaged as, 'an unfinished biological and social phenomenon which is transformed, within certain limits, as a result of its entry into, and participation in, society' (p.12). This foundationalist view of the body appears essential when analysing the ageing body, for it can be argued that the biological bases of the ageing body are the stimuli for the construction of the social identification of the ageing body, which carries with it connotations of futility and death.

We must begin by noting that despite continued embodiment, to grow old is in some ways to become invisible. Those of the older generation literally retire, that is, 'withdraw, go away, retreat, seek seclusion or shelter, recede, go (as) to bed' (*Concise Oxford Dictionary*). Disengagement theory, influential in gerontology in the 1960s and 1970s, argued that ageing was accompanied by a gradual disengagement from social life with sometimes an increasing preoccupation with the self (Cumming and Henry 1961). Accused of functionalism, of describing what happens rather than seeking the cause (and we will see that the sociology of the body suggests a cause), this theory has fallen somewhat into disrepute, but the isolation of the elderly that it talks of is replicated in the academic world, where studies of ageing have been insulated from mainstream sociological theory (Fennell, Phillipson and Evers 1993). In the sociology of the body there is little theorising about the sociology of the ageing body; the body discussed is implicitly a vigorous body which is, save where it is anorexic, full of vigour. When using the sociology of the body to understand ageing and dementia we must therefore look at that which is unsaid, for the ageing body is there as a negative, as a shadow.

We live at a time and in a society where, 'the quintessentially modern individual is young and never dies' (Shilling 1993, p.196). Moore (1994), in the context of analysing how gender is to be understood, argues that: 'One of the most difficult sets of processes or relationships to grasp when it comes to a discussion of the construction of engendered subjects is how the social representations of gender affect subjective constructions, and how the subjective representation or self-representation of gender affects its social construction' (p.53). So too with ageing: how do the social representations of ageing affect subjective constructions, and how do the subjective representations of ageing affect its social construction? The answers to these questions remain, in the general neglect of ageing as an academic subject, unknown. What we can do is make suggestions.

First, let us examine the Body Beautiful. The ageing body has since Ancient Greece been regarded as unsightly and thence best concealed from the public gaze. It does not carry the connotations of heroism and strength of the younger body. There is today what has been described as an almost neurotic desire to remain youthful, with old age holding a 'special terror': 'People cling to the illusion of youth until it can no longer be maintained, at which point they must either accept their superfluous status or sink into dull despair' (Lasch quoted in Shilling 1993). The ageing person confronts the reality of this terror and despair. Where youth, beauty and goodness are regarded as inter-related, the loss of youth can be equated with loss of 'goodness'. This inter-relationship is interesting, for 'goodness' has multiple meanings: there is the 'goodness' which comes from conforming to higher laws and mores, and the 'goodness' which denotes health and vitality, and there is the 'goodness' which implies a positive contribution to society. The absence of 'goodness' therefore implies immorality and negativity. Emotional reactions to the physical images of 'deep old age' involve repulsion and fear, and a need for distance. For many older people their ageing face resembles nothing more than a mask which disguises the 'them' they always were; they feel no different 'inside'. This suggests a distinction between the self and the body, and thus an experiential critique of the post-modernist view of the equivalence of mind and body. 'The image of the mask or disguise which is involuntarily assumed by many of us as we get older' (Featherstone and Hepworth 1990, p.260) leads many to engage in a struggle to avoid the negative stereotyping and loss of independent identity which accompanies ageing. It is, according to Turner (1992), body-image that plays the determining role in the evaluation of the self in the public arena.

Second, let us examine the Body Physical. The, 'theoretical prudery with respect to human corporality' (Turner 1984, p.30) reflects a real-world prudery which prevents our examining much of the messiness of corporality. Anthropologists, for instance, despite carrying out the most intricate examinations of societies simple and complex, rarely report one of the major necessities of all societies: toilet arrangements. Indeed post-modernism's body-without-organs perpetrates this long tradition of ignoring the awkward reality of the gurgles, windiness, smelliness and other numerous activities which are seen as betrayals in the deodorised world of the late twentieth century.

Our bodies dismay us. Over time a body ceases to perform as well as it used to. It slows down, becomes more susceptible to illness. It may bring realisation of its own essential corporality, of knowledge that it is a Body With Organs, presenting itself in a manner deemed undignified and unacceptable in society in general. The ageing body which loses control over continence reduces its owner to social isolation (McGrother et al. 1987), depression or dementia, and hastened death (Vetter et al. 1981). It is a body which, too, has to face up to its own mortality – no textbook in gerontology is complete without a chapter entitled 'Death and Dying' (see, for example, Fennell et al. 1993). In this the ageing body demonstrates to the rest of society the futility of self-identity in the body. In demonstrating the inescapable reality of death an existential uncertainty is provoked (Shilling 1993). It is, in the case of people with a dementing-type illness, a sign that all the care invested in the corporality of their modern bodies is ultimately a worthless investment, for it is apparently the brain (that as yet unexamined part of the body within the sociology of the body) which appears to herald ultimate demise, and what happens to the brain appears to be beyond control.

The ageing body thus becomes a multiply alienated territory. For the older person who feels 'just the same inside', the face that looks back from the mirror is that of another person, an alien. It is a body from which other members of society have to be protected, for it reminds them of their own feared decrepitude (Douglas 1991). It is also a body which has to be protected by society (and this is where the body as locus of control can be found), for as soon as one passes one's 60th or 65th birthday, activities which the day before were regarded as normal suddenly become endangering (Wynne-Harley 1991). This is taken to extremes for those with dementia who 'wander', who are deemed, just like infants, incapable of distinguishing harmful from other situations.

Turner's (1984) exposition of anorexia nervosa may with justice be applied to the ageing body. 'Capitalism has commodified hedonism and embraced eudemonism[1] as a central value,' Turner wrote (p.112). Under capitalism we are under a duty, through consumption, to enjoy ourselves, but this is an enjoyment which can be achieved only through conforming to the necessity to consume

---

1   'Eudemonism' is defined in the Concise Oxford Dictionary as a, 'system of ethics basing moral obligation on the likelihood that actions will produce happiness'.

and to present ourselves as an object for consumption. This compulsion to be an object falls very much upon women so that, 'in late capitalism there is for the individual a representational crisis of self-management' with the result that, 'we might expect, especially for women, the emergence of a presentational illness' (p.113). Such illnesses are built around the need to be thin and to be beautiful. This means that, 'the illnesses of women have one important thing in common – they are, at least sociologically, products of dependency... As diagnostic categories, these illnesses (agoraphobia, anorexia, and so on,) also express male anxieties about the loss of control over dependents as women [leave] the household for work and [are] allegedly exposed to public seductions' (p.113).

Here we must accuse Turner of an ageist bias, for his focus is only on women of child-bearing age. Older women whose child-bearing years have passed may feel much heavier the burden of having to present themselves as an object for consumption. The evidence of their failure to conform to the demands of an appearance of youthfulness and fecundity is written visibly upon their faces. A life-course analysis of presentational illnesses is required, in which we would of necessity include dementia. However, Turner's analysis must apply equally to ageing.

We can similarly draw parallels with the AIDS epidemic. Murphy (1992) claims parallels between the AIDS epidemic and what he terms the 'epistemic epidemic', that is, the loss of certainty within academia. He asks: 'What does it mean that AIDS occurs in America now? How do aspects of the epistemic epidemic affect the ways we interpret and manage the AIDS epidemic?' (p.156). With AIDS we have ageing encapsulated within a short time-frame. The person with AIDS shows what will happen to us all eventually: 'The body with AIDS has been seen as the site of death and contagion, of prejudice, and moral penalties (Murphy 1992, p.157). AIDS marks the body with impending death, he argues, making it identifiable for others. There is a long incubation period for AIDS (progressive immunodeficiency from HIV infection to AIDS has a median incubation time of 9.8 years), so that one's own body comes to be feared as it might unleash the dreaded infection any day. So, too, with dementia, where one in five of us is likely to be affected. But the hysteria surrounding dementia is evoked not at the level of the individual but at that of society, where concern is focused on the costs of caring for people with dementia. 'The ill demonstrate with their bodies that health does not last' (p.167), as do the aged. But AIDS is seen as a punishment for having lived unwisely – it is a 'penalised body', whereas ageing and dementia are punishments for having lived too long.

This brings us when discussing ageing to the inevitable elision between old age and death. To repeat what we have said above, and what has indeed been said many times before, ageing is, 'one of the major markers of that fine existential line' between life and death (Hazan 1994).

Death and the body and the search for a 'cure'

Hazan (1994) following Bourdieu (1991), argues that we need contrasting conceptual categories to bring a sense of order to experiences which would otherwise be unfathomable: we need to know that we are 'not something' in order to know what we are. Our knowledge of death therefore helps us know we are alive, leading to what he calls that perennial human preoccupation of worry over the boundary between life and death. Ageing is, Hazan says, one of the major markers of that fine existential line, so knowledge about, and discussion of, ageing is infused with an 'undercurrent of fear and anxiety'.

The reasons for this are located by Shilling within the sociology of the body. Death is here seen as, 'a particular existential problem for people as a result of modern forms of embodiment, rather than being a universal problem for human beings which assumes the same form irrespective of time or place' (1993, p.177). He constructs his arguments about, 'the importance of death to the relationship between self-identity and the human body' (p.185) as follows:

1. From Peter Berger's work he takes the idea that death, 'is an acute social problem...because of its potential to challenge people's sense of what is real and meaningful about their embodied selves and the world around them' (p.179). The 'unfinishedness of human embodiment', gives the existential problem of the capacity of the mind, bounded within a biological container whose demise is certain, to project itself into, and make plans for, the future.

2. From Anthony Giddens's work he uses the idea that modernity has swept away traditional meaning systems. Where the self traditionally was, 'received automatically through ritual practices', in high modernity self-identity and the body become 'reflexively organized projects' which have to be, 'sculpted from the complex plurality of choices...without moral guidance as to which should be selected' (p.181). The body itself is increasingly controlled. The world of modernity is one, 'which is orientated to the successful achievement of control', but death represents, 'the precise point where human control ends', leading to ontological uncertainty and 'anxieties of an utterly fundamental sort' (p.184).

3. The work of Norbert Elias and Pierre Bourdieu can be read, he suggests, as saying much about a modern tendency to adopt a heightened reflexivity towards one's body, and with this the prospect of death becomes highly disturbing. At its most basic, value is attached to the *living* body so old age brings with it for most social classes a decline in the symbolic value of the body, so that in a world

geared towards the accumulation of value, death represents the ultimate loss of value.

4. To these issues must be added the change in death from being an 'open, communal event' to one which is now a relatively hidden, private and individualised experience, segregated from the rest of society. From Elias he takes the point that individuals are unable to confront the reality of their own mortality, and reminded of it by the presence of those nearing death they seek to extend the boundaries between themselves and the dying. As another's death is a reminder of our own, we cut ourselves off from the dying both emotionally and spatially, leaving death to be medicalised.

5. While avoiding the dying, individuals seek to defer their own death through 'survival strategies' involving care of the body. However, 'when these projects begin to go wrong…as they inevitably must, when the body refuses to be reconstructed in line with the designs of its owner, then this investment in the body can itself serve to make the prospect of death particularly real and terrifying' (p.192).

The body and death are symbiotic, and in late twentieth century society the death of the body, now synonymous with mind and soul, heralds a terrifying oblivion, the inevitability of which is avoided and fought against, the reality of which causes those capable of doing so to avert their faces in fear.

Discussion

In sum, the sociology of the body suggests that in the course of the last century people living in the richer countries have turned to their bodies as a means of developing and affirming their identities. Self-identity and the body are inextricably intertwined. To be, today, means to consume and to be consumed through the sculpting of the healthy body. This leads to an existential crisis, as the biological basis of the body determines that this project is doomed to failure. The aged within society carry this stigma, like an illness, upon their faces and their bodies. The elderly become a living eschatological metaphor. They must therefore be separated from the rest of society. 'A host of socio-psychological forces operate to remove aged people from the rest of society and to assign them to a symbolic and physical enclave' (Hazan 1994, p.3). They are socially isolated, as if they have a disease, and indeed they are, in the age of the perfect body, diseased. Old age itself therefore becomes a disease, one which is incurable.

But in the age of modernity everything has to have a cause, and a cure. Even to suggest that a cure for ageing might be sought would inevitably be seen as quackery, as the twentieth century equivalent of the alchemist's gold. However, if one aspect of ageing could be traced to a factor which could be amenable to treatment, then the ultimate dream would appear within reach – the investment of all that effort in the maintenance of the body would no longer be futile. The existential dilemma which embodiment brings would cease. It is here that we see the sociological necessity of the transmogrification of senility into a disease. If senility is a disease for which a cure can be found, then the ultimate dream of humankind could be in reach: a cure for old age and death, and thus the certainty of continued embodiment. The sociology of the ageing body brings together the body as a biological entity and a body upon which identity is 'inscribed' through societal forces. The ageing body is feared, for it shows that all humankind's investment in the body is ultimately useless; deterioration and death cannot be avoided. A 'cure' for ageing and for death has not yet, perhaps cannot ever be, found. However, dementia, in which the body becomes an empty, mind-free tomb and thus symbolic of death, has, through its medicalisation, come to serve as a proxy for death. The search for a 'cure' for dementia therefore is no more and no less than an alchemical odyssey into wish fulfilment: 'cure' dementia and death will be 'cured'.

This, then, is why senility was so easily reclassified as a disease: in doing this we have been offered the possibility of a cure for death.

The older person in the dementing body

Society *needs* dementia to be medicalised, as if it is classified as a disease it holds out the prospect of a cure for ageing and for death. Social constructionism is dialectical: society constructs and is constructed by its members, often to the detriment of the latter. Let us now examine the second part of the dialectic: the response of the older person labelled as 'demented'.

The sociology of the body alerts us to:

- ° the body as alien territory, governed by the medical profession
- ° the body as territory to be governed and controlled, which has to conform to society's expectations
- ° the body as social territory, which must conform to certain expectations
- ° the mind–body inter-relationship
- ° the body as giver of identity.

When these concepts are applied to the ageing body they lead us to examine whether the person with dementia loses contact with his/her body, forgets its existence, so to speak. Are we seeing a body which in effect is without a brain, a perspective which dominates the medical view of dementia? Case study evidence supports this view. We hear of people who have 'forgotten' how to sit down or how to swallow. We hear of those who take great pleasure in smearing faeces everywhere, their having 'forgotten' its unacceptable place in society (and thus appearing to be beyond the control of the 'gaze' until it reasserts itself and takes the miscreant out of society and chemically or physically subdues the dementing (free-of-constraint) person).

Alternatively, are we when examining dementia observing a retreat from the realities of living in an ageing body? If people, in the age of beauty, feel the white-haired person reflected in the mirror each morning is not only a stranger, but a stranger who holds out the appalling possibility of social derision and isolation, can we not suggest that for some the body is indeed alien, not belonging to them and thus something to be retreated from in horror? Johnson (1987) argues that the body is in the mind, with cognition arising out of this bodily experience. The body therefore becomes a subjective experience. But for the ageing person, especially the old-old, in their ninth or tenth decade of life, his/her body becomes alien territory, something to be retreated from. With dementia, and especially when, as often happens, it is accompanied by incontinence, this isolation from the self is reflected in an increasing isolation from society. Research with socially isolated ill persons (albeit younger than those of this study) has shown that social isolation leads to a loss of a sense of the self, whilst at the same time the focus becomes almost exclusively upon oneself (Charmaz 1983). If this occurs in older people, we can suggest that with ageing comes a retreat from the body, and with this retreat comes a loss of sense of self.

A third possibility arises. The person with dementia is essentially out of control. All those subtle processes of control identified by Foucault slowly break down as the person with dementia asserts his/her inclination to wander the streets in 'inappropriate' clothing (nightwear, and so on,), to smear faeces over walls, to behave as they feel like behaving, free of social constraints towards conformity. The desiring body of the younger years, seen as desiring of sexual and sensual freedom, breaks through the net of constraints. Rather than dementia as a time of decline, it could perhaps be reconceptualised as an assertion (and we do not know how consciously) of the ability, when too tired of wearing them, to throw off the shackles.

Conclusion

The literature focusing on the social construction of the body is useful in drawing our attention to the demands for conformity currently exerted in post-industrial societies. Particularly in those social settings where moral doctrines are dictated not so much by accepted religious leaders, but by the architects of consumerism, the body has become the temple, the locus for self-analysis as a person able to contend with the pressures to 'look good'.

To deviate from socially prescribed norms of physical worthiness is to disregard the canons of acceptable behaviour. In a patriarchal society, particularly, to be over-weight is tantamount to heresy; in a culture dedicated to the apotheosis of youth, to be old signifies an open denial of prevailing secular moral principles. Cosmetic surgery can help to exorcise the malevolent presence of morally wayward attributes for people who feel especially vulnerable to breaching the tenet of the body as a cult object.

Perhaps the rich and famous who choose not to conform in this way may be regarded as 'characters'; power and authority held by individuals can also serve to offset social disapproval of old age. Where mental virility can be exhibited, physical signs of senility may be regarded as less socially stigmatic. But this is only because the observable presentation of the self gives out signals of healthiness. In societies where the medical terminology of 'disease' is used to interpret and explain socially deviant behaviour, no one can escape '*le regard*' – the gaze. Being fat, being criminal, being old are all symptoms of 'being sick'. Most of us, if we become old, will not be rich, famous or powerful. To behave contrary to orthodoxy will be interpreted as a symptom of disease. To 'forget' the rules of acceptable social behaviour will not be construed as a positive disposition but as a form of chronic delusion.

It is ironic that after decades of medical pre-eminence in attempts to analyse and interpret 'the human condition', there is now a recognition of the need to provide evidence-based practice. In our discussion of dementia, we are challenging through reference to an extended exemplar the hegemony of this cultural dominance and seeking to explore the potential for applying a different conceptual lens to the study of certain altered states of mind.

CHAPTER 8

The Social Construction of Dementia

We began this book with a reference to Armstrong's analysis of *The Political Anatomy of the Body* (1983), for our initial analysis of the Project which inspired this book suggested the appositeness of applying his conclusions to the Project. Armstrong uses a Foucauldian analysis to argue that in the 20th century society has been redefined so that it now resembles an organic system, a body whose cells comprise its human members. Disease thus comes to be perceived as a social phenomenon, for the illness of one can challenge the wider society. Where illness had previously been regarded as confined to the individual, in whom signs and symptoms mapped the course of the disease within the space of the body, it has now been redefined as occurring, 'in the spaces between people, in the interstices of relationships, in the social body itself' (Armstrong 1983, p.8). Now 'pathology was seen to travel throughout the social body, appearing only intermittently' (*ibid.*), necessitating a need for an organisational structure which could both survey and monitor the whole community. This has required that all individuals must come under the 'gaze' of the medical profession in order to be regulated. The medical profession and its assistants arrange to monitor all its component cells so as to ensure they conform to the requirements of the overall body politic. Every individual in the country and his/her social space should be made visible to the health service, and the general practitioner should have an intimate knowledge of the patient and his/her family. To this end, health centres have radiated out into the community, or brought the community within their walls. The Edinburgh dispensary achieved this function through what Armstrong terms 'double mapping of locality and relationships'. The medical community had knowledge of the most intimate relationships, it had the full power of the 'gaze', and with this it began to focus on the potentially ill: the healthy and the normal.

When society is a body then those who are not in full 'health' – the ill, the old and the infirm – are seen as infectious and deleterious to the whole. Moreover, some of these, notably those who have developed some form of dementia, are beyond the self-control engendered, in Foucault's world view, in modern societies, for they appear to ignore its most basic rules. They are a challenge to the social body, they threaten it as a cancer would, or as an epidemic of some disastrous illness would. The image of dementia as an epidemic can be seen in the official document, the 'Rising Tide' (NHS Health Advisory Service 1982), which is redolent with an image of dementia as a contagion of epidemic proportions, for it evokes a perception that the whole of society will be so weighed down by the burden of the demented that society's overall health will suffer. The 'demented' therefore have to be controlled, and having lost the capacity to control themselves controls must be provided externally. One way of doing this is through confining sufferers within the walls of institutions, an option made less attractive by its enormous financial costs, so other control mechanisms are required. Community care thus becomes one way of controlling those who would otherwise challenge the orderly nature of society.

We have seen, however, that such a perspective limits us in our understanding of dementia. We need to go further, into social constructionism. This allows us to show that the definitions of dementia to be found in medicine and psychiatry, albeit that they are the dominant definitions in society, are social constructions in that they are based on that which society wishes and needs to believe in. As such they have no prior, objective existence of their own.

Neuroscience has played an important part in providing the rationale for the medicalisation of dementia, yet the sociology of science has allowed us to show that, once neuroscientists set in chain a search for a neurological cause of the syndrome, they can find it and perpetuate it. Physicians may therefore diagnose dementia as a disease because the process of diagnosis is not the scientific art we are led to believe. Physicians may all too easily, under pressure from carers for a 'name' to attach to that which appears to be afflicting their relatives or clients, 'construct' a diagnosis out of evidence which is not evidence. In this physicians conform to the needs of a society which demands that dementia be medicalised, for in an age when the self and the corporeal body are synonymous, the medicalisation of one part of old age holds out the prospect that a 'cure' for old age, and thus death, may ultimately be found.

We have shown that once a disease label is identified which defines an illness according to the behaviour of the sufferer, people's behaviour will be interpreted as conforming to such criteria: the 'gaze' here is a gaze which sees what it thinks it should see, what it expects to see. It becomes blind to any manifestations of behaviour other than those which it wishes to see.

In our analysis of the bio-medical model of disease as it applies to the conditions defined by medical researchers and practitioners as dementia and Alzheimer's disease, we have contested the dominance of one diagnostic perspective. We have tried not to minimise the severity of Alzheimer's disease as an experience for both 'sufferers' and their families. We are certainly not denying that the configuration of memory deficits, oral communication impairment and territorial disorientation presents problems for carers. The social constructionist thesis provides a corrective balance to the interpretation of behaviour which ascribes medical concepts to phenomena which then shift from the individual domain to the public. Certain characteristics become a 'syndrome', with the result that specific episodes in a person's life come to be construed as 'symptoms'. Instances when older people in particular appear to be forgetful and confused are synthesised into a manifestation of a 'disorder'. Alzheimer's description of early onset of these characteristics becomes adopted by earnest medical researchers and reconstituted as a 'disease'.

If medical researchers and practitioners were basing their judgements on firm theory resulting from an extensive body of empirical evidence, then their interpretation of dementia as a disease ought to carry more weight. The positivist search for a cause–effect nexus has to be framed within a social and cultural context. This human quest to discern the first cause, to establish a predictable natural and social universe, creates for itself systems of rationality. These, in turn, produce categories to which experience is allocated. Our inheritance is a dichotomised world view in which we attempt, from our idiosyncratic beliefs, to reconcile apparent opposites: good–bad; mad–sane; diseased whole. The state acts as a mechanism of control over deviations towards socially unacceptable categories. Among several agents of control, organised medical practice plays a significant role in helping to restore 'order' where there is 'disorder'.

Scientific discoveries and technological inventions have contributed to orthodox positivist aspirations that the human body and mind can also be observed, analysed, interpreted and catalogued according to an accepted corpus of theories and laws. Yet the 'mind' is not commensurate with the brain, nor can the 'self' be merely a sum of the constituent psychosomatic 'parts' of each human being. The challenge to the anatomisation of individuals in Western societies comes from holistic therapies and preventive strategies which work from a different set of beliefs about the relationship between humans and the environment. These therapies and preventive strategies derive, in turn, from beliefs about how the universe 'works'. They are no more or less accurate than the distinctive suppositions which lie at the heart of orthodox medical practice. The critique which we present is in line with social constructionist and post-modernist paradigms: that to arrogate to one system of beliefs a 'natural' precedence over any other is to confine observation of human behaviour and experience to a blinkered conceptual lens.

Over 70 years ago Ludwik Fleck, a physician and bacteriologist, argued that scientific facts are socially constructed by distinct 'thought collectives' (Löwy 1988), each composed of individuals who share a specific 'thought style' incommensurable with others. Training in one style hampers one's ability to look at the same object from a different point of view, therefore medical 'specialists' tend to observe the same phenomena. Only a combination of historical, sociological and philosophical perspectives into a multi-disciplinary approach – called by Fleck 'comparative epistemology' – could allow for a proper study of complex phenomena.

Fleck affirmed that no simple causal relationship exists in medicine, and in order to understand such complex phenomena as 'diseases' one needed to apply the principle of indeterminance developed by the theory of relativity. According to this thesis, there can be no grand scientific theory for understanding all the observed phenomena. Therefore there can be no single approach to the understanding of disease. Adopting Fleck's espousal of comparative epistemology as a more valid method of interpreting symptoms, dementia may be seen as a label for certain types of behaviour rather than a tested diagnosis of a disease. There is, then, no such state as 'dementia' – only different types of behaviour considered by medics and paramedics as socially divergent and therefore, from their epistemological vantage point, explicable solely in terms of physiological impairment. Elements of the definition of dementia authorised by the Royal College of Physicians (see Chapter 3) rely heavily on culturally bound criteria of what constitutes acceptable socialisation. It is curious that a professional body dedicated to the pursuit of scientific 'facts' as the only authentic basis for its own discipline, should include in its diagnosis of dementia highly subjective, non-verifiable assumptions about what constitutes social orthodoxy. To make a further conceptual leap in order to suggest a quasi-causal relationship between physiological impairment and contestable 'deviance' is to strain the bio-medical paradigm beyond the boundaries of intellectual credibility. This, presumably, is what Szasz (1974) meant when he announced: 'I hold that psychiatric interventions are directed at moral, not medical, problems' (p.xi).

Is a social constructionist attempt to de-medicalise dementia anything more than a kind of perverse anarchy? Bury (1986) criticised social constructionism for, 'its extreme relativist, even nihilist tendencies' (p.138). He argued that if we are not to apply rational 'modes of discourse' to the study of disease, how are we to judge the merits of the constructivist argument other than from rationality? The answer to this enquiry is two-fold. First of all, we should acknowledge that in the arena of problematic human behaviour there may be competing rationalities which – in the absence of indisputable evidence – should enjoy a reasonable degree of parity in terms of their face validity. The presumption that only a positivist framework can provide the 'true' interpretation of reality derives from a conception of observable phenomena as symptoms of an orderly and ultimately predictable universe. This dominant scientific discourse has been challenged by a number of eminent natural scientists, but notably by Hawking (1995). The quest for immutable laws of nature has engaged positivist thinkers for many centuries. Yet this very quest may be essentially a neurotic fallacy collectivised through religious and, latterly, scientific discourses to *impose* an order upon external phenomena. In this sense, religion and science construct their own subjective universes according to their image of an ideal world. 'Positivism', you might say, is a relativist theory authorised by dominant interest groups. The second response to Bury's analysis of the social constructionist challenge to bio-medical hegemony is that, far from arguing against the application of a rational discourse, we would suggest that the construction of certain behaviour as a disease *caused by* cortical impairment has to be challenged – in the absence of any empirical testimony – as an irrational position judged by its own criteria of proven cause and effect.

Caring for People with Dementia in the Community

We noted in Chapter 1 that this book was inspired by an evaluative project in which we were engaged, assessing whether one small 'demonstration' project achieved its objectives of helping people with dementia continue to live in the community. This experimental service will be referred to hereafter as 'the Project'.

The Project was established in 1988 by a district health authority keen to extend the limits of community care by showing how people with dementia could be enabled to continue living in their own homes. It aimed to:

> ...provide support to elderly mentally ill people in their own homes appropriate to their individual needs at any one time. The desired outcome is that these individuals will be able to continue to live in their own homes for a much longer period than is [sic] hitherto possible due to the lack of suitable support services. (Unpublished Project documents)

Service users were to be: 'Elderly Mentally Ill and/or Mentally Infirm people whose problems were of the severity that their carers can no longer cope within a home setting and who would otherwise then be admitted to hospital, Local Authority Part III Accommodation or a private residential home'.

These appear to be laudable objectives. Maintaining a dependent old person in the community is more problematic, 'if dependency stems from dementia rather than from physical incapacity' (Sinclair 1988). Older people with a dementing illness are more likely than those who are not dementing to enter residential or nursing care permanently (Levin, Sinclair and Gorbach 1989). Many of these, it seems, are unknown to service providers, as up to 50 per cent of all people admitted to residential modes have not previously been visited by community-based care services (Neill *et al.* 1989). Services may, however, actually serve to 'sweep up' people into residential and nursing home care, as people with dementia who have not been in receipt of services come to the attention of service providers, and service providers are alerted to their needs and hence precipitate entry to care (Levin *et al.* 1989). However, the vast majority of people with dementia, even those in its most severe stages, live either in their own homes or those of relatives, often with little or no support from statutory or non-statutory services (Carr 1992). Studies have found that between 53 and 58 per cent of dementia sufferers live alone (Askham *et al.* cited by Askham 1986; Kay, Beamish and Roth 1964).

The Project in practice

The Project was operated by two community psychiatric nurses (CPNs) and a staff of 28 home support workers employed on a part-time basis to provide, 'flexible home-based patterns of care'. Managerial upheavals caused by the restructuring of the health authority led to the Project operating as a semi-autonomous unit, run by the CPN co-ordinators with minimal managerial oversight or guidance. Attendance at monthly management group meetings diminished, so that rather than appearing to be a well-attended planning forum, they disintegrated into sparsely attended meetings at which the CPN co-ordinators provided basic factual information about the Project to an agenda which they had themselves set. This led to a gap in the upward flow of information about the Project to more senior managers, as all information passed upwards was based upon that perceived by the co-ordinators to be of importance. The role of more senior managers appeared to be that of 'fire-fighters'.

The CPNs divided the district (a seaside town which attracted many immigrants from several nearby cities upon their retirement) into two patches according to geography, each taking major responsibility for one. The home support workers were divided into two teams, each under the supervision of a CPN. New clients were referred to a team according to the area in which they lived.

In its first four years the project provided services to 56 people, with the numbers of people receiving its services at any one time fluctuating between 17 and 21. The average duration of receipt of services per ex-client who left for institutional care was 14 months, with a range of 4 to 37 months.

A person's experience of the Project commenced with their being targeted as a potential customer through their initial referral to the Project, following which an assessment of their suitability for inclusion and their needs was made. A package of services was then put together and delivered. Finally, the person would leave the Project through death or as a result of being directed to other services. We will now follow a person's path through the Project so as to gain some understanding of its structures and processes.

The exact aetiology of the process involved in referral to CPNs has remained comparatively poorly understood, with the possibility of complex antecedent interplay between a number of caring agencies making it difficult, if not impossible, to determine which agency has most influence in alerting CPN services to the existence of a person with a need for assistance. Examination of records and forays into the memories of the CPNs suggested that, in the Project's example, 88 per cent of referrals came from within the Health Service and another 12 per cent from social services. Only 5 per cent were self- or relative referrals. Further analysis suggested that referrals to the Project appeared to be dominated by two sources: other CPNs and local hospitals, notably the specialist day hospital. However, further questioning of the Project's CPNs allows us to go one step further back in the referral process, to find the antecedent referral agent, that is, the person who had referred the user to the above referral agents. Table A.1 breaks the figures down into Antecedent Referral Agent, that is, the agent who had referred a user to the person responsible for alerting the Project's attention. This latter person is here entitled the Intermediary Referral Agent. The term Direct Referral Agent is used to denote a person who has contacted the Project directly without using an intermediary.

Table A.1 Referral Sources

Profession	As Antecedent Referral Agent	As Intermediary Referral Agent	As Direct Referral Agent
GP	15	1	3
CPN	–	20	–
Social Worker	8	1	5
Community Occupational Therapist	–	3	2
Home Care Staff	7	–	–
Day Hospital	3	9	2
Other Social Services	1	–	2
Other Health Staff	1	–	5
Relatives	–	1	2
Total	**35**	**35**	**21**

It can be seen that the Project's referrals came via both health and social services, albeit that they were mediated predominantly by the two services having arguably the most direct contact both with service users and the Project staff: other CPNs at the day hospital.

Initially it was intended that people referred to the Project would be assessed by the members of a referral panel comprising a consultant psychogeriatrician, a senior CPN and a mental health social worker. If deemed suitable for the

Project's services, the individual was then visited by either of the Project's supervisors, who compiled a package of services according to the needs assessed. The referral panel fell into abeyance as its members left their posts. The original two-stage operation of: (1) screening being carried out by the members of the referral panel; and (2) assessment of needs being undertaken by the Project's CPNs, thus evolved into one stage, wherein the two CPNs undertook responsibility for assessment.

The Project aimed its services at people who were exhibiting what staff described in interviews as 'particularly difficult behavioural problems', with whom other services 'could not cope' and for whom therefore the Project was a 'last resort'. The sole written illustration of what is meant by these descriptions is found in the advisory notes contained in its referral forms, that is, its target clientele falls into the following categories:

1. Over the age of 65.

2. Diagnosed as suffering from a dementing illness.

3. Living alone or with a carer under great stress.

4. Usually physically active.

5. Presenting such behavioural problems as:

    ° wandering

    ° presenting difficulty in allowing others to gain access to the house

    ° leaving the gas taps on

    ° resistive to the usual forms of support

    ° not taking medication properly.

In sum, users of the service were expected to be physically well, active and continent, and exhibiting behaviour patterns described by the CPN supervisors as problematic.

Assessment criteria

It proved difficult to discover the objective criteria used for assessment. The majority, if not all, of the Project's users were physically active at the time of being accepted for the Project's services. The absence of physical frailty was explained by the CPNs as arising out of their search for people with behavioural problems such as wandering and/or aggressive or other anti-social behaviour, and such problems, they explained, are physically impossible for people who are housebound.

Service provision

Although the Project aimed to provide individualised packages of services, in practice there appeared to be a standard input of services for the 17–20 fully supported users. The standard service was as follows:

1. Home support worker input seven days a week for three hours per morning (usually 9 a.m. to 12 noon) and a further two hours in the evening (usually 4 p.m. to 6 p.m.). This included accompanied visits to coffee mornings once a week and to a social gathering one evening per week.

2. Attendance at the local day hospital for the elderly mentally infirm, and/or respite care.

3. Regular (sometimes daily) services from the CPN.

Home support workers undertook a wide variety of tasks, to the extent of decorating clients' homes. Although the block of hours in the morning were busy, home support workers in interview and during care planning meetings reported difficulties in keeping users amused when evening blocks of care were extended beyond two hours. Interviews with the Project's co-ordinators suggested that the rationale for providing this type of input was based not on service users' needs but on: (1) custom and practice; (2) a need to provide home support workers with a minimum number of hours' work per week; and (3) a belief that it 'works' for service users.

The CPNs inherited, from the original designers of the Project, a policy whereby the budget determined the number of home support worker hours available, and a rule-of-thumb determined the average input of hours of care needed per client and thus the numbers of clients who could be supported.

It was the belief of the CPNs running the Project that the extended period of time during which the service user was in the presence of the home support worker allowed a close relationship to develop, built on trust and understanding. This, they felt, was necessary in order to encourage the service user to become adjusted to 'normal' patterns of daily living, following months, if not years, of self-neglect. To reduce the input following a successful readjustment process was, they argued, to risk regression.

Let us now reduce two people who received the services of the Project to the status of case studies, so as to give the flavour of the Project.

Case study 1

Mrs Y, a widow living alone in a block of flats, was found to be continually requesting the company of her neighbour in the downstairs flat in the evenings, thus causing problems. The home support worker input was therefore increased as shown in Table A.2.

Table A.2. Support worker input, case study 1

Stage 1	Stage 2
9.00 a.m.–12 noon	9.00 a.m.–12 noon
4.00 p.m.–6.00 p.m.	4.00 p.m.–8.00 p.m.

It was felt by the Project's supervisors that since she was well fed and prepared for bed when the home support worker finished her evening shift, there was no need to check on the client's status later in the evening.

Case study 2

Mrs Z lived alone in one of the more exclusive parts of the town. Her neighbours had, on numerous occasions, expressed concern that she had not been placed in an institution, so one of the Project's tasks was to provide reassurance to them. Referred from the day hospital, having been diagnosed as having Alzheimer's disease by the then consultant psychogeriatrician, she tended to 'wander' at night, suffered from delusions and forgot to pay her bills. Since she was afraid to be left alone, yet unwilling to leave her own home, an initial solution to the problems of her crying after her home support workers left for the evening at 6 p.m. was to prepare her for, and leave her in, bed, with the house safely locked. Due to this client's condition, it proved impossible to obtain her opinion about being in bed from 6 p.m. to 10 a.m. Her condition subsequently deteriorated as her illness advanced, and the input of home support worker assistance was increased to nine hours a day, seven days a week, as shown in Table A.3.

Table A.3. Support worker input, case study 2

Assessment	First Revision	Second Revision
10.8.89	19.11.90	8.4.91
10 a.m.–1 p.m.	9.30 a.m.–1 p.m.	9.30 a.m.–12.30 p.m.
4.00 p.m.–6.00 p.m.	5.00 p.m.–7.00 p.m.	4.00 p.m.–10.00 p.m.

Entering nursing home care

Of the 34 people who had ceased being the Project's clients within its first four years, eight had died, two had had their care taken over by relatives, and 25, or 45 per cent, were discharged to hospital, nursing home or residential home, after receiving the Project's services for an average of 14 months.

Fifty-two per cent did so 'following a supervisor's assessment' and 32 per cent following the request of a carer. The consultant psychogeriatrician, in post for the last 16 months of the evaluation, was not involved in the decision to admit people to residential or nursing home care. When questioned about the Project, he emphasised his satisfaction with the supervisors' work and, acknowledging that he lacked scientific evidence, felt that if the Project staff had done all they could do and were still struggling to cope with a person, then the time had come for that person to be admitted.

It proved extremely difficult to 'tease out' the precise causes of why people were deemed to be at a stage where they could no longer be cared for in the community. Entries on file, in nine cases, stated only that 'supervisor's assessment' had led to an admission to a nursing home, whilst in another two instances no information as to reason for admission was entered on the file. In other cases, only proximate reasons were given in the files as to why a person had entered care, such as carer 'ill' or 'unable to cope' (two cases) or another person, such as a carer, relative or landlord, requesting an entry to residential care (seven instances). When interviewed about the decision-making process concerning entry to care, a complex situation emerged.

Questioned as to why a decision was made to refer someone to residential care, the reply from one CPN was: 'It is very difficult to know. Nine times out of ten it will be a physical illness, with the result that the client will need 24 hour nursing care... The other thing is that the carer will take them off [this scheme]'. At other times, despite the CPNs' considering a person needed to enter care, the family carer was adamant that they wished to keep their relative in their own home, and the Project conceded to those wishes.

Askham and Thompson (1990) found that the need for continual guarding was a major factor in determining entry to care. This was rarely a factor in precipitating entry to institutional care of the users of the Project's services. Rarely, except in emergencies, did staff work after 8 p.m. In the context of arguing for further resources, the CPNs stated that they were losing clients to residential care because 24 hour cover was not provided, as some of them could not be left alone at night. Staff could make night-time calls, but in times of crisis only. Interviewed at other times, however, the CPNs were satisfied that:

> ...if you get your care plan right in the day, the nights are not as problematic as some people think. You keep people busy in the day, you tire them out, give them good meals and social contact and make sure they are warm, make sure they use the toilet before going to bed and make sure the sheets are clean and that they are clean and, nine times out of ten, they are relatively safe to leave at night. There is an element of risk, of course, but it is an acceptable element.

Furthermore, should there be a worry that a person could be restless, it was thought that a tranquilliser could be used, especially, they rationalised, as they with their nurse training, 'could monitor its side effects'.

We see a gradual loosening of criteria for inclusion in the scheme. In the first year of the Project, the target group of service users was redefined more loosely as: 'People who are suffering from functional or organic psychiatric illness who, on referral, are over the age of 65 years, living alone or with a Carer under great stress'. It was noted that: 'It is difficult to explicitly set out the criteria for when a person would receive this service and this would necessarily be a decision made on a case by case basis'. Criteria for inclusion in practice became one where the individual with dementia was a cause of disruption to the local social and health community, either directly (through displaying unacceptable behaviour) or indirectly (through the practices of carers which were seen to offend others).

The CPNs became the sole knowledge-holders of dementia. They aimed to provide, 'a comprehensive nursing service for people suffering from psychiatric illness in old age', but they also aimed to promote mental health in old age, independence, and communication with other agencies; and to improve carers' 'self-image' 'through support'. The objectives of the service included: provision of innovative care systems through 'individual planned programmes of care'; training for staff; professional conduct; provision of advisory and supportive services for clients, carers and other agencies 'involved in the care of the elderly'; and provision of an educational framework for statutory and non-statutory bodies. The CPNs therefore attempted to establish themselves as *the* experts in the care in the community of people with dementia. They worked hard at publicising their work, travelling to other health authorities around the country, speaking at conferences and publishing details of their experiment in nursing journals. This, of course, is standard practice amongst those seeking professional status.

A prime requirement of such status is possession of a body of knowledge to which others require access but which they cannot gain directly. However, the body of knowledge they were trying to make their own was not knowledge specific to *nursing*, for it was based firmly and thoroughly within that body of beliefs discussed above: that of the medical profession.

Postscript

Following the end of funding, the Project's services were absorbed into the wider psychogeriatric services of the area.

References

Abbott, P. and Wallace, C. (1991) 'The sociology of caring professions: an introduction.' In P. Abbott and C. Wallace (eds) *The Sociology of Caring Professions.* London: Falmer Press.

ADRDA (1982) *A Disease of the Century: The Case for Alzheimer's Disease.* Chicago: ADRDA.

Alzheimer, A. (1907) 'Über eine eigenastige Erkrankung der Hirnrinde.' *Allgemaine Zeitschrift für Psychiatrie 64,* 146–8.

Amster, L.C. and Krauss, H.H. (1974) 'The relationship between life crises and: mental deterioration in old age.' *International Journal of Ageing and Human Development 5,* 51–55.

Appell, J., Kertesz, A. and Fisman, M. (1982) 'A study of language functioning in Alzheimer's patients.' *Brain and Language 17,* 73–91.

Armstrong, D. (1983) *The Political Anatomy of the Body.* Cambridge: Cambridge University Press.

Askham, J. (1986) 'Do we provide enough of the right care?' *Community Care No.2,* 30 Oct, 1–3.

Askham, J. and Thompson, C. (1990) *Dementia and Home Care.* Mitcham: Age Concern England.

Atkinson, J.M. and Heritage, J. (eds) (1984) *Structures of Social Action.* Cambridge: Cambridge University Press.

Atkinson, P. (1995) *Medical Talk and Medical Work.* London: Sage.

Baggott, R. (1994) *Health and Health Care in Britain.* London: Macmillan.

Barbato, C. and Feezel, J.D. (1987) 'The language of ageing in different age groups.' *The Gerontological Society of America 27,* 4, 527–531.

Barker, J. (1991) *Pharmaceutical Journal,* Jan 26.

Barley, S.R. (1988) 'The social construction of a machine.' In M. Lock and D.R. Gordon (eds) *Biomedicine Examiners.* Dordrecht: Kluwer.

Baron, R.J. (1992) 'Why aren't more doctors phenomenologists?' In D. Leder (ed) *The Body in Medical Thought and Practice.* Dordrecht: Kluwer Academic Publishers.

Bayles, K.A. and Kaszniak, A.W. (1987) *Communication and Cognition in Normal Ageing and Dementia.* London: Taylor and Francis.

Becker, H. (1963) *Outsiders: Studies in the Sociology of Deviance.* New York: Free Press.

Bell, S. (1987) 'Changing ideas: the medicalisation of menopause.' *Social Science and Medicine 24,* 6, 535–542.

Benson, D.F. (1986) 'Alzheimer's disease: the pedigree.' In A. Scheibel and A.T. Wechsler (eds) *The Biological Substrates of Alzheimer's Disease.* New York: Academic Press.

Benson, D.F. (1994) 'Alzheimer's disease: the pedigree.' In A.B. Scheibel and A.F. Wechsler (eds) *The Biological Substrates of Alzheimer's disease.* New York: Academic Press.

Berg, M. (1992) 'The construction of medical disposals.' *Sociology of Health and Illness 14,* 2, 152–180.

Berg, M. (1995) 'Turning practice into a science: reconceptualising post-war medical practice.' *Social Studies of Science 5,* 437–476.

Berger, E.Y. (1980) 'A system for rating the severity of senility.' *Journal of the American Geriatrics Society 28,* 234–236.

Berger, P. and Luckmann, T. (1967) *The Social Construction of Reality.* London: Allen Lane.

Bergmann, K. (1975) 'The epidemiology of senile dementia.' *British Journal of Psychiatry 9,* 100–9.

Bernstein, B. (1974) *Class, Codes and Control.* London: RKP.

Berrios (1994) Chapter 2 in Hupert, Brayne and O'Connor *op. cit.*

Blais, R. (1993) 'Variations in surgical rates in Quebec: does access to teaching hospitals make a difference?' *Canadian Medical Association Journal 148,* 1729–1736.

Bond, J. (1992) 'The politics of caregiving: the professionalisation of informal care.' *Ageing and Society 12,* 5–21.

Bourdieu, P. (1991) *Language and Symbolic Power.* Cambridge: Polity Press.

Bowles, N.L. and Poon, L.W. (1985) 'Ageing and retrieval of words in semantic memory.' *Journal of Gerontology 40,* 71–77.

Boyle, P. (1994) 'Epidemiology of benign prostatic hyperphasia?' *British Journal of Clinical Practitioners Symposium,* May 74, 18–22.

Breitner, J.S.C. and Folstein, M.F. (1984) 'Familial Alzheimer's disease: a prevalent disorder with specific clinical features.' *Psychological Medicine 14,* 63–80.

Bromley, D.R. (1988) *Human Ageing.* London: Penguin.

Brown, P. and Yule, G. (1983) *Discourse Analysis.* Cambridge: Cambridge University Press.

Burns, A. *et al.* (1990) 'Cause of death in AD'. Age and Ageing.

Burns, A. *et al.* (1990) 'Accuracy of clinical diagnosis of Alzheimer's disease.' *British Medical Journal 301,* 1026.

Bury, M. (1982) 'Chronic illness as biographical disruption.' *Sociology of Health and Illness 4,* 167–82.

Bury, M. (1986) 'Social constructionism and the development of medical sociology.' *Sociology of Health and Illness 9,* 137–169.

Calas, M.B. and Smircich, L. (1992) ' Re-writing gender into organisational theorising: directives from feminist perspectives.' In M. Reed and M. Hughes (eds) *Rethinking Organisation: New Directions in Organisation Thinking and Analysis.* London: Sage.

Caporel, L. (1981) 'The paralanguage of care-giving: baby talk and the institutionalised aged.' *Journal of Personality and Psychology 40,* 5, 876–884.

Carr, J.S. (1992) *Tayside Dementia Services Planning Survey.* Stirling: University of Stirling Dementia Services Development Centre.

Charmaz, K. (1983) 'Loss of self: a fundamental form of suffering in the chronically ill.' *Sociology of Health and Illness 5*, 2, 168–195.

Chia, R. (1994) 'The concept of decision: a de-constructive analysis.' *Journal of Management Studies 31*, 6, 781–806.

Close, G.R. Rushworth, R.L. Rob, M.I. and Rubin, G.L. (1993) 'Variation in selected childhood surgical procedures.' *Journal of Paediatric Child Health 29*, 6, 429–433.

Clouser, K.D. (1985) 'Approaching the logic of diagnosis.' In K.F. Schaffer (ed) *Logic of Discovery and Diagnosis in Medicine.* Berkeley, CA: University of California Press.

Cochrane, A.N. (1972) *Effectiveness and Efficiency.* London: Nuffield Foundation.

Cohen, A. and Eisdorfer, C. (1986) *The Loss of Self.* New York: Norton.

Cohen, G.D. (1983) 'Historical views and evolution of concepts.' In B. Reisberg (ed) *Alzheimer's Disease.* New York: New York Free Press.

Conrad, P. and Schneider, J.W. (1980) *Deviance and Medicalisation: From Madness to Sickness.* St Louis: Mosby.

Corsellis, J.A.N. (1979) 'On the transmission of dementia: a personal view of the slow virus problem.' *British Journal of Psychiatry 134*, 553–559.

Coulter, A., McPherson, K. and Vessey, M. (1988) 'Do British women undergo too many or too few hysterectomies?' *Social Science and Medicine 27*, 9, 987–994.

Coulter, J. (1985) 'Two concepts of the mental.' In K.J. Gergen and K.E. Davis (eds) *The Social Construction of the Person.* New York: Springer Verlag.

Coupland, N., Coupland, J. and Giles, H. (1991) *Language, Society and the Elderly: Discourse, Identity and Ageing.* Oxford: Blackwell.

Crapper, D.R., Karlik, S. and Devon, V. (1978) 'Aluminium and other metals in senile (Alzheimer) dementia.'

Cumming, E. and Henry, W.E. (1961) *Growing Old: The Process of Disengagement.* New York: Basic Books.

Cummings, J. and Benson, D. (1985) 'Aphasia in dementia of the Alzheimer's type.' *Neurology 35*, 394–397.

Curran, S. and Wattis, J.P. (1989) 'Round-up: searching for the cause of Alzheimer's disease.' *Geriatric Medicine*, March, 13–14.

Cutlip, W.D., and Leary, M.R. (1993) 'Anatomic and physiological bases of blushing: speculation from neurology and psychology.' *British Neurology 6*, 181–185.

Daniel, S.L. (1990) 'Interpretation in medicine: an introduction.' *Theoretical Medicine 2*, 5–8.

Davis, D. (1996) 'The cultural constructions of the premenstrual and menopause syndromes.' In C.F. Sargent and C.B. Brettell (eds) *Gender and Health: An International Perspective.* New Jersey: Prentice Hall.

De Alarcon (1971) 'Social consequences of mental illness in old age.' In D. Kay and A. Wall (eds) *Recent Developments in Psychogeriatrics.* London: Royal Psychological Association.

Deleuze, G. and Guatarri, F. (1977) *Anti-Oedipus, Capitalism and Schizophrenia.* New York: Viking.

Denzin, N.K. (1992) *Symbolic Interactionism and Cultural Studies: The Politics of Interpretation.* Oxford: Blackwell.

Derrida, J. (1970) 'Structure, sign and play in the discourse of the human sciences.' In R. Macksey and E. Donato (ed) *The Structuralist Controversy.* Baltimore: Johns Hopkins Press.

Diesfel, H.F., Van Houe, L.R. and Moerkens, R.M. (1986) 'Duration of survival in dementia.' *Acta Psychiat. Scand 73,* 366–371.

Douglas, M. (1991) *Purity and Danger.* London: Routledge.

Dowie, J. and Elstein, A. (1993) *Professional Judgement: A Reader in Clinical Decision-Making.* Cambridge: Cambridge University Press.

Dreyfus, H.L. and Dreyfus, S.E. (1986) *Mind Over Machine.* New York: Free Press.

DuBeau, C.E. and Resnick, N. (1992) 'Controversies in the diagnosis and management of benign prostatic hypertrophy.' *Advanced Internal Medicine 37,* 55–83.

Dubos, R. (1965) 'Hippocrates in modern dress.' *Proceedings of the Institute of Medicine of Chicago 25,* 9, 242–251.

Eddy, D.M. (1984) 'Variation in practice: the role of uncertainty.' *Health Affairs 3,* 74–89.

Einstein, A.R. (1967) *Clinical Judgement.* Huntingdon, NY: Krieger Publishing Co.

Eisenberg, L. (1988) 'Editorial: the social construction of mental illness.' *Psychological Medicine 18,* 1–9.

Emery, O. (1984) 'Language and ageing.' *Experimental Ageing Research 1,* 3–60.

Engelhardt, H.T. (1985) 'Typologies of disease: nosologies revisited.' In K. F. Schaffner (ed) *Logic of Discovery and Diagnosis in Medicine.* Berkeley, CA: University of California Press.

Evans, G., Hughes, B. and Wilkin, D. (1981) *The Management of Mental and Physical Impairment in Non-Specialist Homes for the Elderly; Research Report No.4.* Manchester: Psychogeriatric Unit, University Hospital of South Manchester.

Falk, P. (1994) *The Consuming Body.* London: Sage.

Featherstone, M. and Hepworth, M. (1990) *The Body: Social Process and Cultural Theory.* London: Sage.

Feinstein, A.R. (1967) *Clinical Judgement.* Baltimore: Williams and Wilkins.

Fennell, G., Phillipson, C. and Evers, H. (1993) *The Sociology of Old Age.* Milton Keynes: Open University Press.

Ferenczi (1922) 'Psychoanalysis and the mental disorders of general paralysis of the insane.' In M. Balint (ed) *Final Contributors to the Problems and Methods of Psychoanalysis.* London: Hogarth Press.

Ferrer, I. (1992) 'Dementia of frontal lobe type and amyotrophy.' *Behavioural Neurology 5,* 87–96.

Fischoff, B. and Beyth-Marom, R. (1993) 'Hypothesis evaluation from a Bayesian perspective.' In J. Dowie and A. Elstein (eds) *Professional Judgement: A Reader in Clinical Decision-Making.* Cambridge: Cambridge University Press.

Fleck, L. (1935) *Genesis and Development of a Scientific Fact.* Benno Schwabe: Basil. English translation by F. Bardley and T. Trenn, University of Chicago Press.

Folsom, J.G. (1967) 'Intensive hospital therapy for the geriatric patient.' *Curr. Psychiat. Ther. 7,* 209–215.

Folsom, J.G. (1968) 'Reality orientation for elderly patients.' *Journal of Geriatric Psychiatry 1*, 291–307.

Foss, L. (1994) 'Putting the mind back into the body: a successor scientific model.' *Theoretical Medicine 15*, 291–313.

Foucault, M. (1973) *The Birth of the Clinic.* London: Tavistock.

Foucault, M. (1977) *Discipline and Punish.* London: Tavistock.

Fox, N.J. (1993) *Postmodernism, Sociology and Health.* Buckingham: Open University Press.

Fox, P. (1989) 'From senility to Alzheimer's disease: the rise of the Alzheimer's disease movement.' *Millbank Quarterly 67*, 1, 58–102.

Fraser, M. (1987) *Dementia: Its Nature and Management.* Chichester: John Wiley.

Freund, P.E.S. (1990) 'The expressive body.' *Sociology of Health and Illness 12*, 4, 452–457.

Freund, P.E.S. and McGuire, M.B. (1991) *Health, Illness and the Social Body.* New Jersey: Prentice Hall.

Friedson, E. (1986) *Professional Powers.* Chicago: University of Chicago Press.

Garfield, S.L. and Blek, L. (1952) 'Age, vocabulary, level and mental impairment.' *Journal of Consulting Psychology 16*, 395–398.

Garruto, R.M., Yanagihara, R. and Gajdusek, D.C. (1985) 'Disappearance of high incidence amyotrophic lateral sclerosis and Parkinsonism on Guam.' *Neurology 35*, 193–198.

Gergen, K.J. (1985) 'Social constructionist inquiry: context and implications.' In K.J. Gergen and K.E. Davis (eds) *The Social Construction of the Person.* New York: Springer Verlag.

Gianotti (1975) 'The borderlands of dementia.' In N.E. Miller and G.D. Cohen (eds) 'Clinical aspects of Alzheimer's disease and senile dementia.' *Aging 15.* New York: Raven Press, pp.61–80.

Gilbert, N. and Mulkay, M. (1980) 'Contexts of scientific discourse.' In Knorr, Krohn and Whitley (eds) op cit. 269–294.

Gilbert, N. and Mulkay, M. (1991) 'Theory choice.' In M. Mulkay (ed) *Sociology of Science: A Sociological Pilgrimage.* Milton Keynes: Open University Press.

Glover, J.A. (1938) 'The incidence of tonsillectomy in school children.' *Proceedings of the Royal Society of Medicine XXXI*, 1219–1236.

Goffman, E. (1968) *Asylums.* Harmondsworth: Penguin Press.

Goffman, E. (1969) *The Presentation of Self in Everyday Life.* London: Allen Lane.

Good, M.J. and Good, B.J. (1994) 'Disabling practitioners: learning to be a doctor in American medical education.' *American Journal of Orthopsychiatry 59*, 2, 303–309.

Gordon, D.R. (1988) 'Clinical science and clinical expertise.' In M. Lock and D.R. Gordon (eds) *Biomedicine Examiners.* Dordrecht: Kleuwer.

Gravell, R. (1988) *Communication Problems in Old People.* London: Croom Helm.

Green, R.F. (1969) 'Age–intelligence relationship between ages 16 and 64.' *Developmental Psychology 1*, 618–627.

Griffiths, R.A., Good, W.R., *et al.* (1987) 'Depression, dementia and disability in the elderly.' *British Journal of Psychiatry 150*, 482–493.

Gruenthal, E. (1927) 'Kleinisch-anatomisch Vergleichende.' *Z. Ges. Neurol Psychiat 111*, 763.

Gubrium, J.F. (1986) *Old Timers and Alzheimer's: The Descriptive Organization of Senility.* Greenwich, Conn.: JAI Press.

Gubrium, J.F. (1987) 'Structuring and de-structuring the course of illness: the Alzheimer's Disease experience.' *Sociology of Health and Illness 9*, 1–24.

Gurland, B.J. *et al.* (1980) 'The epidemiology of depression and dementia in the elderly.' In J.O. Cole and J.E. Barrett (eds) *Psychopathology in the Aged.* New York: Raven Press.

Gurland, B. *et al.* (1984) 'The SHORT-CARE. An efficient instrument for assessment of depression, dementia and disability.' *Journal of Gerontology 39*, 166–169.

Gurland, B. *et al.* (1989) (1982) 'Criteria for diagnosis of dementia.' *Communit. elderly. Gerontologist. 22*, 180–186.

Gurland, B.J. (1981) 'The borderlands of dementia.' In N.E. Miller and G.D. Cohen (eds) 'Clinical aspects of Alzheimer's disease and sen dementia.' *Ageing 15*. Raven Press, N.Y., pp.61–80.

Hanssen, M.V. and Wold, T. (1994) 'A survey concerning the attitudes of urologists toward prostatism patients.' *Scand. J. Urol. Nephrol*, Sept 28, 3, 257–264.

Harding, S. (1991) *Whose Science? Whose Knowledge?* Milton Keynes: Open University Press.

Harré, R. (1983) *Personal Being.* Oxford: Blackwell.

Harré, R. (1990) 'Some narrative conventions of scientific discourse.' In J. Shotter and K.J. Gergen (eds) *Texts of Identity.* London: Sage.

Harré, R. (1991) *Physical Being.* Oxford: Blackwell.

Hawking, S. (1995) *A Short History of Time.* London: Bantam.

Hayter, J. (1974) 'Patients who have Alzheimer's disease.' *American Journal of Nursing 5*, 14–20.

Hazan, H. (1994) *Old Age: Constructions and Deconstructions.* Cambridge: Cambridge University Press.

Helgason, T. (1977) 'Psychiatric services and mental illness in Iceland.' *Acta Psychiat. Scand.* Suppl. 268.

Helman, C.G. (1988) 'Psyche, soma and society: the social construction of psycho-somatic disorders.' In M. Lock and D.R. Gordon (eds) *Biomedicine Examiners.* Dordrecht: Kleuwer.

Henderson, A.S. (1986) 'The epidemiology of Alzheimer's disease.' *British Medical Bulletin 42*, 1, 3–10.

Henderson, A.S. and Huppert, F.A. (1984) 'The problem of mild dementia.' *Psychiatric Medicine 14*, 5–11.

Herzlich, C. and Pierret, J. (1985) 'The social construction of the patient: patients' illnesses in other ages.' *Social Science and Medicine 20*, 2, 145–151.

Heston, L.L., Mastri, R., Anderson, V.W. and White, J. (1981) 'Dementia of the Alzheimer type.' *Archives of General Psychiatry 38*, 1085–1090.

Hewa, S. and Hetherington, R.W. (1994) 'Specialists without spirit: limitations of the mechanistic biomedical model.' *Theoretical Medicine 16*, 2, 129–139.

Heyman, A., Wilkinson, W.E., *et al.* (1983) 'Alzheimer's disease: genetic aspects and associated clinical disorders.' *American Neurology 14*, 507–515.

Holtgrewe, H.L. *et al.* (1989) 'Transurethral prostatectomy: practice aspects of the dominant operation in American Urology.' *Journal of Urology 141*, 2, 248–253.

Huff, J. (1988) 'The disorder of naming in Alzheimer's disease.' In L. Light and D. Burke (eds) *Language, Memory and Aging.* Cambridge and New York: Cambridge University Press.

Hughes, B. (1995) *Older People and Community Care.* Buckingham: Open University Press.

Hughes, D. (1977) 'Everyday and medical knowledge in categorising patients.' In R. Dingwall, C. Heath, M. Reid and M. Stacey (eds) *Health Care and Health Knowledge.* London: Croom Helm.

Hunt, M. (1990) 'Narrative in mild and moderate dementia of the Alzheimer's type.' In R. Lubinski (ed) 1198–114.

Hunter, D.J., McKee, C.M., Black, N.A. and Sanderson, C.F. (1994) 'Urinary symptoms: prevalence and severity in British men aged 55 and over.' *Journal of Epidemiology and Community Health 48*, 6, 569–575.

Huppert, F.A., Brayne, C. and O'Connor, D.W. (1994) *Dementia and Normal Aging.* Cambridge: Cambridge University Press.

Illich, I. (1979) *Limits to Medicine.* London: Marion Boyars.

Ineichen, B. (1987) 'Measuring the rising tide: how many dementia cases will there be by 2001?' *British Journal of Psychiatry 150*, 195–200.

Johnson, M. (1987) *The Body in the Mind.* Chicago: University of Chicago Press.

Jorm, A.F. (1990) *The Epidemiology of Alzheimer's Disease and Related Disorders.* London: Chapman and Hall.

Katzman, R. (1976) 'The prevalence and malignancy of Alzheimer's disease.' *Archives of Neurology 33*, 217–218.

Kay, D.W., Beamish, P. and Roth, M. (1964) 'Old age mental disorders in Newcastle upon Tyne Part 1.' *British Journal of Psychiatry 40*, 146–158.

Kay, D.W., Beamish, P. and Roth, M. (1964) 'Old age mental disorders in Newcastle upon Tyne.' *British Journal of Psychiatry 110*, 146–158.

Kay, D.W. and Bergman, K. (1980) 'Epidemiology of mental disorders amongst the aged in this community.' In J. Birren and J. Sloane (eds) *Handbook of Mental Health and Ageing.* New Jersey: Prentice Hall.

Keen, J. (1992) *Dementia.* London: Office of Health Economics.

Kempler, D. (1991) *Dementia and Communication.* St Louis: Decker.

Keskimaki, I., Seppo, A. and Teperi, J. (1994) 'Regional variation in surgical procedure rates in Finland.' *Scandinavian Journal of Social Medicine 22*, 132–138.

King's Fund (1986) *Living Well into Old Age – Applying Principles of Good Practice to Services for People with Dementia.* London: K. Edwards Hospital Fund.

Kirmayer (1988) 'Mind and Body as Metaphors.' In Lock and Gordon (eds) (1988) *op. cit.*

Kite, M.E. and Johnson, B.T. (1988) 'Attitudes to older and younger adults: a meta-analysis.' *Psychology and Ageing 3*, 233–244.

Kitwood, T. (1989) 'Brain, mind and dementia, with particular reference to Alzheimer's Disease.' *Ageing and Society 9*, 1–15.

Kitwood, T. (1990) 'The dialectics of dementia with particular reference to Alzheimer's disease.' *Ageing and Society 10*, 177–196.

Kitwood, T. and Bredin, K. (1992) 'Towards a theory of dementia care.' *Ageing and Society 12*, 269–287.

Knorr, K. *et al.* (eds) (1980) *The Social Process of Scientific Investigation*. Dordrecht: Reidel.

Knorr-Cetina, K.D. and Mulkay, M. (1983) *Science Observed*. Beverly Hills: Sage.

Kurhn, T. (1962) *The Structure of Scientific Revolutions*. Chicago: University of Chicago Press.

Lacan, J. (1968) *The Language of the Self*. Baltimore: Johns Hopkins Press.

Lachman, R., Lachman, J. and Taylor, D.W. (1982) 'Reallocation of mental resources over the productive lifespan.' In F. Gaik and S. Trehub (eds) *Ageing and Cognitive Processes*. New York: Plenum, pp.279–308.

Laing, R.D. (1967) *The Politics of Experience and the Bird of Paradise*. Middlesex: Harmondsworth.

Laplane, D. (1992) 'Thought and language.' *Behavioural Neurology 5*, 33–38.

Lapresle, J., Duckett, S., Galle, P. and Cartier, L. (1975) 'Documents cliniques.' *C.R. Soc. Biol. 169*, 282–285.

Larsson, T., *et al.* (1963) 'Senile dementia: a clinical, svecomedical and genetic study.' *Acta Psychiat. Scand.* Suppl. 167.

Lash, S. (1991) 'Genealogy and the body: Foucault/Deleuze/Nietzsche.' In M. Featherstone, M. Hepworth and B.S. Turner (eds) *The Body: Social Process and Cultural Theory*. London: Sage.

Latour, B. and Woolgar, S. (1979) *Laboraatory Life: The Construction of Scientific Facts*. London: Sage.

Latour, B. (1979) *Laboratory Life: The Construction of Scientific Facts*. London: Sage.

Latour, B. (1987) *Science in Action*. Milton Keynes: Open University Press.

Layder, D. (1994) *Understanding Social Theory*. London: Sage.

Leder, D. (1990) *The Absent Body*. Chicago: University of Chicago Press.

Leder, D. (1992) 'Clinical interpretation: the hermeneutics of medicine.' *Theoretical Medicine 2*, 9–24.

Levin, E., Sinclair, T. and Gorbach, P. (1989) *Families, Services and Confusion in Old Age*. Aldershot: Avebury.

Light, L.L. and Burke, D.N. (1989) *Language, Memory and Ageing*. Cambridge: Cambridge University Press.

Little, A., Hemsley, D. and Bergmann, K. (1987) 'Comparison of sensitivity of three instruments for the detection of cognitive decline in elderly.' *British Journal of Psychiatry 150*, 808–814.

Lishman, W.A. (1978) *Organic Psychiatry*. Oxford: Blackwell.

Lishman, W.A. (1994) 'The history of research into dementia and its relationship to current concepts.' In Huppert, Brayn and O'Connor *op. cit.*

Lock, J.D. (1990) 'Some aspects of medical hermeneutics.' *Theoretical Medicine 7*, 41–49.

Lock, M. and Gordon, D.R. (eds) (1988) *Biomedicine Examiners*. Dordrecht: Kluwer.

Löwy, I. (1988) 'Ludwick Fleck on the social construction of medical knowledge.' *Sociology of Health and Illness 10*, 133–155.

Lupton, D. (1995) *The Imperative of Health*. London: Sage.

Lu-Yao, G.L., McLerran, D., Wasson, J. and Wennberg, J.E. (1993) 'An assessment of radical prostatectomy.' *JAMA 269*, 20, 2633–2666.

Lu-Yao, G.L., Barry, M.J., Chang, C.H., Wasson, J.H. and Wennberg, J.E. (1994) 'Transurethural resection of the prostrate among medicare beneficiaries in the U.S.' *Urology, 44*, 5, 692–8.

Lyotard, J.F. (1971) *Discours, Figure*. Paris: Klincksieck.

Mackie, M. (1987) *Constructing Women and Men: Gender Socialisation*. Toronto: Holt, Rinehart and Winston.

Malterud, K. (1995) 'The legitimacy of clinical knowledge.' *Theoretical Medicine 16*, 2, 183–198.

Mangham, I.L. (ed) (1987) *Organisation, Analysis and Development: A Social Construction of Organisational Behaviour*. Chichester: John Wiley and Sons.

Manning, P. (1991) 'The significance of Goffman's changing use of the theatrical metaphor.' *Sociological Theory 9*, 1, 70–86.

Martin, N.G., Kehren, U., Battistutta, D. and Mathews, J.D. (1991) 'Iatrogenic influences on the heritability of childhood tonsillectomy.' *Acta Genet. Med. Gemellol. Rome 40*, 2, 165–172.

McDermott, J.R., Smith, A.I., Iqbal K. and Wisniewski, H.M. (1979) 'Brain aluminium in ageing and Alzheimer's disease.' *Neurology 29*, 809–814.

McGrother *et al.* (1987) 'Do the elderly need better incontinence services?' *Community Medicine 9*, 1, 62–67.

McKhann, G., Drackmin, D., Folstein, M., Kafzman, R., Price, D. and Stadlan, E.M. (1984) 'Clinical diagnosis of Alzheimer's disease.' *Neurology 34*, 939–944.

McLaughlin, A.I.G. *et al.* (1962) 'Pulmonary fibrosis and encephalopathy associated with inhalation of aluminium dust.' *Br J of Ind Med 19*, 253–263.

McMullin, E. (1985) 'Diagnosis by computer.' In K.F. Schaffner (ed) *Logic of Discovery and Diagnosis in Medicine*. Berkeley, CA: University of California Press.

McPherson, K., Wennberg, J.E., Hovind, O.B. and Clifford, P. (1982) 'Small area variations in the uses of common surgical procedures.' *New England Journal of Medicine 307*, 1310–1314.

Meacher, M. (1972) *Taken for a Ride: Special Rest Homes for Confused Old People*. London: Longman.

Mead, G.H. (1934) *Mind, Self and Society*. Chicago: University of Chicago Press.

Meltzer, B.N., Petras, J.W. and Reynolds, L.T. (1975) *Symbolic Interaction: Genesis, Varieties and Criticism*. London: Routledge.

Mendelsohn, E. (1977) 'The social construction of scientific knowledge.' In E. Mendelsohn, P. Weingart and R. Whitley (eds) *The Social Production of Scientific Knowledge*. Dordrecht: Reidel.

Menzies Lyth, I. (1988) *Containing Anxiety in Institutions*. London: Free Association Books.

Miller, E. (1977) *Abnormal Ageing: The Psychology of Senile and Presenile Dementia*. London: Wiley.

Mills, A.J. (1992) 'Organisation, gender and culture.' In A.J. Mills and P. Tancred (eds) *Gendering Organisational Analysis.* Newbury Park, Calif: Sage, pp.93–111.

Mills, A.J. and Murgatroyd, S.J. (1991) *Organisational Rules.* Milton Keynes: Open University Press.

Moore, H. (1994) *A Passion for Difference.* Cambridge: Polity Press.

Morgan, R.F. (1965) 'Note on the psycho-pathology of senility: senescent defence against threat of death.' *Psychology Reports 17,* 305–306.

Morris, R.G. and Kopelmann (1986) 'The memory deficits in Alzheimer-type dementia.' *Quarterly Journal of Experimental Psychology 381,* 575–602.

Mulholland, C., Harding, N. and Bradley, S. (1995) *Variations in Admissions to Acute Hospital Beds: Report for the DHSS, N. Ireland.* Belfast: DHSS.

Mulkay, M. (1991) *Sociology of Science: A Sociological Pilgrimage.* Milton Keynes: Open University Press.

Murphy, J.S. (1992) 'The body with AIDS: a post-structionalist approach.' In D. Leder (ed) *The Body in Medical Thought and Practice.* Dordrecht: Kluwer Academic Publishers.

Myers, G. (1990) *Writing Biology: Texts in the Construction of Scientific Knowledge.* Madison: University of Wisconsin Press.

Neill, J., Sinclair, I., Gorbach, P. and Williams J. (1989) *A Need for Care: Elderly Applicants for Local Authority Homes.* Avebury: Aldershot.

Nelson, A. (1994) 'How could scientific facts be socially constructed?' *Studies in the History and Philosophy of Science 25,* 4, 535–547.

NHS Health Advisory Service (1982) *The Rising Tide: Developing Services for Mental Illness in Old Age.* Sutton, England: NHS Health Advisory Service.

Nicolson, M. and McLaughlin, C. (1987) 'Social constructionism and medical sociology: a reply to M.R. Bury.' *Sociology of Health and Illness 9,* 2, 107–126.

Norman, A. (1987) *Rights and Risk.* London: Centre for Policy on Ageing.

Oakley, D.P. (1965) 'Senile dementia: some aetiological factors.' *British Journal of Psychiatry 111,* 414–419.

Parsons, T. (1951) *The Social System.* London: RKP.

Payer, L. (1990) *Medicine and Culture.* London: Gollancz.

Pfeiffer, R.I., Afifi, A.A. and Chance, J.M. (1987) 'Prevalence of Alzheimer's disease in a retirement community.' *American Journal of Epidemiology 125,* 3, 420–436.

Pickering, A. (ed) (1992) *Science as Practice and Culture.* Chicago: Chicago University Press.

Polkingthorne, D. (1988) *Narrative Knowing and the Human Sciences.* Albany: University of New York Press.

Pollit, P., O'Conner, D. and Anderson, I. (1989) 'Mild dementia: perceptions and problems.' *Ageing and Society 9,* 261–275.

Post, F. (1944) 'Some problems arising from a study of mental patients over the age of sixty years.' *Journal of Mental Science 90,* 554.

Powell, L.S. (1985) 'Alzheimer's disease: a practical psychological approach.' *Health Needs of Women as They Age 20,* 2–3, 53–62.

Price, D.L. *et al.* (1982) 'Basal forebrain cholinergic systems in Alzheimer's disease and related dementias.' *Neuroscience 1,* 84–92.

Proctor, R.N. (1991) *Value-Free Science? Purity and Power in Modern Knowledge.* Cambridge, Mass: Harvard University Press.

Radley, A. (1990) 'Artefact, memory and a sense of the past.' In D. Middleton and D. Edwards (eds) *Collective Remembering.* London: Sage, pp.46–58.

Ramanathan-Abbott, V. (1994) 'Interactional differences in Alzheimer's disease.' *Language and Society 23*, 31–58.

Rawls, A. (1987) 'The interaction order "sui generis".' Goffman's contribution to social theory. *Sociological Theory 5*, 136–149.

Reisberg, B. (1981) *Brain Failure.* New York: Free Press.

Robinson, R.A. (1968) 'The organisation of a diagnostic and treatment unit for the aged.' In K. Geigy (ed) *Psychiatric Disorders in the Aged.* Manchester: University of Manchester.

Rohwer, R.G. (1984) 'Scrapie infection agent is virus like in size and susceptibility to inactivation.' *Nature 308*, 658–662.

Roos, N.P., Wennberg, J.E. and McPherson, K. (1988) 'Using diagnosis – related groups for studying variations in hospital admissions.' *Health Care Financial Review 9*, 53–62.

Roth, M. (1994) 'The relationship between dementia and normal ageing of the brain.' In F.A. Huppert, C. Brayne and D.W. O'Connor (eds) *Dementia and Normal Aging.* Cambridge: Cambridge University Press.

Roth, M. and Wischick, C.M. (1985) 'The heterogeneity of Alzheimer's disease and its implications for the scientific investigation of the disorder.' In T. Arie (ed) *Recent Advances in Psychogeriatrics.* Edinburgh: Churchill Livingstone.

Rothschild, D. (1937) 'Pathologic changes in senile psychoses and their psychological significance.' *American Journal of Psychiatry 93*, 757–784.

Rovner, B. *et al.* (1990) 'Stability over one year in patients admitted to a nursing home dementia unit.' *International Journal of Geriatric Psychiatry 5*, 77–82.

Royal College of Physicians (1981) *Organic Mental Impairment in the Elderly.* London: Royal College of Physicians.

Sabat, S. (1991) 'Turn-taking, turn-giving and Alzheimer's disease: a case study conversation.' *Georgetown Journal of Languages and Linguistics 2*, 161–175.

Sabat, S. and Harré, R. (1992) 'The construction and deconstruction of self in Alzheimer's Disease.' *Ageing and Society 12*, 443–61.

Salthouse, T.A. (1982) *An Experimental Psychology of Ageing.* New York: Springer Verlag.

Sanders, J., Schenk, V.W.D. and Van Veer, P. (1939) 'A family with Pick's disease.' *Verh. Kon. Nederl. Akad. Weteuschlappen 2*, 124–128.

Sarap, M. (1993) *An Introductory Guide to Post-Structuralism and Post-Modernism.* New York: Harvester-Wheatsheaf.

Schaffner, K. (ed) (1985) *Logic of Discovery and Diagnosis in Medicine.* Berkeley: University of California Press.

Scheibel, M.E. and Scheibel, A.B. (1975) 'Structured changes in the aging brain.' In H. Brody *et al.* (eds) *Aging, Clinical, Morphological and Neurochemical Aspects of the Aging Central Nervous System. Vol I.* New York: Raven Press.

Seidman, S. (1992) 'Post-modern social theory as narrative with a moral intent.' In S. Seidman and D.G. Wagner (eds) *Post-Modernism and Social Theory*. Cambridge, Mass: Blackwell.

Selkoe, D.J., Liem, R.K., Yen, S.H. and Shelanski, M.L. (1979) 'Biological and immunological characterisation of neurofilaments in experimental neurofibrillary degeneration induced by aluminium.' *Brain Research 163*, 235–252.

Semin, G.R., and Gergen, K.T. (eds) (1990) *Everyday Understanding: Social and Scientific Implications*. London: Sage.

Shepherd, M. (1984) 'Psychogeriatrics and neo-epidemiologists.' *Psychol. Med 14*, 1–14.

Sheppard, M. (1991) *Mental Health Work in the Community*. London: Falmer Press.

Shilling, C. (1993) *The Body and Social Theory*. London: Sage.

Shotter, J. (1985) 'Social accountability and self specification.' In K.J. Gergen and K.E. Davis (eds) *The Social Construction of the Person*. New York: Springer Verlag.

Shotter, J. (1993a) *Conversational Realities: Constructing Life Through Language*. London: Sage.

Shotter, J. (1993b) *Cultural Politics of Everyday Life: Social Constructionism*. Buckingham: Open University Press.

Shotter, J. and Gergen, K.J. (eds) (1989) *Texts and Identity*. London: Sage.

Sinclair, I. (1988) 'Elderly.' In I. Sinclair (ed) *Residential Care: The Research Reviewed*. London: National Institute for Social Work, pp.241–292.

Sinnott (1977) *Gerontologist 17*, 459–63. cited in Gurland 1981 (*op. cit.*)

Sonder, E. (1993) 'Alzheimer's disease and older women.' *Journal of Women and Ageing 5*, 139–154.

Squire, L.R. (1987) *Memory and Brain*. Oxford University Press.

Stacey, M. (1988) *The Sociology of Health and Healing*. London: Hyman.

Stuart-Hamilton, I. (1994) *The Psychology of Ageing*. London: Jessica Kingsley Publishers.

Szasz, T. (1974) *The Myth of Mental Illness*. London: Harper and Row.

Tanenbaum, S.J. (1993) 'Outcomes research and public policy.' *New England Journal of Medicine 329*, 17, 1269–1270.

Terry, R.D. (1976) 'Dementia, a brief selective review.' *Archives of Neurology 33*, 1–3.

Thal, L.J. (1984) 'Current concepts of pathogenesis of senile dementia of the Alzheimer type.' *Ger. Med. Today 3*, 1, 86–89.

Thorndike, E.L. and Gallup, G.H. (1944) 'Verbal intelligence in the American adult.' *Journal of Genetic Psychology 3*, 75–85.

Torak, R.M. (1978) *The Pathologic Physiology of Dementia*. Berlin: Springer.

Townsend, P. (1981) 'The structured dependency of the elderly.' *Ageing and Society 1*, 15–28.

Turner, B. (1984) 'Medical power and social knowledge.' In Falk (1994) *The Body and Society*. Oxford: Blackwell.

Turner, S. (1991) 'Social constructionism and social theory.' *Sociological Theory 9*, 1, 22–23.

Turner, B.S. (1992) *Regulating Bodies: Essays in Medical Sociology*. London: Routledge.

Ulatowska, H., *et al.* (1988) 'Discourse performance in subjects with dementia of the Alzheimer's type.' In H. Whittaker (ed) *Neuropsychological Studies in Non-Focal Brain Damage.* New York: Springer.

Van der Cammen, T.J., Simpson, J.M., *et al.* (1987) 'The memory clinic: a new approach to the detection of dementia.' *Br. J. of Psych.*

Vetter, N.J., Jones, D.A., and Victor, C.R. (1981) 'Urinary incontinence in the elderly at home.' *Lancet 2,* 1275–1277.

Victor, C.R. (1994) *Old Age in Modern Society: A Textbook of Social Gerontology.* London: Croom Helm.

Vygotsky, L.S. (1971) *Thought and Language.* Massachusetts: MIT Press.

Waters, M. (1994) *Modern Sociological Theory.* London: Sage.

Whalley, L.T., Carothers, A.D., *et al.* (1982) 'A study of familial factors in Alzheimer's disease.' *British Journal of Psychiatry 140,* 249–256.

Wiener, M. and Marcus, B. (1994) 'A socio-cultural construction of depressions.' In T.R. Sarbin, and J. Kitsuse (eds) *Constructing the Social.* London: SAGE Publications.

Wilcock, G.K. (1988) 'The challenge of Alzheimer's disease: no longer a silent epidemic.' *Health Trends 20.*

Wilkin, D. and Thompson, C. (1989) *Users' Guide to Dependency Measures for Elderly People.* Sheffield: University of Sheffield.

Wilson, D.C. (1955) 'The pathology of senility.' *American Journal of Psychiatry 111,* 902–906.

Wisniewski, K., Jervis, G.A., Aritz, R.C. and Wisnienski, H. (1979) 'Alzheimer's neurofibrillary tangles in diseases other than senile and presenile dementia.' *Annals of Neurology 5,* 288–294.

Wittgenstein, L. (1980) *Culture and Value.* Oxford: Blackwell.

Woolgar, S. (1988) *Science: The Very Idea.* London: Tavistock.

Wright, A.F. and Whalley, L.J. (1984) 'Genetics, ageing and dementia.' *British Journal of Psychiatry 141,* 20–38.

Wright, P.W. (1988) 'Babyhood: the social construction of infant care as a medical problem in England in the years around 1900.' In M. Lock and D.R. Gordon (eds) *Biomedicine Examiners.* Dordrecht: Kleuwer.

Wulff (1981) *Rational Diagnosis and Treatment: Introduction to Clinical Decision Making.* Oxford: Blackwell Scientific Publications.

Wurtman, R.J. (1985) 'Alzheimer's disease.' *Scientific American 252,* 2, 48–56.

Wynne-Harley, D. (1991) *Living Dangerously: Risk Taking, Safety and Older People.* London: Centre for Policy on Ageing.

Yates, J. (1990) *Private Eye: Heat and Hip: Surgical Consultants: the NHS and Private Medicine.* Edinburgh: Churchill Livingstone.

Young, I.M. (1992) 'Breasted experience: the look and the feeling.' In D. Leder (ed) *The Body in Medical Thought and Practice.* Dordrecht: Klewer Academic Publishers.

Zola-Morgan, S., Cohen, N.J. and Squire, L.R. (1983) 'Recall of episodic memory in amnesia.' *Neuropsychologia 21,* 487–500.

Subject Index

References in italic indicate figures or tables.

Author Index

Abbott, P. 42
ADRDA (Alzheimer's Disease and Related Disorders Association) 74
Afifi, A.A. 37
Amster, L.C. 52
Appell, J. 67
Armstrong, D. 1, 7, 130, 131, 142
Askham, J. 41, 42, 61, 148, 153
Atkinson, J.M. 71
Atkinson, P. 107

Baggott, R. 43
Barbato, C. 71
Barker, J. 7
Barley, S.R. 18
Baron, R.J. 114, 120, 131
Bayles, K.A. 71
Beamish, P. 52, 148
Becker, H. 3
Bell, S. 5
Benson, D.F. 66, 95
Berg, M. 113–14, 121
Berger, E.Y. 75
Berger, P. 5, 12, 13–16, 137
Bergmann, K. 35, 52
Bernstein, B. 70
Berrios 97–8
Beyth-Marom, R. 111
Blais, R. 116
Blek, L. 66
Bond, J. 33, 42, 57
Bourdieu, P. 137
Bowles, N.L. 66
Boyle, P. 116, 117
Bradley, S. 116

Brayne, C. 95
Bredin, K. 8, 41, 60, 61, 63–4
Breitner, J.S.C. 49
Bromley, D.R. 35
Brown, P. 71
Burke, D.N. 65, 68
Burns, A. 37
Bury, M. 18, 75, 145

Calas, M.B. 128, 129
Caporel, L. 71
Carr, J.S. 148
Chance, J.M. 37
Charmaz, K. 140
Chia, R. 107–8
Close, G.R. 45
Clouser, K.D. 111, 115
Cochrane, A.N. 45
Cohen, A. 66, 73
Cohen, G.D. 66
Cohen, N.J. 68
Conrad, P. 5
Corsellis, J.A.N. 50
Coulter, A. 45
Coulter, J. 27
Coupland, J. 71
Coupland, N. 71
Crapper, D.R. 48, 50
Cumming, E. 133
Cummings, J. 66
Curran, S. 34–5, 41
Cutlip, W.D. 60

Daniel, S.L. 118
Davis, D. 71
De Alarcon 52
Deleuze, G. 129
Denzin, N.K. 11, 16–17
Derrida, J. 22
Devon, V. 50
Diesfeldt, H.F. 40
Douglas, M. 135
Dowie, J. 110
Dreyfus, H.L. 120

Dreyfud, S.E. 120–1
DuBeau, C.E. 117
Dubos, R. 6
Durkheim, E. 3

Eddy, D.M. 45
Einstein, A.R.
Eisdorfer, C. 73
Eisenberg, L. 19–20
Elias, N. 137–8
Elstein, A. 110
Emery, O. 67
Engelhardt, H.T. 105
Evans, G. 54
Evers, H. 133

Falk, P. 127, 132
Featherstone, M. 134
Feinstein, A.R. 104, 105, 109, 111–12, 115, 116, 117–18
Fennell, G. 133, 135
Ferenczi 47
Ferrer, I. 71
Filstein, M.F. 49
Fischoff, B. 111
Fisman, M. 67
Fleck, L. 102, 125, 144–5
Folsom, J.G. 51
Foss, L. 69, 108–9, 114
Foucault, M. 22, 130
Fox, N.J. 20, 129, 130
Fox, P. 79, 81, 124
Fraser, M. 44, 47, 49, 50, 52, 60
Freund, P.E.S. 3, 4, 36, 130
Friedson, E. 124

Gajdusek, D.C. 51
Gallup, G.H. 66
Garfield, S.L. 66
Garruto, R.M. 51
Gergen, K.J. 27

Made in the USA
Lexington, KY
26 January 2018